Urban Religious Events

Bloomsbury Studies in Religion, Space and Place

Series editors: Paul-François Tremlett, John Eade and Katy Soar

Religions, spiritualities and mysticisms are deeply implicated in processes of place-making. These include political and geopolitical spaces, local and national spaces, urban spaces, global and virtual spaces, contested spaces, spaces of performance, spaces of memory and spaces of confinement. At the leading edge of theoretical, methodological, and interdisciplinary innovation in the study of religion, *Bloomsbury Studies in Religion, Space and Place* brings together and gives shape to the study of such processes.

These places are not defined simply by the material or the physical but also by the sensual and the psychological, by the ways in which spaces are gendered, classified, stratified, moved through, seen, touched, heard, interpreted and occupied. Places are constituted through embodied practices that direct critical and analytical attention to the spatial production of insides, outsides, bodies, landscapes, cities, sovereignties, publics and interiorities.

Global Trajectories of Brazilian Religion,
edited by Martijn Oosterbaan, Linda van de Kamp and Joana Bahia
Religion and the Global City,
edited by David Garbin and Anna Strhan
Religious Pluralism and the City,
edited by Helmuth Berking, Silke Steets and Jochen Schwenk
Singapore, Spirituality, and the Space of the State,
Joanne Punzo Waghorne
Towards a New Theory of Religion and Social Change,
Paul-François Tremlett

Urban Religious Events

Public Spirituality in Contested Spaces

Edited by Paul Bramadat, Mar Griera,
Julia Martínez-Ariño and Marian Burchardt

BLOOMSBURY ACADEMIC
LONDON • NEW YORK • OXFORD • NEW DELHI • SYDNEY

BLOOMSBURY ACADEMIC
Bloomsbury Publishing Plc
50 Bedford Square, London, WC1B 3DP, UK
1385 Broadway, New York, NY 10018, USA
29 Earlsfort Terrace, Dublin 2, Ireland

BLOOMSBURY, BLOOMSBURY ACADEMIC and the Diana logo are trademarks
of Bloomsbury Publishing Plc

First published in Great Britain 2021
Paperback edition published 2023

A catalogue record for this book is available from the British Library.

Library of Congress Control Number: 2021932294

ISBN: HB: 978-1-3501-7546-4
        PB: 978-1-3502-3846-6
        ePDF: 978-1-3501-7549-5
        eBook: 978-1-3501-7548-8

Series: Bloomsbury Studies in Religion, Space and Place

Typeset by Integra Software Services Pvt. Ltd.

To find out more about our authors and books visit www.bloomsbury.com
and sign up for our newsletters.

Contents

Figures

Tables

Acknowledgments

This book grew out of an unusually productive workshop on religion in urban spaces, held in Sitges (Catalonia, Spain), in the late autumn of 2018. Over three days participants explored the complex presence of religion in cities around the world, strengthened scholarly networks, and discussed potential scholarly outcomes. Some of the research shared at this workshop is presented in special issues of *Religion, State and Society* and *Space and Culture*. We would like to thank colleagues at the International Society for the Sociology of Religion (especially Jörg Stolz and Véronique Altglas), for a Workshop Grant without which we could not have convened such a strong group of international scholars.

We also received direct and indirect support from several academic units, including the Faculty of Theology and Religious Studies and the Centre for Religion, Conflict and Globalization, both of the University of Groningen; the Centre for Studies in Religion and Society at the University of Victoria; and the ISOR (Centre for Research in Sociology of Religion) at the Autonomous University of Barcelona.

We would like to thank Anna Clot-Garrell, Rosa Martínez-Cuadros, Víctor Albert Blanco, and Carolina Esteso, who provided valuable and cheerful assistance in the organization and hosting of the Sitges workshop. As well, we were well supported by Therese Mager at Leipzig University, Peter Scales at the Centre for Studies in Religion and Society who helped us with important editorial tasks, and Rachel Brown at the Centre for Studies in Religion and Society, who worked closely with us throughout the final administrative and editorial work on the manuscript. The journey between our Sitges event and the book you are now holding was made easier by the competence and kindness of Bloomsbury editor, Lily McMahon.

Paul Bramadat (University of Victoria, Canada)
Mar Griera (Autonomous University of Barcelona, Spain)
Julia Martínez-Ariño (University of Groningen, The Netherlands)
Marian Burchardt (University of Leipzig, Germany)

October 7, 2020

Introduction: Religious Events in Contemporary Cities

Mar Griera, Marian Burchardt, Paul Bramadat, and Julia Martínez-Ariño

All over the world, public urban spaces—including streets, squares, and parks— are increasingly the sites for the production and performance of innovative religious forms. More and more religious groups are taking religion to the streets in an attempt to defend or challenge existing definitions of public space, to assert symbolic claims to territory and public recognition, or to demonstrate communities' willingness to participate in society. This, arguably, flies in the face of often-widespread public (but also scholarly) assumptions about the trajectories of modern secular democracies, and their quintessential urban expressions. In our view, secularization may no longer be considered a taken-for-granted or hegemonic explanation for religious change, and as such, cities may no longer be considered as sites of inexorable religious decline. Instead, there are "multiple secularities" (Wohlrab-Sahr and Burchardt 2012) that characterize not only societies and transnational social fields but also the different urbanisms, which shape cities and urban agglomerations. Within these urbanisms, multiple actors including political authorities and religious organizations are involved in defining religious and secular spaces for distinct purposes and times, thereby forging a spatial regime that is both hierarchical and power-laden but also flexible and inchoate (see also Berking, Steets and Schwenk 2018).

The Sikh festival of Vaisakhi, the Islamic procession of Ashura, the many and varied Easter Catholic processions, the World Interfaith Harmony Week, the International Day of Yoga, or the countless Pentecostal evangelization campaigns are some of the events that are held in global cities every year. These are phenomena that take religion "outside of congregations" (Bender et al. 2012) and make groups visible, sometimes in contested ways, in public space. In many cases, these occasions have a transnational character both because they are celebrated simultaneously in many places and circulated through social media, and because they link people in one place with their memories of another. Likewise, these events usually create and reproduce global imagined communities on the one hand and strengthen local communities' cohesion on the other. Whether participants are newcomers or long-term urban residents, these events point to what we might call sacred geographies that are increasingly a part of global cultures and contemporary urban identities (Knott, Krech and Meyer 2016).

This book interrogates collective expressions of religion and spirituality in public spaces, with the aim to understand contemporary urban religious formations and illuminate their complexity. Religious events offer a unique opportunity to examine how religion and urbanity are transformed *together* by current social processes (e.g., transnationalization, neoliberalism, or mediatization) (Burchardt and Becci 2013) and how public spaces mediate people's religious experiences and collective expressions (Salzbrunn and Weichs 2013). We consider religious events and rituals as privileged sites to study the transformation of both religion and cities, and the interactions between them.

Research on religious diversity has, until now, mainly focused on demographics, public policy, and places of worship (Ahlin et al. 2012; Bramadat and Koenig 2009). These emphases have illuminated some of the complex forces at work when once hegemonic configurations of religion shift and as (often racialized) religious communities seek ways of establishing themselves in an unfamiliar environment. These lines of inquiry have enhanced our ability to understand some key political and cultural forces operating in contemporary societies, but they have also led researchers to reify religious groups and orthopraxy. Critically engaging urban religious or spiritual events reveals not just the performative interplay between religious and secular spaces, but also the construction of boundaries between religion, culture, and heritage that are the common ingredients of public narratives in modern democracies. Whether a public event is categorized as religious, cultural, or as a celebration of heritage has a tremendous influence on its shape, public perception, and the way it is handled by urban authorities. This also explains why such boundaries are often strongly contested.

The concept of "urban religious events" is at the center of our argument. Drawing inspiration from the literature on the "eventization" of social life (Betz, Hitzler and Pfadenhauer 2011), we define urban religious events as expressions of religiosity that take place in urban public spaces and which share most of the following characteristics: first, they transform a religious ritual or practice into a cultural experience (Hitzler 2002, 202) through the choreographic movement of the bodies of the participants, the creation of sonic atmospheres and/or the use of visual aids; second, they generally heighten the emotional and aesthetic dimension of the ritual (Jakob 2013) and become a sensory experience to participants and audiences; third, they are new forms of re-enchantment which foster the creation of a sense of unity (Betz, Hitzler and Pfadenhauer 2011; Gebhardt, Hitzler and Pfadenhauer 2013) with those involved "face-to-face" but also, often, with imagined global communities (Anderson 1990), which are performing simultaneously the same ritual in other latitudes; and, finally, urban religious events are also "infractions" from a Goffmanian perspective, that is to say events that disrupt, transgress, and transform the "normal flow" of the city, and the ascribed meaning of a certain urban reality (see Griera and Clot in this book). In sum, urban religious events constitute rather new forms of spiritual and religious expressions that put the sensorial experience at the center in order to create vibrant and euphoric collective performances that foster *communitas* while shaping contemporary urban dynamics. Doing so, religious events often include features drawn from time-honored collective practices such as religious rituals, performances and processions. As we argue below, anthropological theories of ritual (Turner 1974) as well as sociological theories of social performance (Alexander 2004) go a long way in explaining the dynamics of religious events. However, we suggest that what turns rituals into events are the ways that they are shifted into a collective and public performance that "appeals to all the senses and stages it in a 'cultural world of experience'" (Hitzler 2002, 202) through particular economies of exchange (of energies, social attention, and cultural recognition) between participants and multiple, mutually overlapping audiences.

Despite sharing certain characteristics, the religious events examined in the chapters of this book differ considerably depending on various factors such as the scope, the content, the meaning, and the context in which they take place. The ritual of lighting the *hanukkiah* in a central square in Barcelona, the celebration of a "festival of religions" in the city of Torino, the production of public altars and shrines in Mexico City, or the tensions that emerged in response to the first International Day of Yoga in Vancouver are some of the public religious events examined in this book. In addition, the chapters, which come out of qualitative research developed in different urban contexts around the world, offer new insights on religion as an analytical category that is at the heart of broader conversations about citizenship, pluralism, secularization, globalization, bureaucratization, and urban space.

The book contains twelve chapters, plus an epilogue that critically engages with the book as a whole. The book is structured in three different parts: "After the Secular City: Religion and Urban Effervescence," "The Politics of Religion in Urban Spaces: Power and Symbolism in the City," and "Public Religious Events, Urban Transcendence, and Embodied Spirituality," each of which contains four chapters. The first part includes chapters that analyze a variety of public religious events across different geographical contexts, which challenge the common notion of cities as exclusively secular spaces. The chapters in the second part examine the political nature of religious events and performances in urban public spaces and the contestations that emerge around them. The chapters in the final part turn our attention to the embodied dimension of urban religious festivals by examining the resonances participants create between enchantments of urban space, on the one hand, and spiritual bodily states, on the other. These three parts provide a good account of the many ways religion and spirituality are imagined, situated, and contested in contemporary cities.

New Urban Religious Landscapes

Urban religion has become the focus of scholarly interest in the sociology and anthropology of religion in recent years. This interest has been nurtured by several theoretical innovations, and in particular the spatial turn (Hervieu-Léger 2002; Knott 2015b), the visual turn (Brighenti 2007), and the material turn (Keane 2008; Meyer et al. 2010). How might we best understand the relationship between the vibrant religious landscapes we see in many cities on the one hand and contemporary urban social processes on the other hand?

First, globalization and migration have contributed to the ethnic, cultural, and religious diversification of contemporary cities, which in turn has had an impact in the configuration and animation of local religious fields. The rise of religious super-diversity (Burchardt and Becci 2016; Vertovec 2019) has mainly been illustrated, and also conceived, by referring to the establishment of new religious centers and the articulation of an architecture of religious diversity. Pentecostal churches, Mormon temples, Islamic mosques, Buddhists monasteries, Sikh gurdwaras, or spiritual centers of many kinds have contributed to what we might think of as a new and living sacred geography in most medium and big cities of the world. However, these new geographies are not only traceable by identifying the new formal religious centers (e.g., temples, mosques, churches) but also by observing religious events and performances that are increasingly organized in the cities' public spaces. By participating in these religious events "new minorities contribute to the re-questioning of taken-for-granted uses and meanings of the urban texture" (Saint-Blancat and Cancellieri 2014, 658) and simultaneously express claims for visibility and recognition. The chapter on Brazilian Jiu-Jitsu events and their uses by evangelical coaches and pastors is interesting in this regard. In his chapter, Raphael Schapira shows how these evangelical events serve to imbue the marginal public spaces of Rio de Janeiro's *favelas* with new meanings while exemplifying subjectivities that stand as alternatives to those embodied by drug dealers. Related to these themes, the chapter by Julia Martínez-Ariño offers an account of how contemporary Catalan Jewish communities arising out of migratory flows in the twentieth century articulate claims for recognition, and ask for historical reparation for past wrongdoing against Jews, through the lighting of a large *hanukkiah*—the nine-branched candelabrum—and the construction of a *sukkah* (or hut) in two city squares.

In many cases the growth of certain (relatively new) groups occurs against the backdrop of the sometimes rapid decline of established religious institutions. In practice, in most but not all cases presented in this book, these social processes are embodied in interactions between historically privileged forms of Christianity and either new expressions of the same faith or forms of non-Christian religions. However, it is important to note that not only religious minorities claim a space in these often cosmopolitan urban contexts; historical churches also adopt new strategies to gain public visibility and media attention. Hubert Knoblauch's chapter examining Pope Benedict's visit to Berlin, and the mediatization of the ceremony staged in the Olympic Stadium, clearly shows how the Catholic Church employs the tools of eventization in its public displays of faith. Likewise, in her chapter, Mónica Cornejo argues that the march of the International Day of the Unborn Child in Madrid offers a unique example of how some Catholic groups align with new far-right movements, and foster innovative public repertoires blending festive, popular, and political repertoires with the aim to attract and articulate new audiences and to assert the role of the Catholic Church in contemporary urban religious landscapes.

Second, the global politics of religion and the resurgence of religious identities have led to deprivatization trends and religious communities' desire to gain public visibility (Casanova 1994). These social forces have been problematized by democratic publics through contestations in which religion has been storied mainly as a threat to social order, progress, and cohesion. Examples of such contestations are the opposition to what have been labeled "ostentatious religious symbols" and concerns over special treatments of religious minorities in public institutions. As the chapters show, controversies around public religious events demonstrate the connections between local and historical dynamics. For example, in Paul Bramadat's examination of the cancellation of Vancouver's International Day of Yoga just a week after it was announced, he notes, "This incident may remind us that religious and spiritual claims are not *sui generis* but rather part of larger social discourses that reveal a great deal about this-worldly concerns, interests, and values." This event in Vancouver illustrates the difficulty of drawing clear lines between religion, spirituality, popular culture, and leisure. These are often intermingled dimensions in an urban context marked by what Hubert Knoblauch calls the "popularization of religion," which "underline[s] the fact that the boundaries of marked religiosity claimed by the great institutions are being dissolved in two ways: the lay are actively creating religious communication and the communication of religious organizations is going beyond culturally marked religiosity" (2008, 148). The emergence in many cities of meditative flash mobs and mindfulness marches is a timely example of the popularization of religion. As Griera and Clot-Garrell contend in their chapter, "These new urban spiritual events are creative assemblages that blend together languages and practices from different milieus, such as urban culture, holistic spirituality, popular religion, and social movements, which in turn generate new public interventions and spatial practices." These events also draw attention to public expressions of holistic spirituality that problematize dominant scholarly approaches to spirituality as private.

Third, many cities and states have pursued neoliberal branding efforts to promote their urban cultures. Through these efforts, cities draw on labels and images such as entrepreneurial cities, creative cities, healthy cities, cosmopolitan cities, multicultural cities, etc., in order to accumulate symbolic capital, attract investments, and buttress conviviality. These strategies feed into the dynamics of city rankings as the globally dominant form of hierarchical ordering. However, they also foster what we might call both the "eventization of the sacred" and a process of the "heritagization of religion." In the first trajectory, religious places and public religious rituals become valuable events—spectacles, festivals, pageants, processions—that can be marketed for touristic and local consumption; and in the second process, religion is employed as part of campaigns aimed at reproducing or contesting the nation or state (Astor, Burchardt and Griera 2017). Significantly, struggles to preserve or resurrect religious heritage are often intractably bound to efforts to assert primordial national heritage. In her contribution, Nadezhda Rychkova discusses the multiple meanings contemporary Muscovites attach to the iconic Pushkin Square. She shows how the prayers conducted in that square by a group of Orthodox activists in favor of the reconstruction of a former monastery that had been demolished by the Soviet state mobilize particular notions of a timeless Russian nation and its articulations with urban space and heritage. Forthcoming work by several of our colleagues will extend these conversations about the Americas, Europe, and Israel to analogous phenomena in Asia, Africa, and Oceania.[1]

Understanding Religious Events

The bulk of existing research on contemporary processes of religious transformation focuses on "walled" public spaces such as museums, libraries, or places of worship and has (rightly) emphasized their significance as sites in which one can observe the institutionalization and negotiation of public space and the public sphere. Although there is no doubt that the conventional emphasis on formal spaces, institutions, and policies reveals a great deal, there is a lack of systematic and comparative approaches to understanding how contemporary religious communities use and engage with relatively informal public urban spaces. Hence there is a need to go beyond institutional approaches and reach outside of "walled" public space. In this book, we question the idea that, because of their ephemeral nature, social interactions in public space do not have lasting impacts. Instead, we consider that different kinds of public spaces allow for different uses and may have different enduring consequences, some of which might be counterintuitive.

Religious events and rituals, as Monika Salzbrunn and Raphaela von Weichs (2013, para. 3) suggest, "have a performative and interactive character and attract people who would not necessarily meet outside the event frame." Events generate their own audiences and foster "new forms of sociability, which are being created out of global and virtual networks, along with ephemeral forms of face-to-face interaction" (Griera and Clot-Garrell in this volume). Religious events might spring from *several sources and motivations*. First, they can be long-standing parts of the established repertoires of religious traditions, such as processions at Easter for Catholics or the celebration of the Zikat by Sufis (see Kasmani in this book). Second, they can be products of new repertoires of public presence or of the intertwining between different repertoires. This is the case, for instance, with public prayers organized by Catholic antiabortion groups during political demonstrations (see Cornejo in this volume), the lighting of the *hanukkiah* (see Martínez-Ariño in this book), or the organization of public meditations

or silent marches for peace in many cities around the globe. A third source of
these events are interreligious activities that have proliferated at an accelerating
pace over the last two decades across the world (Griera and Nagel 2018). One of
the interreligious events' main effects is the dramatization of the role of religion
within imaginaries of peaceful (future) coexistence. Finally, religious events in
public space can also form part of larger events, such as intercultural festivals,
national holidays, cultural (or countercultural) festivals, or the commemoration
of national tragedies (see Becci and Okoekpen, Giorgi and Giorda, and
Bramadat in this volume). Our focus in this volume is on contemporary rather
than traditional events such as religious processions, which are often collective
reenactments of some foundational charismatic experience that occurred
in a mythical past. Nevertheless, processions may also become "eventized"
through often-controversial innovations (e.g., changing the conventional
ethnoracial identities of key actors and their aesthetic embellishment), the use
of new technological resources (e.g., Instagram Live and YouTube), or through
new meanings attributed to them by changing social realities (e.g., when a new
political regime reframes a traditional event to promote its immediate interests
and appeal to wider audiences).

Relatedly, it is important to consider that religious events are often
manifestations of religious communities' more or less enduring religious
investments in urban space that aim for a visible public presence (Becci,
Burchardt and Giorda 2017). Such strategies are often grounded in or inspired
by specific political and other motivations, such as a wish to protest a feature
of the prevailing social norms, or claims for recognition of the group by the
dominant society. In his chapter, for instance, Nimrod Luz explores both the way
Palestinians lay claims to Jerusalem by conducting Islamic religious rituals at
the Haram al-Sharif/Temple Mount and the way these rituals emerge from new
forms of pilgrimage that draw thousands of people from across the Palestinian
territories. Such pilgrimages are central practices within Palestinian spatial
strategies that seek to mobilize the site's much-storied sacrality for geopolitical
and religious ends. Hugo Suárez's contribution on the religious life in a popular
neighborhood in Mexico City as well explores urban pilgrimages and much like
Nimrod Luz, he points to the intricate ways in which pilgrimages connect temple
and public ritual, the permanent and the ephemeral, for example through the
carrying of icons and images of the Virgin through the streets.

Moreover, urban religious events have a particular *temporal structure* that
may involve calendrical repetition that thereby marks them as special within
the regular flows of social time. This also implies that, for urban societies, public

events enjoy the status of the extraordinary, often expressed through particular aesthetic arrangements. In his theory of ritual processes, Victor Turner (1969) argues that the temporal structure of rituals involves the separation of individuals from society, a liminal phase characterized by an intensified experience of *communitas* and transformation, and then their subsequent reintegration. Despite some differences, religious events echo Turner's understanding of *communitas* as a kind of temporarily delimited "counter-structure" (Turner 1969, 139) in that events are momentary disruptions of ordinary time and routine flows of everyday urban experience.

Furthermore, religious events are characterized by what Alexander (2004) and others describe as sequencing. Urban religious events usually begin with opening rituals that already gesture toward certain understandings of the events, including ways of reaching out to audiences, references to tradition and textual authority, and so on. There is an inner sequencing of events that may be dictated by time-honored scripts (e.g., in Easter processions) but that may also be an outcome of changed circumstances. Religious events organized by religious diaspora communities are often especially rich in innovation. Among other things, in those events there is also something like a contextual sequencing by which we mean the ways in which religious events are placed—intentionally or unintentionally— against the backdrops of particular political contexts or contestations. That is, for carrying out an Islamic event, it matters whether the public space in question exists in a society characterized by heated anti-immigrant or anti-Islamic campaigns (as in India or Europe, for example) or recent experiences of religiously motivated terrorist attacks. Sequencing is thus part of the broader temporal structure that shapes urban events and their interpretation.

In addition, events may involve spectacular performances and festive atmospheres that transcend established social boundaries, unsettle conventional separations between social groups, and potentially stimulate new and overlapping senses of belonging (see Bramadat in this volume). Again, such a conceptualization of events bears something in common with scholarly notions of ritual or social performance. First, as Turner (1969, 132) argues, rituals involve a temporary homogenization of those participating in them. During rituals, status differences and hierarchies among participants tend to be suspended. While the degree to which this is the case in the often spectacular religious events discussed in this book may vary, we do note that they are typically said to render visible otherwise opaque solidarities among participants. This becomes particularly tangible in Kasmani's discussion of the Sufi ritual of *zikr* carried out by newcomers in Berlin even as participation requires members of this circle to keep their eyes closed as they commune by chanting and rhythmically moving so as to create intimacy and solidarity through saintly devotion. And it is this intimacy as a principle of "religious worlding" that articulates desired modes of being in the city thereby becoming part of its "breathing geographies."

Second, as rituals, events involve the circulation of social energies among participants and audiences. Highlighting this aspect, Alexander (2004, 527) suggests that "ritual effectiveness energizes the participants and attaches them to each other, increases their identification with the symbolic objects of communication, and intensifies the connection of the participants and the symbolic objects with the observing audience, the relevant 'community' at large." The events described and analyzed in this book may be efficacious to very different degrees. Yet all of them do indeed intensify relations with observing audiences, be it in terms of solidarity and recognition, or tension and conflict (see Rychkova and Suárez in this book). Ritual efficacy may also unfold as part of the afterlives of religious events, when the temporary suspension of temporal routines and the disruption of urban spatial flows have come to an end.

It is important to highlight the special experiential quality of religious events, as being particularly significant. The momentous quality of events resides in the fact that they draw participants into the affective dynamics of an emergent collectivity, which mobilizes peoples' sensory capacities, involves some level of collective excitement, and may produce subjective engagements but also disaffection and conflict. As mentioned earlier, religious events leverage a shared sense and feelings of collective effervescence, a moment of being drawn into the emerging flow with its own dynamic capacities and potentialities that transcend routine mental and emotional states. In *The Elementary Forms of Religious Life*, Durkheim ([1912] 2001, 245) cogently describes how interactions that participants experience as extraordinary and that stimulate euphoria are able to produce collective effervescences. It is the experience of such moments of collective effervescence that gives rise to distinctions between the sacred and the profane as qualities of spaces, times, and inner states. Moreover, Durkheim assumed that such emotional experiences may stimulate radical reevaluations of such interactions and inspire shifts of norms or values.

This brings us back to the question of the ritual efficacy of religious events we have raised above. Whether religious events are ritually efficacious—and thus successful in this sense—often depends on the degree to which they incite some level of collective effervescence. Some religious events may well remain formal ceremonies, which—according to Turner (1969)—are merely affirmative of the social order and lack the capacity to change and to stimulate new potentialities.

However, many of the chapters of this book show that public religious rituals might forge new collective articulations animated by feelings of togetherness expressed and reinforced by the ritual. The religious performance is not only the following of a formal script but the representation of a meaningful dramatic interpretation aimed at provoking thaumaturgical and political effects (See Griera and Clot-Garrell, and also Kasmani in this book). As Koukal (2010, 109) argues, "Of all of the various forms of political dissent, the most dramatic as a form of expression is that which places lived bodies in tension with the prevailing social order." However, it is also important to acknowledge that, as Irene Becci and Salomé Okoekpen contend in their chapter, "Even if the organizers proclaim inclusivity and openness, the specific aesthetic, artifacts, and objects displayed in these two festivals are material symbols speaking only to those who belong to specific social classes and thereby possess the cultural codes needed." This reminds us of the social, cultural, and religious boundaries that events might reinforce.

In a different vein, urban spaces are spaces of affect. People live, inhabit, and traverse urban spaces on the basis of the emotional qualities these spaces have for them. People afford particular urban spaces distinct emotional valences and these valences have to do with their roles as women or members of racially, sexually, or religiously marked groups. This also means that people's positionality circumscribes the way they attach emotions to streets, parks, neighborhoods, and other urban spaces. We therefore suggest that there are emotional regimes involving what Arlie Hochschild (1979) calls feeling rules and that these are central components of urban regimes (Burchardt and Griera 2019). The ways religious events are organized, staged, and experienced, and especially the question of whether they are able to produce experiences of collective effervescence are clearly shaped by such emotional regimes. One of the decisive issues in this context is how those who carry out the event and the question of whether they are religious minorities, or minorities within minorities, are placed with the urban cultural hierarchies which define the social value and desirability of public religious performances in the eyes of urban majorities. As Griera and Clot-Garrell observe in their chapter, "The perception of the event is highly dependent on observers' experience, knowledge of the spiritual practices they are witnessing, moral arguments about acceptable uses of the public space, and feelings of safety (or danger)."

Many empirical studies show that the unfolding and impact of religious events often seems unpredictable, and it is this suspension of the mundane horizon of expectations that makes these events appealing to people, draws them in, and inspires an openness for change. At the same time, events are carefully planned, staged, and choreographed with the aim of producing particular effects in audiences through careful preparation, organization, and management. Most of the events analyzed in this book involve, to some extent, organizers, committees, volunteers, parade permits, security guards, staffing, registration, publicity, street closures, equipment rental, liquor licenses, involvement of municipal representatives, fundraising, and other mundane details. Thus, events straddle the line between structure and liminality: between planning, order, and predictability on the one hand, and the extraordinary, spectacular, and transgressive on the other.

Religious Events and Constructions of Public Space: Final Reflections

In their chapter Alberta Giorgi and Mariachiara Giorda draw attention to how newly invented "festivals of religion" are becoming an increasingly prevalent form of displaying religion in urban space. In their analysis, they make the important point that the growing presence of religion in urban space does not eclipse but actually heightens the boundaries between religious and secular spaces in cities: "Rather than blurring the boundaries between the religious and the secular, or between religions, festivals of religions have the effect of standardizing the language of different religions by offering similar platforms for displaying different religious 'contents,' such as rites, theology, celebrations, or leaders and exemplary figures."

Religious events in urban space are significant for understanding constructions of public space in three respects: first, they are—usually—open and accessible to everyone, which enables, invites, and even provokes social encounters of all kinds; second, through religious events, urban citizens engage in "role-taking" (Mead 1934), which allows them to shift their perspectives between those of the audience and those of religious practitioners; third, as a result of their ephemeral nature, religious events illustrate the constitutive circularity of public space. At least in a normative sense, space becomes public to the extent that conventional uses are temporally limited and actors leave the stage to make way for others. It is also through this circularity that the secular nature of public space harmonizes—or conflicts—with religious uses and aspirations. When an explicitly or implicitly religious activity is performed in, or religious actors are temporarily in control of, a space that is generally understood to exist under the aegis of secular governance, it can create in participants a tension which might be experienced as alienation (if they are reminded of their incommensurable separation from other residents) or empowerment (if occupying that secular space even for a brief period underlines their potential power and latitude). Such an event might produce related experiences for passers-by, and for the ordinary users of these secular spaces, who might feel displaced or suddenly aware of the ontological diversities of their city. In other words, public spaces are simultaneously awash with power relations and historical legacies, and (inter) religious events are subject to specific governance power regimes. These events are, thus, spaces for domestication and adaptation, but also for subversion and creativity.

Part One

After the Secular City: Religion and Urban Effervescence

Religion from the Street: Religious Expression in a Popular *Colonia*, Mexico City

Hugo José Suárez
IIS-UNAM

Debates around space, cities, and religion have been a focus of academic interest in a range of contexts (Abruzzese 1999; Becci, Burchardt and Casanova 2013; Garbin and Strahn 2017; Gutiérrez 2005; Gutiérrez, de la Torre and Castro 2011; Hernández 2007; Hervieu-Léger 2002; Portal 2009).[1] The intention of the present chapter is to explore the relation between territory and religion, and to understand the ways in which religiosity is expressed in the urban environment: its forms, its features, and its characteristics. Focusing on the heart of the discussion regarding the visibility (or invisibility) of religious expression in public space (Burchardt and Becci 2013, 12) as well as its various dimensions and implications, I seek to understand the religious geography of a particular case. I depart from the thesis that there are three dimensions to the manner in which space is occupied by faith—that is, the way in which faith constructs the significance of space and, ultimately, resemanticizes it: the *macro*, the *meso*, and the *micro*. Each of these is the result of a specific connection to the sacred, moving from the official and institutional to the collective and, finally, the individual. At the same time, this chapter seeks to show the dynamism of the season of popular religious initiatives within the public space and the corresponding implications of interventions on the part of the authorities.

Toward these ends, I reflect on some of the results of an empirical investigation conducted in the popular *colonia* of Ajusco, Mexico City, from 2008 to 2018. The study's intention was to understand the distinct characteristics of religious experience in a Mexican neighborhood; its multidisciplinary methodological strategy was carried out with irregular intensity during specific periods. The research relied on dozens of thorough interviews, a survey, a photographic registry, and field notes. The data was interpreted with statistical instruments, a qualitative interpretation, and content analysis (Suárez 2015, 2012). For this text, an ethnographic focus was favored in order to take advantage of the multiple field observations.

Colonia Ajusco contains some 30,000 inhabitants within two square kilometers. Beginning in the 1950s, the zone was populated following an expanding urbanization which brought the arrival of thousands from the provinces of Mexico City. Large contingents settled in lightly populated territories; in the case of Colonia Ajusco, the geological substrate was volcanic rock, and thus settlement was challenging, including struggles with both the natural elements and with authorities that would negotiate and authorize the community's legal recognition and the implementation of basic services. Today, Colonia Ajusco is completely integrated into urban life, enjoying all basic services including transport and education. It is considered a "popular _colonia_ of medium density in process of consolidation," understood in the terms of zones that "do not exhibit thorough urbanization and whose housing represents different levels of completion" (Suárez 2000, 394). The socioeconomic level is low, as is the "level of social development" (Evalúa DF 2011); the average length of education is nine years. Home ownership is 72 percent (Alonso 1980; Azuela 1999; INEGI 2010; Zermeño 2005). More than 70 percent of residents have broadcast television, while nearly 30 percent have internet, and 25 percent have cable television; 55 percent of the population is married, and 50 percent works informally or "at home." Politically, 20 percent of the population considers itself leftist—the left has without exception won a majority of votes—and only 4 percent is right wing; 66 percent is not interested in politics. Finally, 70 percent of the population feels proud to live in Colonia Ajusco (Suárez 2015).

The dynamism of religious practices is notable. There are four Catholic institutions (two parishes and two chapels), two Protestant churches, seven Pentecostal centers of worship, two _biblicas no evangelicas_, two _santería_ shops, a cult of Santa Muerte, and numerous expressions of popular religiosity. Sundays count fourteen Catholic masses and thirteen celebrations by other denominations; over 5,000 people participate in different religious events. Literally dozens of pilgrimages churn through the colonia's streets, transferring images from one resting place to another. Likewise, celebrations of patron saints and the Day of the Virgin of Guadalupe (December 12) are events of significant magnitude, mobilizing hundreds, along with the corresponding investment of material and economic resources. The population is largely Catholic (78 percent) but with a high percentage of nonbelievers (14 percent, higher than the national average) as well as practitioners of non-Catholic religions (8 percent). Religious practices and beliefs are important: 86 percent belong to some religion, 92 percent pray with regularity (albeit with varying degrees of frequency; for example, 60 percent pray daily), 48 percent display some religious image in the home, and 31 percent pray the rosary during Guadalupe celebrations in December. Ninety percent believe in God, 75 percent in heaven, 72 percent in miracles, and 77 percent in the Virgin of Guadalupe.[2]

In order to adequately review the religious geography of Colonia Ajusco, this text is divided into three sections. First, I describe the official ecclesiastic institutions that visibly exhibit a physical space from which they minister— churches, parochial centers. The second part deals with expressions of popular religiosity that are not necessarily linked to religious authorities and the responsibility for which rests on the initiative and care of the faithful themselves. I develop three aspects of this phenomenon: fixed spaces (chapels that house the image of the Virgin of Guadalupe or some other saint), circulation (pilgrimages, celebrations, the transfer of images and icons between neighborhoods and homes), and domestic altars. The third section describes the experience of the Monumento a la Piedra, for which I draw upon a decade's worth of data that permits us to perceive its evolution. The Monumento began as a collective religious space and official civic symbol but ended up a forgotten trash heap. Finally, the conclusions will point to new analytical challenges. The content of this chapter should be understood as a reflection complementary to my web page, wherein the data is explained in more didactic form.[3]

Territorial and Institutional Anchors

Religious institutions are clearly situated in the public space by way of churches, centers, and icons corresponding to their respective functions.[4] The best-positioned religious institution is the Catholic Church, which expresses its presence officially through two parishes, La Resurrección (administered by the Jesuits) and Nuestra Señora de Guadalupe (administered by the Congregation of the Oración de San Felipe Neri) as well as two chapels, La Anunciación (administered by the Jesuits) and El Señor de los Milagros (maintained by the local community).

La Parroquia de la Resurrección, established in the 1970s, comprises a large property located on the Colonia's main thoroughfare. In the middle of the property sits the church, surrounded by a small enclosed dirt field for soccer, another for basketball, a parking lot, a patio for celebrations, and four classrooms. The interior has a seating capacity of 350 persons; a wooden Christ with outstretched arms is located at the center, accompanied by paintings of the Virgin of Guadalupe and San Ignacio. Services are not only religious but also social and cultural; the parish hosts medical clinics, dental services, and educational programs, among other things. The Capilla de la Anunciación is more modest, with little space outside the chapel itself. The interior has a capacity of 150. In the center, in front of a wooden wall, the Virgin gazes upon the angel of the Annunciation.

The parish of Nuestra Señora de Guadalupe is wide and comfortable, with a capacity of about 400. In the center is a reproduction of the Virgin of Guadalupe, while to the side is a crucified Christ of considerable dimension. The elegant and thoughtful architectural design consists of three stained-glass windows which feature the Virgin, the Christ, and the Holy Spirit. The space comprises various surrounding rooms and a small soccer court to the rear.

The Capilla del Señor de los Milagros is the most atypical, the result of friction between the Jesuit priests and the popular religiosity of the 1970s. After a confrontation, the administrators of the chapel decided to end their dependency on the Iglesia de la Resurrección and instead report to a church in the neighboring colonia. Located on a side street, its dimensions are significant, occupying a large property with a spacious atrium in order to comfortably house many followers and sacred images. Its interior can hold up to 120. In the center of the altar is the figure of El Señor de los Milagros dressed in white—crowned and adorned with flowers—and angels of smaller dimension. The Señor is flanked by the Virgin of Santa Úrsula, with an arrow piercing her breast, and a crucified Cristo Rey, half naked and bleeding. In the background is an image of the Virgin of Guadalupe. Seven stained-glass windows decorate the nave, three on each lateral wall and one above the entrance, all narrating biblical stories. The administration rests not on bureaucratically assigned functionaries but rather on *mayordomos* (stewards) who rotate their responsibilities. The construction of the chapel was completed with the support of the stewardship and offerings from the neighborhood. One of the protagonists of the project, who died a few years ago, has a plaque in his honor affixed to a wall to celebrate his memory as "the founder." This chapel and the spaces of official Catholicism mentioned above take on distinct pastoral forms which, in their turn, respond to various theological orientations.

Multiple non-Catholic Christian cults and denominations also exist in the colonia. The Methodist church is found on a side street; its exterior presentation is discreet, with a cross and a flame; its slogan appears as an identifying mark: "Rock of salvation." The interior features a wall-mounted panel that shows two calendar schedules with cleaning and decorating tasks for the entire year, along with the names of those responsible for said duties, and information about Church of Mexico activities; a small letter-sized sheet, computer-printed, lists the executive organization of the church, including various administrative offices. The principal hall has about fifty cushioned folding chairs. Two steps up is the altar with a carpeted floor. A sober and simple table of light wood that contrasts with the dark-wood walls is covered by a green mantel with gold fleck, and on the principal flank is a metal plaque with religious symbols and the message "in memory of me" (*en memoria de mí*). A few blocks away, the Anglican Community administers the Iglesia de San Lucas, constructed on a single parcel; its distinction is the church's seal, featuring the biblical inscription, "the truth shall set you free."

The Pentecostal world is present in various forms: Iglesia Cristiana Interdenominacional, Iglesia Evangélica Presbiteriana, Iglesia Cristiana Evangélica Pentecostés Nacional, Iglesia Presbiteriana Reformada, Iglesia Evangélica "Gracia de Dios," Congregación Nacional Presbiteriana Conservadora, and Iglesia Universal del Reino de Dios. Each has its distinct approach to occupying space, both interior and exterior. The Iglesia Universal rents a community center located in a prominent neighborhood space, accompanied by highly visible billboards. The Iglesia Cristiana Interdenominacional hangs a small sign at the entrance of a private home where it announces its schedule of services and, in capitalized red letters, the phrase "God is love." Inside, after crossing a cement patio, a small wrought iron and glass door leads to a main room with about thirty wooden seats and white, unadorned walls. The Iglesia Cristiana Evangélica operates in a garage and is difficult to perceive at first glance. But there are also groups whose gospel is not preached from a fixed location: on Sundays they might set up in a central location of the colonia with nothing more than a sign, a sound kit (electric guitar, microphone, and amplifier), a Bible, and the firm hands of a preacher.

Separately, it is worth noting the Temple of the Latter-Day Saints (Mormons) and the Kingdom Hall of the Jehovah's Witnesses. The Mormon temple is located on the main avenue and is reflective of this religious organization's standard architecture throughout the world. The central building comprises two wings connected by a small passageway with glass doors. Outside, the building is flanked by a wide parking lot, a basketball court, and well-organized gardens with trimmed grass. The Jehovah's Witnesses' house of worship, an elegant and well-lit two-story house, is constructed on a large property along a side street. The name of the organization is inscribed in a sober blue on the building's white external wall.

Practitioners and Their Appropriation of the Street

There is a notable dynamism on the part of practitioners as they take to the streets for their own religious initiatives. This process comprises three dimensions: the static, as in altars, crosses, or street-side shrines; the dynamic, as when sacred images depart on their pilgrimage between homes; and the intimate, as in domestic altars that are directly linked to the prior two dimensions. Beginning with the static dimension, street-side altars[5] are small constructions approximately one meter high that house the image of the Virgin of Guadalupe, or perhaps another virgin or saint. These images are frequently protected within a small vitrine and a door that can be secured with a padlock. Alongside the image, the faithful can place various objects, from votive candles to a glass of water, engravings, or other images. There are nearly sixty such altars distributed throughout the colonia, especially on side streets. They originate from various resident initiatives, as much for religious purposes (e.g., sites where a miracle has transpired) as civic (e.g., constructing an altar to discourage littering). The administration of these altars falls on neighborhood families that inherit the responsibilities, or delegate them to another. Depending on the particular altar, on December 12, the day of the Virgin of Guadalupe, some become spaces to pray the rosary, with seats placed around and the faithful invited to have a drink or a bite to eat. Near others, huge neighborhood celebrations take place, including rodeos, *jaripeo* (bull-riding) with bulls brought in from the countryside, musical performances with full sound systems, fireworks, mariachis, and Eucharist ceremonies. These activities are prepared throughout the intervening year and often at significant expense. The quantity of altars distributed throughout the colonia demonstrates the importance of this kind of resemantization of space, not through institutional programs, but essentially through local, personal support systems and initiatives.

The shrine is a construction with a similar function to the altar, but with greater dimensions. It is usually a room formed by two-meter-tall partitions, occupying roughly eight square meters of surface space. The image of the Virgin of Guadalupe is found in the center in front of two rows of prayer pews. As with the chapels, a shrine's origin, function, and dynamism depend on the residents who are in charge of its care, cleaning, and the organization of surrounding activities.

The colonia includes eight crosses—normally along the main thoroughfares—that commemorate an accidental death, almost always by automobile. Each small cross contains the name of the deceased and the date of the accident. A small altar is sometimes constructed in order to house a vase or votive candle in memory of the dead, although the altar will usually be found empty and unkept. Overall, altars, shrines, and crosses are expressions of popular religiosity that take the streets as faith dictates, converting everyday and ephemeral spaces into religious icons bestowed with intense activity.

In addition to the above, it is worth noting another example of this static dimension of religious expression: five instances of religiously motivated graffiti. These represent a range of images, from legitimate icons like the Virgin of Guadalupe (painted exactly according to formal expectations) to innovations such as the figure of Christ with shaggy hair and a beard—perhaps evoking the guerrilla revolutionary spirit of the 1970s—or the insertion of Aztec images sharing space with Catholic references.

The second dimension of non-institutional religious practice is the dynamism and the circuits of appropriation of space through sacred images. In Colonia Ajusco, there are innumerable images in pilgrimage, moving through the neighborhoods and homes without requesting formal permission from the religious or civil authorities. In fact, 54 percent of the colonia's Catholics have received an image of the Virgin in their home. A range of images take to the streets—without regard to the disruption of traffic, noise, or any other consideration—and follow routes predetermined by their administrators or owners.[6] These pilgrimages can respond to any of three distinct regimes. First, the "ecclesial model" refers to images that belong to a parish and that, on the day of their respective celebration, embark on a significant pilgrimage organized by a festival commission. These festivals are extremely important, involving hundreds of participants; the image travels throughout the neighborhood, visiting various houses of worship and ultimately returning to the church after weeks of having been hosted throughout the colonia. The "intermediate model" applies to images that may be housed in a parish, but whose devotion is organized and promoted by a group unrelated to the official church structure, maintaining instead a more instrumental relationship with the authorities. This is the case for San Luis Rey, the saint of Nahuátzen (Michoacán) which was brought to Colonia Ajusco in the 1970s by migrants from Michoacán. These former migrants continue to maintain San Luis Rey's pilgrimage, from basic logistical questions to economic and symbolic concerns. Third is the "autonomous model," which involves images that belong to private parties who neither request nor permit the intervention of priests in their activities; if officials participate, it is for the specific function of administering the Eucharist. These revolve around individuals who have obtained an image through their own means, for reasons linked to their own life experiences. The owner controls the season, financing, route, and content of the figure's journey.

The dynamism of these pilgrimages resignifies everyday spaces, rendering them sacred. Thus, a simple household garage, which is normally purely practical, becomes—for a few days—the principal place of religious interaction; the Virgin is installed therein, rosaries are prayed in her name, and she receives the faithful. The street, normally a space of banal transit, is suddenly dressed for a festival, with parades and decorations to witness the passing of the sacred image, announced with noisy fireworks and music. In short, the ordinary space becomes the sacred.

The appropriation of space by religious images accompanies the installation of a new temporality that breaks with the official Catholic calendar, or intersects with it only on a few precise dates (such as specific saints' days or December 12, the day of Guadalupe). The rhythm, dates, and schedule to which the marches of the images correspond are given new form by the initiative and will of image owners or caretakers.

Diversity and malleability, at the service of the needs of the faithful, make popular religiosity the most dynamic and autonomous form of territorial resemantization. This is manifested in the final dimension, the intimate territories of the sacred: household altars. In Colonia Ajusco, 81 percent of residents have altars at home, and of these, 88 percent dedicate one to the Virgin of Guadalupe, 28 percent to guardian angels, 20 percent to Pope John Paul II, and 16 percent to patron saints.

The domestic altar is the place of greatest facility of religious innovation. Such altars are usually found in the living room, or in a private business as the case may be. They contain a range of objects of distinct type, origin, and function. At the center of a small table, one finds the dominant religious figure—usually the Virgin of Guadalupe—which can be represented by an engraving or a sculpture. She is surrounded by votive candles, flowers, holy water, or other sacred objects. Alongside her may appear other images of popular Catholic religiosity (San Judas Tadeo, Niño Pa, the Virgen de Juquila) or official propaganda from the Church (like a photograph of the pope or a formalized prayer). But the altar can also include images or icons from any number of sources, from the Buddha and guardian angels to indigenous leaders or revolutionaries (such as Moctezuma, Che Guevara, or Emiliano Zapata). It is also not uncommon to find altars festooned with figures from popular cinema, whose origins might include franchise films like *The Lord of the Rings*, *Harry Potter*, or *Star Wars*.

However, the altar also becomes the space in which family history is nourished and recreated. Photos of deceased loved ones are included, as are images of important family events (baptisms, weddings) or collages that retell the life story of a family member. The various forms of sustaining and giving life to the altar are also autonomous and creative. Candles are lit and objects are incorporated, from water to wine (claiming a way to ask favors of the saints, perhaps learned from a movie), apples with honey and cinnamon are included to bestow abundance, and so on. In short, intimate territories of the sacred are incorporated into the life and everyday spaces of their owners, and they represent channels of communication with the street-side altar, the visits to images held in residences, the pilgrimages through the streets, and finally to significant urban religious events. They are spaces where homeowners are permitted to elaborate their own religious forms and practices, incorporating elements from diverse traditions interlaced with family narratives of significant intensity.

Time: The Life and Death of a Religious Space

Located on one of the colonia's side streets, the Monumento de la Piedra is a testament to the evolution of sacred space, having completely transformed over a period of ten years.[7] The Monumento consists of a massive boulder, approximately five square meters at its base and five meters tall, standing next to a high, windowless wall that suggests a factory. The first graphic report about the Monumento appeared in 2006: *Vestida del sol* (López 2006), a book that assembled images of the Virgin of Guadalupe from around the country. The enormous volcanic rock, a vestige of a colonia that never finished its creation nor the demolition of the many outcroppings that dot its territory (thus leaving uneven spaces throughout), then featured at its summit a tiny church, only fifty centimeters tall, made of tezontle and rendered in fine, minute detail: two frontal towers, each with arrow slits; a main door with a blue belfry; bell towers on the roof painted light blue and topped with tiny golden crosses; and curved windows and balconies. Next to the church was another, smaller belfry above an arch that contained a faithful reproduction of the image of the Virgin of Guadalupe. At a higher, more visible level stood a thick cross, slightly larger than the church itself. To the rear, there was a small two-level house, also made of tezontle, with red roofs, white-framed doors, and windows. Linking the cross, church, and house were cobblestone roads painted white in contrast with the reddish-black of the volcanic rock. The tiny citadel on the rock was adorned with colorful ribbons and plastic flowers. On one of the walls of the boulder there was a spray-painted portrait of the Virgin, with three leafy flowers encrusted in one of the folds left by the volcanic formation. At the foot of the boulder stood a vase of wilting flowers.

Two years later, in 2008, the situation had changed. The boulder was covered in graffiti images of popular religiosity: the Virgin of Guadalupe, San Judas Tadeo, the Santo Niño de Atocha, the crucified Christ, Santa Muerte, the Archangel Saint Michael, San Expedito, and Saint Joseph. Toward the back was an improvised and well-kept sidewalk of stones and plants, along with fresh flowers and votive candles. This was the work of a collective of residents, inspired by the two septuagenarians who had first established the memorial by ordering the construction of the miniature church atop the boulder and bringing in a priest to celebrate the Eucharist every May 3, the day of the Santa Cruz. Later, the community met with young graffiti artists who had requested permission to paint images around the Monumento without leaving a centimeter of blank rock. There was community disagreement over this project, but it moved ahead.

Previously, in 1996, another group of residents without religious motivations had initiated a campaign to convert the boulder into an official monument. To this end, they forwarded various letters and petitions to the mayoral authorities of Coyoacán, requesting intervention; they had hoped to make the Monumento de la Piedra into a homage to the colonia's settlers, who battled difficult geographical conditions in order to make the zone inhabitable. The response took fifteen years to arrive. In 2011, the mayor's office finally intervened, and the boulder walls were painted over in a metallic black. Constructed at the monument's base was a broad brick garden bed with columns of fortified concrete, lined with tezontle. The columns were painted green and the brick was varnished. Colorful vegetation was planted throughout, and a protective chain hung from green tubing was placed around the garden. A spray-painted mural was commissioned on the rear wall, representing the founders working between the volcanic rocks, converting a stony landscape into a flourishing settlement. An official pronouncement was hung—in red capital letters—with the delegation's logo and that of the government (Gobierno del Distrito Federal): "Littering prohibited. Civil Code. Art. 9 Sec. 1. Penalty: Fine of 11 to 20 days' wages or 13 to 24 hours of detention."

A metal plaque signed by the mayor was affixed to the most visible part of the stone, with a text that celebrated the inhabitants of the colonia and highlighted the courage that was exhibited in founding it. The uncomfortable question of what to do with the summit's miniature church, houses, and cross remained. While the residents who had originally requested the official Monumento asked that they be taken down, since the site was now a civic and secular space of homage, the authorities opted for prudence and, to avoid a backlash, left the summit intact. The monument's inauguration, of course, was a political festival complete with the presence of local authorities, neighborhood leaders, surrounding residents, and the press.

By 2015, the deterioration of the Monumento de la Piedra had become critical: the mural on the rear wall, commissioned by the mayor's office, was covered in a riot of urban graffiti; the surrounding area was littered with overstuffed garbage bags and several abandoned automobile tires; the garden bed and the boulder itself were peppered with tags; and on the summit, the citadel and church were completely destroyed. All that remained was the cross, the base of which had corroded to the point of toppling over. The mayoral plaque was rusted and falling apart, overgrown with weeds. Three years later, in 2018, the Monumento was overwhelmed with trash and bushes, left formless, colorless, fenceless. A shapeless knoll, a symbol of urban decay. The ten-year episode of the Monumento de la Piedra makes visible the tensions over place between the civic and the religious, as well as the intervention of authorities and the charmlessness of a sacred territory that has lost its capacity to attract adherents, returning to what it was before the community took up its cause: a dead and abandoned place.

Conclusion

The objective of this chapter has been to show how the street is a privileged place for different forms of religious expression, applying this concept to concrete data selected from research conducted in Colonia Ajusco, Mexico City. What conclusions can be drawn from these descriptions?

We have seen the vitality of religious life in Colonia Ajusco and the various means of appropriating space: the street is a dynamic place of innovation and creativity. An initial aspect that one must consider is the division between the multiplicity of institutional initiatives and those of the faithful. Institutions respond to leaders established at the centers of religious diffusion, evangelization, and the respective ecclesial bureaucracy that accompanies them (whether national or international); the faithful, on the other hand, act according to their specific and organizational needs regarding practices of faith in everyday life. Thus, while on the one hand there are church institutions with their homogeneous architecture—such as we see with the Mormons—on the other hand, we find an altar with the Virgin which could result from a miracle, a desire for well-being—good fortune in business, for example—or simply an attempt to discourage littering. Both institutions and the faithful as practitioners stamp their religious seal on public space, but in different ways.

A second conclusive element has to do with the three dimensions of the relations between space, territory, and faith. The *macro* is that which depends on the authorities, which reproduces legitimate icons and pre-established forms that respond to the relevant religious traditions; it is controlled, planned, and nourished by an established ecclesial apparatus. The *meso* is religious expression in the street, communicated via altars and shrines, which serve as intermediate places that engender the resemantization of space, marking an individual or collective form of expression in a local public space. The *micro* refers to family altars located within the home, where autonomy and innovation is total (if canonical), which act as repositories of family memory and the nourishing of faith. The link between these three religious dimensions are the images themselves, whether virgins or saints, which move from the domestic altar to the parish, especially on festival days and during pilgrimages. The images are what permit visits and routes among the three spaces to nourish relations between the community faithful, religious authorities, and the secular world. The festival is thus the occasion for encounters between the image belonging to the *macro* space—that which resides in houses of worship—and the *micro*—the little icon that resides in the home.

While these three dimensions are not contradictory, they can stand either in tension or harmony, depending on the circumstances. For example, if the faithful enter houses of worship to interact with images, votive candles, offerings, or any expression not controlled by authorities, they will provoke a reaction from the clergy. To give an example, a tag once appeared on the exterior of La Resurrección parish, which, as we have seen, is the principal religious organization in the neighborhood. In response, a banner was hung, featuring the images of the Virgin of Guadalupe and Christ on the cross and offering the following message: "Dear friend, who paints, draws on, and damages these walls, please respect this place, because it is sacred." At the same time, on other occasions, official space can be a privileged place for the discovery of images that circulate from the private to the public realm, facilitating a fluid interaction within the context of a single, transversal, religious universe.

It should be pointed out that the popular religious creativity detailed in these pages does not unfold in the same way in colonias of higher social status. An unpublished investigation shows that street-side altars in the Colonia Hipódromo-Condesa (in the mayoralty of Cuauhtémoc) and the Colonia Santa Catarina (in the mayoralty of Coyoacán) tend to be formal and decorative, as opposed to festive and devotional. We can therefore perceive a regime of religious expression in the public space that is directly linked to social class conditions.

From the experience of the Monumento de la Piedra, we can derive a number of lessons. On the one hand, we can observe the tension between the secular and the sacred within the context of space. Among the colonia's residents, there were two competing intentions: some proposed the construction of a national icon that recognized the citizens, their efforts, and their culture, while others sought to convert the boulder into a place where the sacred was made manifest. We must remember that the authorities do not have a specific regulatory strategy for urban religious expressions such as these, and that in the case described here the official response was essentially confronted with a specific popular demand; furthermore, faced with a potential conflict between residents, and given that some wanted to eliminate any sacred image from the site, the authorities opted for an unusual compromise between the religious and the civic. On the other hand, the intervention of the authorities—a result of the request and insistence of a group of residents and not necessarily of an intention to secularize the public space—altered the relation between the faithful and the religious symbol they had constructed. Civic symbols do not inspire commitment, nor do they mobilize residents around the care and nurture of the place. Quite the contrary, it is left up to the authorities to assume this kind of responsibility. The faithful, accustomed to taking ownership over sacred places, can be relied upon to keep such places clean and vital. Moreover, the boulder demonstrates a process of sacralization and de-sacralization, a sort of territorial disenchantment, the loss of the illusion that the space once generated—its religious attraction for the faithful.

Finally, these pages may bring us to value the possibility of focused research in specific territories, sustained over time and thereby able to accumulate comparative results, permitting us to perceive processes of evolution and transformation. Thus can graphic expression, in support of informational figures (which, as stated earlier, accompany this text on a web page), allow other analytic dimensions—beyond the pedagogical—which may yield new opportunities for interpretation.

Staging Green Spirituality in the Parks of Lausanne and Geneva: A Spatial Approach to Urban Ecological Festivals

Irene Becci and Salomé Okoekpen
Institute of Social Sciences of Religions (ISSR)
University of Lausanne, Switzerland

In the urban contexts of contemporary Western societies, public parks occupy a peculiar position.[1] Throughout history, they have been mediators of a whole imagery of nature for urban dwellers. This imagery is shaped on the one hand by the strategic location of parks in cities (Corbin 2016, 2018) and by social struggles over their use. As a case in point, geographer Matthew Gandy has found that the London Abney Park, which in the nineteenth century served as a garden that hosted the first European nondenominational cemetery, fulfilled a "mix of ceremonial, didactic, and moral functions to meet the aspirations of middle-class Londoners" (2012, 2) before being progressively abandoned to overgrowing vegetation. This enabled new imageries and possibilities of use for marginal groups. The kinds of developments in which both natural and social action are articulated are often overlooked in current studies, which concentrate either on human action or on nature. In this chapter, we will combine a spatial approach, taking the natural location of a park very seriously, with a study of social practices in the realm of ecological activism. More specifically, we will look at how ecological festivals taking place in the public parks of two francophone Swiss cities, Lausanne and Geneva, promote a particular religious (or in emic terms, spiritual) approach to nature. Our empirical observations will serve to understand what specific spirituality is staged and performed despite a very universalizing discourse. Our analysis will also demonstrate in which ways boundaries are set and put forward through aesthetics and infrastructure.

Since the sociology of religion adopted the insights of the "spatial turn" introduced in the 1970s by the seminal writings of Henri Lefebvre (1974) and

Michel Foucault (1984), "sacred space," too, has started to be conceived in relational terms. Sociologist Martina Löw writes that space indeed arises "from the activity of experiencing objects as relating to one another" (2008, 26) and even argues that "spaces develop their own potentiality which can influence feelings" (44) through the creation of an "atmosphere" mediated by sight, smell, hearing, taste, and emotions. Within cities, different spaces are constantly socially and topographically defined as secular or "sacred" (Smith 2004; Stringer 2015) through interactions between people, but also between people and natural elements. In recent years, nonmainstream and marginalized religious (or spiritual) actors have increasingly used city parks to express ecological concerns and promote practices based on particular understandings of the connection between nature and humans. Some eco-festivals in urban parks promote claims of a "spiritual" approach to nature and ecology. Such claims can be traced back to the inception of ecological movements, when holistically oriented ideas were promoted by deep ecology (Næss 1972) or ecosophy (Guattari 1989). Later they developed into so-called dark green religion—that is, a set of body practices and social discourses signifying a feeling of profound belonging and connection to nature, considering the earth and its life-system as sacred and interconnected (Taylor 2010). Situated only at the margins and in countercultural movements, such discourses, views, and values about the earth and nature criticized the rationalistic and profit-oriented capitalist way of life introduced by the Industrial Revolution.

In this text, we will use ethnographic data, including a small survey about eco-festival attendees' involvement in ecology, politics, and religion (based on our original questionnaire),[2] to argue that "dark green religion" is playfully "popularized" (Knoblauch 2009) during events such as eco-festivals. Such developments are rather surprising, considering that scholarly literature emphasizes the secular profile of environmental activists. According to international sociological surveys, Western ecological activists tend to have no religious affiliation and a progressive political orientation. Their high education (Hamilton 2011) and income levels (Greenhill et al. 2014) and their rather young age (with an average of just over thirty) are factors that are usually associated with less attachment to religion (Stolz et al. 2014). In our view, through its popularization, "dark green religion" is developing into a *subtle green spirituality,* supported by a rhetoric of openness and inclusion which avoids subjecting personal conduct to severe rules, instead espousing principles that smoothly guide everyday action toward a higher awareness of environmental impact. In our view, eco-festivals serve as a visible arena in which ecological activists—the majority of whom are women—adopt a form of spirituality that we qualify as *subtle,* in contrast to the "dark" green and "deep" ecological approaches, to indicate that practices of spirituality permeate ecological discourses in a subtle manner. Through their settings, these eco-festivals in urban parks create a space apart where the staging and popularization of a subtle green spirituality is made possible. In what follows, we will illustrate how this happens by putting the actors and space at the heart of our analysis.

Approaching Festivals as Popular Mediators of Eco-spirituality

The two francophone Swiss eco-festivals presented in this text are,[3] along with other events and actors, part of a larger local and transnational environmental network. Since the beginning of the new millennium, eco-festivals have emerged in the Swiss urban context as a new kind of large public cultural events. They share various features with events such as the "fête de la musique" (which takes place in June), including live music, family activities, a large array of culinary choices, and plenty of open-air bars. Their announced objective—to promote ecological action—is made clear through their websites, posters, and general aesthetic.

From a sociological point of view, festivals can be considered as events (Gebhardt 1987, 2000; Getz 1989, 2005)—that is, unusual and unique experiences (Cudny 2016). Even when they are *planned*, each event is "unique, and stems from the blend of management, program, setting, and people" (Getz 2005, 16). The festivals observed in our research embrace several types of events, as identified by Getz (2008, 404); they are, in a way, cultural as well as political events, with spaces for entertainment, business, scientific education, and, finally, recreation.

The eco-festivals we studied take place within cities in order to gather people around local ecological transition initiatives in a short period of time.[4] Interestingly, city dwellers are prone to be particularly interested in socially and politically emancipatory actions as well as scientific knowledge. As cities have, however, also promoted industrial productivity, the acceleration of mobility, and instrumental rationality, ecological festivals are situated in a particular location: urban parks. It thus seems that city parks have become, in the era of eco-festivals, a place apart, or—to use a notion theorized by Michel Foucault—a heterotopic space ([1967] 1986). After having discussed our study, we will elaborate on this idea in our conclusions.

Our two observation sites are the *Festival de la Terre* (Earth Festival) in Lausanne and the *Alternatiba Léman* in Geneva. The *Festival de la Terre* has been taking place at the beginning of every summer in the town of Lausanne since 2005, while the *Alternatiba Léman* festival has been held since 2015 at the end of each summer in the city of Geneva; the urban parks that host these two festivals are only sixty kilometers away from each other. While it is useful to reflect on the distinctive characteristics of each festival and park, in this chapter we will draw important lessons from their compared analysis. Both festivals are supported by their local municipalities. Moreover, they share four additional features: their bottom-up organization, their focus on ecology, their location in city parks, and their comparable size (30,000–50,000 attendees).[5] They also attract a similar type of audience and appeal to an overlapping network of activists.[6]

Gebhardt's (2000) work points to specific dimensions of events that are relevant to our two field observations. Events are programmed as unique experiences exceeding everyday life, occupying "an exceptional 'location'"[7] (19) and creating "total experiences" (20) intended to be touching and lasting beyond the moment itself. Disrupting the usual uses of the city parks, both *Alternatiba Léman* and the *Festival de la Terre* propose a lived experience in a common location that is temporarily rendered exceptional. As their goal is to encourage citizens to engage in a bottom-up sustainability transition,[8] they propose alternative ways of dealing with daily activities and create synergies between various stakeholders. Moreover, according to Gebhardt, events convey feelings of togetherness amongst participants, and as such only "a very fine internal differentiation can be observed"[9] (2000, 21) among participants. A survey we conducted among the participants of both festivals in 2018 allowed us to verify this statement and corroborated our field observations.[10] We identified an eco-friendly, spiritual but non-affiliated milieu strongly oriented to the political left, with a majority of highly educated white upper-middle-class urban dwellers. In fact, even though the festivals (which we will now introduce) are freely accessible open-air events, there are spatial arrangements and signs steering and filtering people toward places or practices, invoking notions of sacredness.

The *Festival de la Terre* takes place in the context of a worldwide initiative which connects with dozens of other countries. The activities planned there aim at "celebrating the earth"[11] through concerts, exhibitions, art, dance, music, food, naturopathy, ecopsychological experiences, various yoga classes (Prana Mudra Yoga, Kundalini, Santraj), presentations of alternative ways to live in bodily harmony with nature, workshops, conferences, and rituals encouraging solidarity, joy, holistic sexuality, and creativity. The usually calm and sober garden area of the park is loudly animated by thousands of visitors strolling through from midday till late into the night. *Alternatiba* is a citizen movement born in Bayonne (France) in 2013 as a reaction to the release of the fifth IPCC report on climate change (Brusadelli et al. 2016). As a popular bottom-up organization, the organizers' goal is to "initiate the social, energetic, and ecological transition without delay" by means of a "cross-border community."[12] The *Alternatiba Leman* is a locally organized event within this transnational network. Its central idea is to involve local actors and gather attendees from Geneva and the surrounding area, including neighboring France. The event takes the shape of an ephemeral tent, or "village des alternatives," in Geneva's city center parks, showcasing local initiatives and projects through stands, conferences, concerts, and activities such as walks through nature, shiatsu massages, laughter yoga, and workshops on nonviolent communication.

The content of the two chosen festivals varies slightly, as the first emphasizes harmony, linking well-being with ecology, and the second focuses more on NGO actions and political activism in favor of sustainability transition measures. Within both of these environmentally committed events, an increased set of religious discourses and practices are emerging in close relation to the natural environment of the parks in which they take place. Mainly brought in by an overlapping network of stakeholders linking religion/spirituality and ecology, this form of spirituality is shared amongst the visitors and performed during the festivals.

In order to study these events empirically from 2015 to 2019, we took a series of methodological stances.[13] First, we started with participant observation: we wandered through the streets of the festivals, stopped at stands, collected flyers, interacted with the exhibitors, participated in several activities offered within the festival (conferences, concerts, workshops, introduction to a practice, etc.), recorded notes, took photos, and filmed several scenes.[14] Overall, we recorded about one hundred hours of conferences and speeches at workshops, took hundreds of pictures, jotted down notes in dozens of booklets, conducted innumerous ethnographic conversations, and gathered hundreds of flyers and leaflets. In 2018, we distributed a one-page self-administered questionnaire among the visitors to gain a better overview of the profiles of the attendees at these two festivals. We also conducted fifteen interviews with workshop organizers and speakers who engaged with issues such as ecospirituality and/or the "inner transition." Moreover, we held numerous ethnographic conversations with attendees, practitioners, and respondents while distributing the questionnaire, attending concerts, or visiting food stands. In this text, we mainly focus on the analysis of our fieldnotes and the interviews to triangulate the results with a spatial approach to the festivals.

Staging Subtle Green Spirituality through Space and the Senses

As we mentioned above, festivals introduce an eventful space-time, as they create a particular spatiotemporal entity. We will now illustrate how the practices enacted during the observed festivals disrupt the usual use of the urban parks where they occur, thereby opening up space for spiritual ecological explorations. Adding to this description, we will show how these created spaces are marked by a rhetoric of openness, even though access to them is filtered into different levels of participation. We study bodies and senses as cultural and social constructs, offering us an experience and a representation of space (Knott 2015b, 156).

The Montbenon Park in Lausanne and the different parks used by *Alternatiba Léman* in Geneva[15] play a number of public roles. During the daytime and particularly in summer, families, students, migrant communities, lovers, and urban dwellers of every age hang around lazily to eat lunch, read a book, or take a nap in the afternoon. Late at night, especially on weekend nights, the parks become a meeting point for louder youth groups gathering to drink alcohol or smoke. Following the writings of Jonathan Smith (2004), some remarks on how the sacred topographically emerges in these places are needed. In the parks that host the festivals, monuments certainly mark the space with secular authority and even a sacred aura. In Montbenon (Lausanne), secular monuments are glaringly present; with its nineteenth-century courthouse and statue of William Tell[16] (the archetypal Swiss hero), Montbenon is a symbol for juridical power, while contemporaneously also a center for contestation and culture through an early-twentieth-century former casino building which today hosts the national cinema archives, concert halls, and a stylish brasserie.

Bastions Park, where *Alternatiba Léman* took place in 2018 and 2019, is a centrally located wooded area in Geneva. Initially designed for the public as the city's first botanical garden, it is one of Geneva's oldest public parks. The park hosts historic university buildings, the cantonal library, human-sized chessboards, and the famous Wall of the Reformers. This promenade, where students take breaks and relax, is thus also a must-see for tourists exploring the Calvinist history of the city. Considered Geneva's most popular park, Bastions fulfills a public function by hosting festivals and events such as the *Fête de la Musique* and the Christmas Market, both of which attract many visitors. In addition, the park partially serves as a niche for "urban outcasts" (Wacquant 2008), offering urban dwellers the opportunity to experience nature in the city. During the two summer eco-festivals, the daily, profane flow of actions and practices is disrupted. While the trees, flowers, grass, and fountains of the park are silent sources of restful enjoyment year-round and stand in sharp contrast to the frenetic urban rhythm (Long and Tonini 2012), during the eco-festivals, they become the stage for peculiar rituals. Both events rely on an impressive infrastructure of stages, food trucks, stands, and tents and domes with cozy interiors, as well as artistic installations and colorful decorations of garlands, flowers, and banners. The usual daily life of the park is disrupted at the acoustic, visual, olfactory, and discursive levels. In order to identify this staging in detail, we will analyze how visitors arrive at the festivals.

There are three ways to enter the *Festival de la Terre* in the given setting of the park sites. One way is to arrive by elevator, exiting at the seventh floor of a parking garage, the lower entrance of which is only a few hundred meters from the central railway station. Once you exit the elevator on the top level, any memory of the parking garage immediately vanishes (as does the building itself) as its architectural structure lies beneath the park hill. The non-place (Augé 1995) of the parking garage (which is unattractive and a bit scary) is transformed into a significant space, one loaded with cultural symbols and sociality, simply by stepping out of the elevator and onto a huge terrace offering a breathtaking view of Lake Geneva bordered by the Alps, with Mont Blanc towering in the background. The second and third entrances to the festival are situated in front of a historic building.

Under a colorful paper arch, a couple of volunteers welcome visitors and announce that no fees are required to enter the *Festival de la Terre* but that "conscious participation" is encouraged, indicating the possibility to leave a donation in a large transparent box containing coins and banknotes. The message communicated by the volunteers at the entrances raises awareness that everything we do has an impact and that nothing is free: everyone's unique contribution is needed. The *Festival de la Terre* features a particular aesthetic arrangement and follows a specific visual identity, a continuity from one year to the next. Once visitors pass through the welcome gate, they encounter a series of stands. There, artisans sell different types of products such as organic food, clothes, accessories, and cosmetics, and various organizations—be they non-governmental, governmental or, in one case, linked to the main local Protestant and Catholic churches—propose activities such as creative recycling (crafts and art projects using recycled materials), self-help, and games for children.

A similar disruption can be observed at the *Alternatiba* festival. Upon entering the park of the festival through the main entrance, visitors leave behind the hustle and bustle of the city, the traffic, and the imposing buildings of the

Place de Neuve. They are first welcomed by planter boxes marked "Perma Love Culture," an opportunity for visitors to recognize edible plants. Farther along, colorful and creative banners and signs give the tone of the event: "Break free from fossil fuel," "Climate justice: YES to the food sovereignty initiative," or "Atom [atomic energy] or life: the choice is yours."[17] A chestnut tree lane provides shade for the calm and playful gathering, where visitors might discuss permaculture, an alternative economy, education, or ecological building strategies. Altogether, the organizers' vision has been to institute an alternative village, using tents for conferences, exhibitions, and workshops, tables and benches for eating and drinking, and stages for almost nonstop live music.

The two festivals therefore take over these urban parks with their infrastructures, statues, and trees to create an ephemeral green utopia. These staged ecological gatherings in the luxuriant green of the parks recall Foucault's "enacted utopia" ([1967] 1986) as festive sustainable counter-sites to contemporary urban life. In so doing, they offer participants and visitors a space in the city for transformative experiences of intertwined environmental activism and spirituality. Even if the organizers proclaim inclusivity and openness, the specific aesthetic, artifacts, and objects displayed in these two festivals are material symbols speaking only to those who belong to specific social classes and thereby possess the cultural codes needed. Weeks ahead of time, posters in the city and on the university campus announce the dates and programs for both festivals; even the cities' official websites include information about them, showing their desire for the festivals' openness. Upon arrival, however, a certain cultural capital is needed to recognize references to oriental practices and the holistic or philosophical vocabulary inspired by deep ecology. As most indications are used playfully and as symbols, with very few explicit explanations, social distinctions are made apparent. Such a selection process is particularly visible in the spatial organization of the festivals.

In the upper section of the *Festival de la Terre* and the entrance of the *Alternatiba Festival*, the impression is that of an alternative, easily accessible market. This is the easiest level of participation. When visitors approach the large gates assembled by the organizers of the *Festival de la Terre* in Montbenon Park, they hear the sound of drums or loud music "that will make you travel very far but also deep within."[18] When they step onto the esplanade, they smell chai or incense coming from the stands. Their eyes cannot ignore the huge dream catcher on the horizon when gazing toward Mont Blanc, nor the 100-square-meter "dome" erected for the occasion on a lawn decorated with flower and stone mandalas. There, the highlights of the festival occur, labeled as artistic or spiritual: workshops such as drum construction or kite making and activities such as playing djembe, yoga, or meditation. Once inside, visitors have passed the spatially filtering area and entered a special type of momentum (Eade and Garbin 2007; Knott 2015a). This is the medium level of participation. The spectrum of activities is quite large, including sustainable initiatives and projects, such as the Sea Shepherds, Fairphone,[19] the production of one's own cosmetics and washing powders, vegan food, and even neo-shamanistic rituals, or meetings with the spirits of the forest. At the very least, when they participate in one of the festival's proposed activities, visitors are actually performing what scholars call "contemporary spirituality" (Fedele and Knibbe 2013). For instance, we participated in shamanistic visualization sessions, guided meditation, and healing rituals for "Mother Earth" while seated on oriental rugs in the dome, facing complex colorful paintings or totems. On the lawn outside, we performed a "planetary dance": two shamans played drums in the middle of a circle of about fifty dancing participants, all sweating, singing, and shouting under the midday sun. This is the most committed level of participation, which requires bodily participation and a certain time commitment. Access to these spiritual activities is more or less filtered through time, space, and discourse. In fact, visitors will not accidentally bump into a spiritual ritual while wandering through the festival, as some intimacy is created not only by the tents (which accept a limited number of persons) but also through the language. A semantic field of contemporary spirituality is delimited with the use of notions such as "planetary dance," "visualization," "ritual," "spirits," "chakra dance," and "mantra singing"—codes which are not commonly used in the public space or in ordinary urban life.

This physical and time-based commitment, the separation of spaces, and the specificity of the language used act as filters and serve to sacralize these moments, isolating them in a sense from the profane world. These "gates" then make it possible to relieve any potential tension between spiritual activities and the ecological fair happening outside the dome or small tents. Numerous spiritual activities and rituals assume imageries filled with references to "other" distant and exoticized cultures without addressing such cultures as potential visitors. This became obvious when, one morning, one of our team members arrived late to a shamanic drum session and bumped into three persons arguing at the entrance of the dome. Three young people, visibly affected by alcohol, had been prevented from entering the tent. One organizer and a private security guard hired for the event were explaining to them why they were asked not to be loud, and that they were suspected of having the intention of stealing. What was striking about the encounter was that the three young men were the only racialized persons in the vicinity. They were used to spending their after-party time in the park and were amused to read that the festival was about totems, spirits, and rituals. Ironically, their stated origins were in Africa and Brazil, while many of the festival activities centered on an exoticized Amazonian culture and jungle animals. The organizers invited them to join the djembe building workshop instead, a suggestion confirming that a smooth selection process was indeed at work.

In such an instance, the supposed capacity of public events to draw participants into the affective dynamics of an emergent collectivity seems to fail. This selection of participants is not visible at first glance. However, the festival contains various frontiers that became operational when needed in order to set aside certain activities as "sacred" for a chosen audience. At the same time, by remaining public, this sacredness seems open, since it is possible at any moment to stop an activity and exit the space. Through this opening, this spirituality appears as a bridge between profane daily life and the sacred natural world. Clearly, the event is planned, staged, and choreographed with the aim of producing the effect of a sacred earth amidst the audience through careful preparation, organization, and management. In the end, however, planning, order, and predictability are also disrupted by the extraordinary, spectacular, and transgressive. As the editors of this book write in the introduction, this "unfolds within a dual horizon straddling the line between structure and liminality." The spatial arrangements of spirituality have a different dynamic at the Geneva festival, but our observations there brought us to a similar conclusion.

As a nonpartisan meeting, *Alternatiba* presents local initiatives ranging from agriculture, economy, and finance to health, wellness, and inner transition. We first observed how activities related to the latter—such as workshops dealing with ethical and spiritual questions—were located in a somewhat isolated nearby park. They were indicated on the festival's map under the heading of "inner transition,"[20] which we found particularly interesting. Within the festival, this was the place where a "spiritual" offer was proposed and a specific relationship to nature was staged through rituals, yoga, meditation, energetic balancing, and mandala drawings. A few church-related actors were also present, but in a discreet way or in connection to their social and ecological activities.[21] In the festival's last two editions, the separation was made quite clear in the spatial organization of Bastions Park, as visitors were only allowed to discover (for free, and in a playful manner) heartfulness meditation, laughter yoga, and nonviolent communication at the other end of the boardwalk, in a quieter zone.

The two areas of the festival—environmental activism and inner transition—were reflected by two opposing trends among the organizers and were already apparent when we attended *Alternatiba Leman*'s general assembly in 2016. One group of organizers was oriented toward what they called "inner transition," an approach to ecology that places a strong emphasis on personal and individual change, and the other was mainly composed of civil society actors and political activists (Becci and Grandjean 2018). The latter was strongly action-oriented and openly criticized the former for prioritizing *talking* instead of *doing*. Throughout our years of observations (2015–19), we noticed that the inner transition space was slowly moved toward the margins of the park, rendering it less accessible and farther away from places where visitors converged for organic food, drinks, and music. It has since remained on the festival's outskirts. The different levels of participation detailed here depend on these two orientations.

An interview conducted with the woman who integrated the inner transition issue into *Alternatiba* in 2015 provided us with a more precise view and understanding of this tension. This woman, then in her sixties, had found herself unemployed in her fifties and created an organization named *Eco-Attitude* after a "life-changing experience" she had in the New Age community of Findhorn, Scotland, and a number of other eco-villages in India. In the late 2000s, she tried in vain to unite local interested individuals and organizations on eco-neighborhood projects in Geneva. The *Alternatiba Leman* project first seemed to embody her will to unite and create a synergy between different local stakeholders on ecological issues. Willing to bring an inner transition space, which she defined as essential and missing, she joined the core project and experienced how unifying it was. However, she stressed the difficulties she encountered while working with what she called "militant groups"/"activist groups." As she said, "These people are not used to looking inside themselves; they are often violent in their rhetoric and in the way they silence those whom they do not agree with."[22] As she could not make herself heard, she left the committee but kept coordinating the space, uniting various stakeholders and organizing conferences on ecopsychology. In the following years, additional conflicts arose from this tension, and, in 2016, she left *Alternatiba Leman* feeling wounded. Today, she is active in the *Extinction Rebellion* movement. Reflecting on the gathering and organization of the inner transition space, she recalled how friendly it was, yet the organizations involved did not have a strong-enough bond to undertake further collaborations. Indeed, after she left, the various stands and workshops remained, but without any reference to the role of "inner transition" in the fight against climate change. As we observed during the festivals in 2018 and 2019, several stands and organizations promoting inner transition values changed location and highlighted other elements of their activities, thereby keeping a strategic low profile.[23] The *Alternatiba Leman* case shows how tensions emerging between the sociopolitical ecological activists and the inner transition stakeholders ended up pushing the more spiritual–ecological discourse toward the margins, on both the spatial and discursive levels.

These observations underline how these eco-festivals and the urban parks in which they take place are far from being free of social control. Indeed, gaining full visibility and space are achieved through performing certain ideas and discourses on ecological activism and spirituality. Although less visible, notions of spirituality are still present in *Alternatiba Leman*, as our 2018 survey and recent observations showed. Visitors are inclined to appreciate spiritual aspects of the movement and to participate in spiritual activities, as long as they are "subtle," smooth, and non-invasive.

As suggested above, both festivals temporarily transform the parks, juxtaposing supposedly incompatible spaces and creating a heterotopic space in which a type of spirituality can be experienced in relation to nature. There is indeed a tension between the park as the place it is planned to be and the space it becomes during the festival. In both parks, the space is transformed through ornaments, decorations, narratives, and ritual practices, which we can interpret following the distinction between the experience of a space and its representative value suggested by Michel De Certeau (1980) and Henri Lefebvre (1974). This clash is intriguing and revealing for our purposes, as it helps us understand the ways in which, in a secular context, a shift toward the practice of new spiritual rituals occurs.

In his essay on heterotopia Michel Foucault ([1967] 1986) mentions the distinction between sacred and profane places. Heterotopic spaces, he suggests, are disruptive to the established order as they are not inserted within it, but exist outside of it. To make his idea clear, he mentions the example of the mirror, which we find particularly relevant for the suggestion we would like to make—that eco-festivals in urban parks be considered heterotopias. Foucault writes:

> [In] the mirror, I see myself there where I am not, in an unreal, virtual space that opens up behind the surface; I am over there, there where I am not, a sort of shadow that gives my own visibility to myself, that enables me to see myself there where I am absent: such is the utopia of the mirror. But it is also a heterotopia in so far as the mirror does exist in reality, where it exerts a sort of counteraction on the position that I occupy. From the standpoint of the mirror I discover my absence from the place where I am since I see myself over there. (Foucault [1967] 1986, 4)

In contemporary societies, according to Foucault, heterotopias are places "in which individuals whose behavior is deviant in relation to the required mean or norm are placed." The urban park eco-festivals are heterotopias inasmuch as they are "not oriented toward the eternal, they are rather absolutely temporal" (Foucault [1967] 1986, 7). They are also "capable of juxtaposing in a single real place several spaces, several sites that are in themselves incompatible" (Foucault [1967] 1986, 6).

Conclusion

The two festivals we have analyzed jointly are events that attract, over several days, a particular audience to an urban and public green space: young, urban, politically progressive, and spiritual—but not religious—participants. Despite their appearance as being open and accessible, these urban events are in fact attended by a rather uniform audience, thereby strengthening the idea of participating in one common effort. When strolling around these two festivals, one notices an air of harmony; political NGOs opposing nuclear energy are placed beside stands offering organic food. From these sites, one easily glides to a meditation session or an energetic massage. The juxtaposition of these activities in a playful and open way generates a harmonious suite of environmentally themed options.

The diversity of actors involved in the festival is ordered spatially so that attendees can situate the realm to which each activity belongs, whether it is well-being, consumption, recycling, etc. This spatial mapping of activities is presented as a harmonious arrangement that is organized functionally. Religious and spiritual actors also find their place within the festival, putting them at a similar level of importance for environmental action compared to other participants. In the Lausanne festival, ecological activism is framed as an open spiritual discourse that seeks to connect living beings with nature. For attendees who might find themselves tasting a vegan dish, learning how to construct a house from earth and straw, or discovering how natural contraception works, the combination of these activities under the canopy of *écologie* (in French) makes sense. The festival nonchalantly offers to combine these actions with reflections on "feeling connected" to nature, be it through an inner transition exercise, dancing to the rhythm of a drum, or sensory experiences. These practices join together to compose environmental action. Moreover, some of these spatial settings create a sense of sacredness, such as large labyrinths or tents with carpets, paintings, and totems that close during sessions. These activities bring a particular added value to environmental action. They can be continued on one's own after the festival or by joining one group or another, or they can simply be practiced during the event.

This spiritual offer comes as an invitation to get closer to "dark green religion" for a day, a moment, in a festive way. The network of "dark green religion" is popularized through such events. The resulting set of discourses and practices is what we have named a *subtle green spirituality*, a spirituality offering an extra value and meaning to environmental action without requiring the adoption of a precise religious or philosophical tradition. It stresses the idea of harmony and connectedness between spiritual and environmental action, rejecting an environmentalism that is only based on technological, political, or economic factors. This rhetoric of openness and inclusion eschews severe rules and embraces principles that smoothly guide everyday actions toward a higher awareness. Thus holistic spirituality, which has its own niche within these festivals, coexists with a discourse of spirituality that subtly permeates the ecological movement.

An analysis of these two festivals has therefore allowed us to identify how, at least in these sites, a spiritual approach to nature is popularized through practices more than through discourses. The bottom-up movement of the various NGOs that work together during these festivals paves the way for attendees to combine political action with spirituality. The spatial closeness of secular and spiritual activities during the festivals allows participants to bridge (to some extent) tensions between the political and religious realms within environmentalism. The latter appears in this way to be composed of diverse strands that are all needed nowadays, as the climate change crisis reaches a critical point. The presence of spiritual activities, and more rarely the discursive register referring to spirituality (which in this context is public and supported by local secular authorities), illustrates the pertinence of spiritual concerns within ecological action for attendees. Spiritual initiatives are introduced as voluntary, open, and contingent. Altogether, they disseminate the idea of a single entity, the earth, that is alive and with which individuals must "connect"—consciously and sensitively rather than just intellectually. For urban dwellers attending the festival, the park becomes a symbolic recipient of an imaginary of enchanted nature and an active contributor to a form of politically committed spirituality.

Constructing a Religioscape: The Case of Pushkinskaya Square in Moscow

Nadezhda Rychkova

Russian Presidential Academy of National Economy and Public Administration

On November 16, 2016, I was crossing the Pushkinskaya Square in Moscow when I noticed two women kneeling before a granite stone set in the center of this square. I was surprised and decided to come closer. The women were singing "God, save the tsar"—the national anthem of the Russian Empire. There was a cross, some icons, and an icon lamp by the stone. When they finished singing, I asked them what was going on. This was how I found out about the Orthodox community devoted to the revival of the Strastnoy Monastery, which was located on Pushkinskaya Square until 1937.

A reflection on this place raises several questions, namely: Who visits this square? What is their purpose? How do they create their own space? If religious and nonreligious groups use this place, how do they relate to each other? What do the material objects located on the square mean for each group? In this chapter, I address these questions by employing the concept of shared places coined by Robert Hayden (2016). This allows us to trace practices implemented by the construction of a religious landscape as well as to describe and analyze the strategies and tactics of interaction with space in multi-confessional environments and beyond. The author of this model mainly focuses on urban environments in the postimperial, postcolonial, and post-Soviet spaces. In the post-Soviet space, for instance, urban environments are shared (or contested) places, claimed by both religious and nonreligious groups. One such place is Pushkinskaya Square, claimed in the Soviet era and in modern times by different groups of Muscovites.

Studying religion in urban public places and spaces has become mainstream in present-day religious studies. As Marian Burchardt and Irene Becci (2013, 1) fairly claim:

There are two reasons why it seems particularly urgent to examine the conjunctures between religion and urban spaces under the current conditions. … [First,] the fact that many cities turn out to be vibrant centres of religious innovation forced social scientists to interrogate and partially reject earlier generalized assumptions about the secularizing effects of urbanization. Urban change seems to reshape religious lines of difference rather than to eclipse them. The second reason stems from the observation that religious life in major cities is often quite different from that in the rural areas, regions or societies that surround them.

The attention to various manifestations of religion in cities has led to criticism of the theory of secularization that has long dominated in sociology and anthropology of religion (Uzlaner 2019). Researchers have begun to talk about a new era, termed "postsecular" by Jürgen Habermas.

The transition between these periods in Russian history coincided with the change of political regimes, which had an impact on the peculiarities of these processes. Indeed, secularism takes on a variety of features in different countries. On the one hand, Soviet secularism was forced, and on the other, "A Soviet experience, by the virtue of its totalitarian claims, gave rise to an alternative system of sacred ideals and practices, a kind of 'atheistic religion' with corresponding dogmas, mythology, hagiography and practices—'religion', partly based on the heritage of traditional religions" (Agadjanian 2012, 101). Soviet officials oppressed traditional religions, separated church and state, and expropriated a great deal of religious property, proclaiming it public. Some churches were demolished, while others were converted into anti-religious museums, or so-called clubs. Christians were persecuted and repressed for their faith. After the collapse of the Soviet Union, however, state policy was transformed and religion returned to public life.

This concept of "return" is a topic of discussion in the academic community. Current research shows that, firstly, the secular did not disappear, but that "the configuration of the religious and secular in society has changed" (Agadjanian 2012, 103).[1] Secondly, using the term "return," one might expect a return of a presecular type of religion, which is obviously not the case. One instead observes "the other type of religion which is themed in a new way" (Agadjanian 2012, 103). Thus, we live in a

postsecular era which doesn't signify desecularization, meaning abolishing the results of secularization and returning to the old times. Revival is not possible, because a situation of post-secularity corresponds to a new socio-cultural situation. The world is not divided into the 'religious' and 'non-religious'—

these spheres are combined; they penetrate each other up to the point of indistinguishability. Now nothing is literally secular or religious; everything can be sacred and everything can be profane. … Religion can be present everywhere together and along with the secular, but not in its old forms. (Kyrlezhev 2004)

To better understand the unique "return" of religion in post-Soviet Russia, it is necessary to go back to the Soviet secular era, in particular to the 1960s, when religion began to be present in the public sphere, but "in a new status, as a part of the Soviet secular—of culture—and in many contexts of the national culture ('national sacred')" (Kormina and Shtyrkov 2015, 14). In 1965, the All-Russian Society for the Protection of Monuments of History and Culture was established to protect objects of cultural heritage, most of which were churches and monasteries. Zhanna Kormina and Sergey Shtyrkov note: "According to the logic of cultural workers, the communication between a Soviet person and former objects of a religious cult should not cause religious sentiments, but rather aesthetic and patriotic ones" (2015, 16). Architects and restorers also took an active part in the protection of cultural heritage, including the Strastnoy Monastery.[2] During that time, religious buildings became tolerated because they were perceived as cultural heritage rather than places for religious rituals.

History of the Place

Since the collapse of the Soviet Union, the Orthodox Church has acquired many religious buildings. This is done in three ways that are uncovered in my research: the first is revival, or the rebuilding of demolished churches or monasteries on their original site; the second is the construction of new churches; and the third is the reclaiming of buildings that formerly belonged to secular organizations. The gradual transfer of church buildings began in 1991, and in 2010, Federal Law 327, which expanded the concept of "religious property" and facilitated the procedure for its transfer, was adopted. "From 2013 to 2017, the state returned 482 objects to religious organizations."[3] However, these three processes (revival, construction, and reclaiming) do not always happen peacefully, especially in big cities, where groups of activists protest against changes to the cityscape or the customary order of things. Thus, in 2017, a group of Saint Petersburg residents protested against transferring the Saint Isaac's Cathedral from the State Russian Museum to the Russian Orthodox Church (Goncharenko 2017). A massive outcry led to the official decision to keep the cathedral a nonreligious building. Another example of a confrontation between the secular and religious was the project to build a new church in the city park of Ekaterinburg (Rainsford 2019). In May 2019, a group of activists successfully campaigned against the project. This case demonstrates one of the popular ways of influencing authorities' claims to change the urban landscape. Citizens did not want to have a church; they wanted to have a park. In postmodern Russia, aside from state authorities, the Church is oftentimes a key actor in the struggle for urban spaces. In this case, the fight for the space played an important role.

In 2005, Muscovites learned of a municipal government investment contract for the reconstruction of the transport infrastructure in Pushkinskaya Square—one of the most famous squares in Moscow. The project included the construction of an underground parking garage and a shopping center at the square. With the support of the All-Russian Society for the Protection of Monuments of History and Culture[4] and other social movements, activists formally requested the preservation of the modern landscape of the square, particularly the foundation of the Strastnoy Monastery and the burial sites of religious nuns located beneath the surface. In 2006, Orthodox believers created the Community of Strastnoy Monastery and began to gather for public prayers at Pushkinskaya Square.[5] They eventually succeeded in preventing the construction of the parking garage and have since continued to hold prayer meetings, their sights set on a more developed agenda.

Today, the members of the community campaign for (1) a revival of the monastery and (2) a restoration of its sacred status. To accomplish the former, they write letters to religious and state authorities and collect signatures, and for the latter, they gather for public prayers, or so-called standings. Every Saturday at 2:00 p.m. as well as on parish feast days, the members of the community read a prayer—Akathist to the Most Holy Theotokos Strastnaya—and perform a sacred procession around the site of the former monastery. In 2012, a commemorative stone was placed in Pushkin Square with the following inscription: "The Strastnoy Monastery by the name of the Most Holy Theotokos Strastnaya Icon stood here. It was founded in 1654 and destroyed in 1937. In memory of the Strastnoy Monastery and the 200th anniversary of the first Divine Liturgy in the name of the liberation of Moscow from Napoleon's army in 1812." While construction was underway at the square, the nuns' burial sites were damaged, prompting the community to gather the remains and make a necropolis on the square. Nonetheless, one of the monastery buildings has managed to survive intact to this day. Formerly the monastery rental house, it has now been converted into an office building. It has not yet been returned to the Orthodox Church, and the community is preparing a lawsuit.

Religion has thus "returned," but as Dmitry Uzlaner rightly argues, "it does not 'return' to an empty space, but to the landscape created by the processes of secularization" (Uzlaner 2013). Indeed, the modern Pushkinskaya Square (the nonofficial center of Moscow, as opposed to the Red Square) is itself a case in point. In 1931, Strastnaya Square, named after the monastery, was rechristened Pushkinskaya; in 1937, Strastnoy Monastery was demolished. In 1950, the monument of Alexander Pushkin located opposite the monastery site was transferred to the empty square and turned 180 degrees, while the "Rossiya" cinema was built in 1961. Thus, was Pushkinskaya Square created—the square that Muscovites born after the 1950s know and love.

Since 2006, a "religioscape" (Hayden 2016) has gradually become visible in the secular landscape of the square. I will use this concept of "religioscape" to refer to material religious objects spread throughout the square. The first of these to appear were several icons and a cross on the wall under the stairs leading to the "Rossiya" cinema. Then, in 2012, the commemorative stone with the small Strastnaya icon[6] was set in the center of the square, behind the Pushkin monument.[7] The monument was itself placed above the burial sites, while two Orthodox baptismal crosses were recently attached to a tree where a commemorative chapel is to be constructed.

Methods

This study draws on qualitative data collected from members of the Strastnoy community, but also from other Muscovites or stakeholders who use the square. Since 2016, I have participated in numerous prayer meetings and other activities, such as gatherings of community activists and postprayer standing tea parties. In addition, I have had informal meetings with certain participants and have visited other events devoted to (or organized at) Pushkinskaya Square. For instance, "Pushkinskaya Square which we didn't lose" was a meeting with contemporary Russian poet and public activist Lev Rubinstein, Russian journalist Tatyana Malkina, and an anti-Putin political activist. The discussion was dedicated to the events of Perestroika, most of which were held on Pushkinskaya Square. According to Rubinstein, "At that time, Pushkinskaya Square became such a place of free speech, action, [and] expression." Furthermore, I have observed contemporary political rallies that have taken place on the square.

Along with my ethnography, I have conducted and recorded in-depth interviews throughout the research period. These interviews have focused on different issues: the organization of the Strastnoy community, its goals and internal relationships, and the history of the monastery and of the movement. (Most talks have been recorded over tea.) Moreover, I have joined the Strastnoy Monastery group in the Russian social network "VKontakte" as well as a group chat in WhatsApp, where members discuss not only problems with the monastery but also issues of Orthodox life. Finally, I have used information from media and social networks.

Using different methods has afforded me a deeper understanding of those people who come to a group vigil only once and remain in the community for a long time; it has helped me to learn about the participants' aspirations. Participating in prayer meetings and sacred processions—rather than merely observing them—has allowed me to share the embodied experience with my informants. Furthermore, studying both the religious community and other groups for whom Pushkinskaya Square is an important place has helped me maintain a research balance, taking arguments from all actors into account.

The Religious Community on the Public Square

In pre-Revolution Russia, the main unit of church socialization was the parish, formed within the community of a church. However, contemporary parishes are often formed differently (not only around the church but also around the priest, among other ways), calling for an analysis that involves the specificity of the postsecular time in which they have been established or developed.

The Strastnoy Monastery community formed around a place—Pushkinskaya Square—where the Strastnoy Monastery stood until 1937. Among the members of the movement "For the Revival of Strastnoy," there is a common phrase, "to go to Strastnoy" or "to be on Strastnoy," which means to participate in a prayer meeting at Pushkinskaya Square next to the commemorative stone. The community is officially registered; it has its own website where current information is posted about upcoming events, the history of the monastery, plans for revival, and so on. There is also a community on the social network "VKontakte" which features posts on prayer meetings with pictures and the priest's sermon amid the advertisements. The community is under the pastoral care of Orthodox priest Aleksii Gomonov, from the neighboring church of the Assumption of Our Lady in Putinki. However, he is not a unifying leader, meaning that the community members would just as readily gather under the leadership of any other priest. In fact, the community has secular leadership. From the start, there have been three leaders who, while not elected by members of the organization, were recommended to assume this position by the priest.

A community leader has several public functions: to represent the community at various events, to send out letters to state institutions, and, most importantly, to organize prayer meetings, notifying members and leading meetings when the priest is absent. Father Aleksii usually leads meetings during parish (*prestol'nye*) feasts,[8] but on Saturdays, the community leader presides over meetings. It is also important to mention a special ritual—the communal reading of the akathist, when all participants take turns reading the text aloud. Indeed, even during a visitor's first experience with Strastnoy, one becomes a full-time participant. New participants receive an akathist text and are welcomed to pray along with others. There is thus nobody left who is not praying. Participants pray together, thus implementing Sobornost', a phenomenon analyzed by Alexandr Agadjanian based on the example of two other urban Orthodox subcultures (Agadjanian 2011).

After reading the akathist, participants embark on a sacred procession around the former territory of the monastery. The procession itself is organized as follows: the men walk first, carrying a "For the Revival of Strastnoy Monastery" poster; the women walk behind them, many holding icons or wearing them around their necks. During the procession, participants constantly sing the "Hail Mary" prayer, or "Christ is risen" if the procession takes place right after Easter. An additional unifying act is the remembrance of the dead of Strastnoy Monastery, which takes place next to the burial sites at Pushkinskaya Square. Among the dead are religious nuns executed during the Soviet era (so-called New Martyrs) and contemporary participants, including Roman Tsekhanskii, architect and author of the revival project.

The final episode of the procession is a sermon if a priest is present, or, if not, a speech from a community leader. The priest always connects the day of the saint whose akathist is read with the circumstances around the monastery, or with the current struggle for its revival. The community leader usually discusses current affairs concerning the revival. Afterward, there is a community fellowship gathering. If it is a parish feast, everyone proceeds to the church cafeteria for tea and the exchange of news. The most popular form of fellowship involves stories about Orthodox miracles. On Saturdays, the fellowship gathering usually takes place right on the square. Participants exchange stories about their pilgrimages, the revival of other churches, and so on.

How do people learn about prayer meetings, and who attends them? As I have already mentioned, this community is not equivalent to a parish. Not everyone attends services at the Assumption of Our Lady in Putinki, meaning that "the Eucharist [is not] the central moment of the mystical unity of [the] religious group" (Breskaya 2011, 217) as happens in parishes. Father Aleksii is not a patron (*duhovnik*) of everyone who comes to the prayer meetings. On Saturdays, most of the participants do not even enter the church, and fellowship gatherings only take place on Pushkinskaya Square. Orthodox believers learn about these prayer meetings from their friends. An example of a typical story is: "One friend from my church told me that on Saturdays they prayed here, so I came and stayed." Sometimes passersby join in the prayer during a standing, returning regularly thereafter. At present, the core of the community consists of fifteen to twenty people. The largest number of people that I have observed congregates for the Strastnaya icon feast on August 26 of every year; in 2019, there were about 100 people assembled. Sometimes only two to three people participate in the Saturday group vigil.

Most of the participants are over forty years old. About ten young people come to pray occasionally. They find out about the prayer meeting from the priest due to their involvement in the Orthodox youth club "Peter and Fevronia," hosted by the church of the Assumption of Our Lady in Putinki. The gender distribution, both in the core of the community and in its expanded membership, is about two women for every man. The main reason why people stay—or leave and cannot come back for some time—is the supposed power of this place, or its nontrivial essence. One of my interlocutors explained to me that he had not come to Strastnoy for a long time because after the prayers, he felt physically sick. Many people face various temptations, but the ultimate goal for every community member is to cope with hardships and continue praying for the monastery.

The difference between the Strastnoy community and other forms of religious sociality is the fact that the members act in a space that does not belong to them fully. The community sits on the boundary between the secular and the religious world, acting on a presumably secular territory. Its members must interact with outsiders during prayer meetings, engage them to participate, or narrate the history of the place and the movement, performing a public function. This additional crucial detail, which only emerges due to historical shifts such as those of the Soviet era, is a trait of contemporary postsecular time.

The Pushkin Monument in the Religioscape of the Square and the Narratives of the Community

The main goal of the community is the revival of the monastery, and one of the first steps toward this is the construction of a bell tower where the monument of Pushkin currently stands. The monument, according to the community members, should be moved back to its original place. As I mentioned at the beginning of this chapter, the Pushkin monument was only transferred to the square in 1950; from 1880 until then, it had been located on Tverskoy Boulevard. Therefore, in the context of the myriad stories told by community members, narratives involving the Pushkin monument occupy a special place. I am mainly interested in why these narratives spread through the community, why people share them, and how community members interact with their environment and society.

The Pushkin monument is the main marker of the square—the main attraction and symbol. For example, on December 5, 1965, dissidents organized a protest at Pushkinskaya Square, the first ever public political demonstration in the postwar Soviet Union. It was organized in support of writers Andrei Sinyavsky and Yuli Daniel. The dissidents continued to assemble at the square every year, first on December 5 (Soviet Constitution Day) and then on December 10 (Human Rights Day). In contemporary Russia, anti-censorship rallies are organized in this same place—Pushkinskaya Square—with the monument of Pushkin pictured on the posters.[9]

Undoubtedly, the generations of citizens born in the 1950s and later are accustomed to this location for the monument. Pushkinskaya Square, and the monument in particular, has been a common and important meeting place for local youth for decades. For many of my interlocutors, Pushkinskaya Square is an integral part of Soviet history in Moscow, linked to the private memories of many Muscovites and deserving to be preserved. However, it is important to note that the Pushkin monument was a popular spot for assemblies, friends, and lovers to meet even before it was moved—when it was still on Tverskoy Boulevard. In the 1920s, there was a couplet that reflected this:

Na Tverbule u Pampusha
Zhdet menia milenok Grusha.
(Chukovskii 1962)

(On the Tverbule [Tverskoy Boulevard],
next to the MonPush [monument of Pushkin]
My lover Grusha is waiting for me [the names are merged together])
(translation into English by N. N. Rychkova)

Recently, in a Facebook group called "About you and about Moscow," a discussion about the Pushkin monument, its "authentic" location, and this couplet took place. One of the users posted a picture of the place where the monument was formerly located and added a caption: "On the Tver[skoy]boul[evard], next to the pam[yatnik—monument] of Push[kin]." The post gathered 195 comments. Muscovites were divided over the name, the monument, and Tverskoy Boulevard. Some said the post showed exactly how one could recognize a Muscovite, while others replied that only a migrant could distort the language so badly. However, I am much more interested in some of the other comments, which discussed the absence of the Pushkin monument in its former place: "This is not the place anymore, this is now 'On Tverskoy boulevard WITHOUT the monument of Pushkin.' Pushkin has not been on Tverskoy Boulevard since August 14, 1950 (oh, August!)" (Facebook user). One commenter posted a popularized view of Strastnoy Monastery and the monument of Pushkin from the side of Tverskoy Boulevard, demonstrating how the square once looked. Without a doubt, older generations of Muscovites, who remember Pushkin on Tverskoy, see the monument's current location as illegitimate. Their attitude to the relocation is poetically expressed in the Valentin Kataev book, *My Diamond Crown*:

> For the people of my generation, there are two monuments of Pushkin. Both identical Pushkins are placed across from each other, separated by the noisy square, streams of automobiles, traffic lights, and police officers. One of the Pushkins is ghostly. He stands in his original, legitimate place, but only the old Muscovites can see him. For the others he is invisible. In the unfilled emptiness of the beginning of Tverskoy Boulevard they see a real Pushkin, surrounded by lights and a bronze chain. And today's Pushkin for me is just a ghost. (Kataev 1978)

The most important word in this quote is "invisible," which defines the whole space of Pushkinskaya Square. The space of Pushkinskaya Square is heterogeneous; there is visible and invisible in it. The former is available to all, yet unreal. The latter is available to some—"legitimate," "authentic"—and maintained through memories only.

Here I must step back for a moment and return to 1937, which was a pivotal year both for the monastery and for Pushkin. In 1937, the Soviet government organized an event for the centennial of Pushkin's death. The reasons for the Soviet establishment's veneration of Pushkin are discussed in a book by Jonathan Platt, entitled *Greetings, Pushkin!: Stalinist Cultural Politics and the Russian National Bard* (Platt 2016). The centennial was a huge campaign involving all Soviet citizens; the Pushkin memorial days were held in all places, from big cities to distant villages. On February 10, 1937, there was a demonstration in Moscow next to the Pushkin monument. Video footage from that day shows that Pushkin could be seen at the very place where he would eventually be relocated in 1950: a huge poster of his likeness was hung on the bell tower of Strastnoy Monastery. The process of the symbolic substitution of religion with education and secular culture (and Pushkin's works in particular) had begun. This is illustrated in a chastushka (small Russian folk song) which, as Aleksander Panchenko (2011) states, could be performed during commemorations in the Pushkin Museum:

> Otkatilsia ot derevni
> Zvon otvergnutykh tserkvei,
> My teper' no voskresen'iam
> Khodim v Pushkinskii muzei.
> (Panchenko 2011, 406)
> (The bells of rejected churches
> Have left a village
> Nowadays, on Sundays
> We visit the Pushkin Museum)
> (translation into English by N. N. Rychkova)

As Panchenko (2011) points out, this chastushka reflected the issues "discussed during the meetings and conferences of 'rural Pushkinists'" (406). A simple idea remained, propagated by the Soviet government: to fight religious superstitions by means of enlightenment and universal literacy. This could be achieved, for instance, by reading the works of Pushkin, a national poet. In this respect, the positioning of a poster of Pushkin on the bell tower of Strastnoy can be interpreted as a victory of the Soviet over the religious. It is worth mentioning that the most common use of repurposed church buildings during the Soviet era was as cultural centers. Today, this idea of substituting religion with culture is often discussed among the members of the community:

> The Soviet power, it exchanged faith for culture. It is always said, Pushkin's poetry, it's the breath of God, breath of God. He wrote it with inspiration that came from God … He's a minister of the word, and who is our God? Logos, the Word, and Pushkin is a minister of the word. His poetry supported those Soviet kids … And his poetry unveiled cherubs, seraphim—this is very interesting. Hence, Pushkin is here for a reason. Some say he's here as a sacrilege (woman in the community, about fifty years old). (recorded by N. N. Rychkova, 2016)

Pushkin's poetry appears to be a guide to the world of religious symbols; it protects and might even be compared to prayers. Hence, Pushkin's location up until this time—a time when order can be restored—is the best thing that could have happened to the square. In some texts, he is a guardian of this place. He is present for a reason, for he is a kind of minister for God, as some community members understand him:

> The monument of Pushkin, as it may appear, sacrilegiously occupies the place of a church ... of Aleksey, the Man of God. At the same time, it has served as a guardian. In the darkest period, in 1950, it was moved on rails during the night, surrounded by the NKVD forces. [The square] was preserved from the enormous projects which were repeatedly published in the newspaper—they were supposed to take the Strastnoy Monastery's place. Pushkin didn't allow these projects to happen. As a matter of fact, these days we never drop the idea of returning the monument of Pushkin back to its original place [, nor the importance of] his proper orientation in a prayer posture facing the east (former leader of the community, about sixty years old). (recorded by N. N. Rychkova 2018)

Another important detail that this former community leader has mentioned, as quoted above, is the correct orientation of the monument, which should face east. East and west here are not just cardinal directions, but a representation of cultures. The leader's statement reflects the ideas of many Orthodox believers about a hostile Western world "which deviated from true Christianity" and has harmed the Russian people "by imposing on them a foolish culture of mass consumption, intentional corruption, propaganda of premarital ties and abortions" (Akhmetova 2010, 179). Symbols of Western culture on the square include, on the one hand, a musical theater (see more in the next sections), where, according to community members, Western musicals are shown. On the other hand, there is a McDonald's restaurant, which is now seemingly worshiped by the great Russian poet.

> This monument—it's Opekushin[10] [the sculptor] who won the competition against some strong opponents, and his winning idea was a monument of Pushkin. He [the statue] used to bow to Strastnoy in a praying pose, and now ... The authorship of that sculptor has been apparently violated, and he's now bowing to McDonald's (woman in the community, about forty-five years old). (recorded by N. N. Rychkova, 2017)

This kind of reference to the name of Opekushin and violation of authorship is one more way to achieve the relocation of the monument to its original place. For this purpose, community members sent a letter to the sculptor's granddaughter, asking her to support their initiative. In the letter, they emphasized not only the corruption of the artistic imagery, but also the sacrilegious treatment of the holy place. The letter concluded by stressing the necessity of the revival of moral and historical justice in respect to the monument of Pushkin. Here, the letter's authors emphasized one last reason for the relocation of the monument: to pay respect to the sculptor's authorship rights.

The Strastnoy community thus uses the following narratives to justify displacing the Pushkin monument from their sacred place: (1) Pushkin is a praying devotee, a guardian of the square. He has now fulfilled his mission. (2) Pushkin himself represents old Moscow. He should be put back in his original place, which is empty without him; Moscow does not seem the same otherwise. (3) Pushkin is the creation of Opekushin, who intended for him to face east. He should be returned to his original place and position out of respect for the authorship rights of the great sculptor.

Though not yet achieving the desired displacement, these narratives involve actional practices of displacement. The first one is the symbolic relocation of the monument of Pushkin to its historical place, with a sign stating, "Here is the place of the monument of Pushkin" on Tverskoy Boulevard. On the website of the Strastnoy community, there is a picture posted with the caption: "Muscovites react to the empty place where the Pushkin monument originally stood." In the photo, former community leader plays the role of "a Muscovite."

However, as suggested above, only a portion of older Muscovites really believe that Pushkin occupies the wrong place. For others, modern Pushkinskaya Square—complete with the Pushkin monument—is a significant place. As a case in point, during the event "Pushkinskaya Square that we didn't lose," poet Lev Rubinstein called Pushkinskaya Square the center of the street, a nonofficial city center, and a place of power. This meeting, where attendees shared their memories about historical events, illustrated one last feature of Pushkinskaya Square's past: the history of social and political movements. Muscovites present there did not support the idea of the revival of the monastery nor the moving of the monument of Pushkin to its original place, favoring instead a more measured approach. As expressed by Rubinstein: "My parents met at the monument of Pushkin, which was on the boulevard. Tverbul, it was called. At Pampush. And I grew up, therefore, next to a different monument. That is, at the same monument, but in a different place. And this is all very interesting, it needs to be known and written about." To preserve memory about events, as Rubinstein suggested, it is necessary to convert the private memory of people into the memory of culture through books, commemorative signs, and so on (Assman 2018). The idea of preserving memory is popular among the members of the Strastnoy community, but there is a difference between restoring the landscape of the presecular era and preserving a historically established place.

One more practice of displacement exercised by the Strastnoy community is a prayer meeting held on the feast of Saint Aleksey, the Man of God, at an altar (*prestol*) right in front of the Pushkin monument. This new location for the prayer meeting first appeared in 2019; in 2017 and even in 2018, the meeting was still held in front of the commemorative stone. This new placement of the saint's icon next to the Pushkin monument serves as a displacement, however temporary, of a secular (or rather, Soviet) monument with a religious symbol.

To elucidate, this action indicates a scheme of symbolic displacement over time, reflecting the struggle over Pushkinskaya Square. When it occupied the square, Strastnoy Monastery was an instrument of religiosity; then, in 1937, a portrait of Pushkin was posted on the bell tower of Aleksey, the Man of God. That action was a displacement of religiosity, and the demolition of the bell tower followed by the erection of the monument of Pushkin became the sign of the establishment of secularity. Organizing the prayer meeting next to the monument and placing the icon of Aleksey, the Man of God in front of Pushkin could be considered the displacement of secularity. Likewise, should the monument of Pushkin be relocated and the monastery revived—or the bell tower reconstructed, at least—it will probably be considered the establishment of religiosity. Thus, that place will become visible as holy again.

The Cinema and Religion

The second symbol of the secularscape (and Western culture) on the square is the "Rossiya" cinema (now converted into a musical theater). According to the narratives of the community members, the altar of Strastnaya church was located exactly where the stairs leading to the cinema are now. This fact is the reason why, in the first years, the prayer meetings were held there.

The biggest event that takes place at the cinema is the Moscow International Film Festival. During this festival, the stairs are covered with a red carpet, ready to receive theater and film personalities, but the square only remains available for certain groups of people. The days of the festival comprise the only period when the religious community (among other groups) sense the presence of state authorities exercising "sociospatial exclusion" (Low 2014, 24) (limitation of entry to the square), demonstrating who really owns the place.[11] Authorities coordinate all activity on the square. As one of my interlocutors told me, in 2019, the community was requested to remove the wooden cross located on their necropolis. The community leader stated:

The cross was located on the square. [And why was it removed?] Because this year, when the film festival took place, it was opening, and someone complained that the whole area was seized by priests. They, well, we showed them the documents. And they removed the cross, because we had no documents for the cross, of course. [And who requested that?] The authorities. [And who exactly?] It does not matter. That is, the people who officially oversee this space (current leader/man in the community, about fifty years old). (recorded by N. N. Rychkova, 2019)

Different groups have their own perspectives on how the square should look during certain events. The Strastnoy commemorative stone and the necropolis monument are already built into the architectural ensemble of Pushkinskaya Square and have legal grounds to be situated there. However, a variety of unofficial additions—such as a cross and wooden chapel which stood next to the necropolis for some time—have been outlawed and removed at the request of the authorities, as suggested by the above quote (see also Martínez-Ariño 2019).

It is interesting to note that community members regard the film festival and musical theater performances as blasphemous in relation to the sacred place. Indeed, the "blasphemy" of the Pushkin monument standing near the community's altar and the blasphemous performances occurring on the other side of the altar represent radically different value systems. The monument of Pushkin is viewed as a temporary guardian of that place, while the theater and festival are its defilers.

However, since humility is one of the main tenets of Orthodox Christianity, members of the community try not to allow themselves harsh judgments. The notions of humility[12] and permanent prayer purification of the place are almost always present in the speeches of the priest after each prayer meeting. In his opinion, the peculiarity of holy places attracts both God and Satan. The main aim of the community is to pray there in order to achieve the eventual construction of a chapel, and to maintain the purity and the holiness of the place. The monument of Pushkin has seemingly defended the square from new buildings, while the envisioned chapel can protect from profanation. An invisible monastery, imagined during the standing, can become real only when the holy place, which is currently too filthy, is cleansed by prayer. Once this has been achieved, all people—not only the community—will understand the need for the monastery.

This cleansing through prayer is not necessarily well received, however. Despite governmental support from the Russian Orthodox Church, many grassroots initiatives organized by Orthodox communities are not supported by the city dwellers and are sometimes even ridiculed. It also happens vis-à-vis the activities of the Strastnoy Monastery community. Members of the community appear as a marginalized group or, according to Michel de Certeau, a "weak" group. This is expressed in the community members' narratives and in reactions from other groups:

> I say to the director [of one of the companies]: "Well, you deal with deputies, well, you need to close [this square]—innocent children are dancing, they are dying, they do not know that this is a terrible place." And he says to me, "People laugh at you." And I say, "Why?" And he says, "Because you hold sacred processions" (woman in the community, born in 1965). (recorded by N. N. Rychkova, 2017)

To complement the above, I present a fragment of one of the priest's speeches. In this particular speech, he discussed the plan to build the chapel and compared this with a typical prayer meeting: "It was one thing when laughable grandmothers, aunts, and uncles with bells in their hands stood quietly somewhere and said something there; they did something incomprehensible."

In both of these quotes, members of the community reproduce the attitude of ordinary people, of outsiders. In both quotes, they use derivatives of the word "laugh," highlighting their marginal status. A review of posts on social media confirms their marginality; for example, one Facebook photo that shows kneeling members of the community has a string of sarcastic comments from users. As suggested by the comments, people are aware of what is going on in the square; however, they use the word "sect" to designate members of the community. This emphasizes the community's marginal status, even in everyday religious discourse, because a sect is always opposed to the official religion.

Conclusion

Currently, the topography of postmodern cities is becoming more secular and more religious at the same time. It is easy to see that new churches, mosques, and synagogues are being built next to business centers made of glass and concrete. However, in addition to these separate buildings, one can also see the coexistence of the secular and religious in one place. For example, in Moscow, chapels and mosques are organized inside airports and railway stations. Religious publicity can also be seen throughout the Russian capital—in new Orthodox monuments, on commemorative plaques on buildings where churches once stood, on billboards during Orthodox holidays, in the streets and squares during religious rituals. However, the public manifestation of religion in a country where only 53 percent consider themselves religious (Kochergina 2017) is met with disapproval, condemnation and, in some cases, active protests. Thus, some places are owned neither by secular nor by religious groups.

My research shows that Pushkinskaya Square in Moscow is one of these "shared" spaces, identified as a unique place by the groups that claim rights to it. For secular people, the square's peculiarity is expressed in its specific energy, which attracts people; for religious Muscovites, this peculiarity is expressed in the idea of the sacredness of the place, which has been achieved through prayer.[13] Currently, the square serves primarily as a place for walking, meetings, rallies, and major city events. However, the Strastnoy Monastery community continues to hold prayer meetings at this place, thus attempting to return the square to the function it performed in the presecular era. Thus, the landscape of the square functions differently in the memories of different groups. In that respect, the case I have presented is not unique. Places and spaces that have changed their affiliation (see also Said 2000) have colorful histories. Certain events from these histories are carefully selected by one group or another to suit its purposes.

Hence, Pushkinskaya Square has two spaces: a secular, visible, and constant space and a religious, invisible, and fragmented space (see also Saint-Blancat and Cancellieri 2014). The main goal of the Strastnoy Monastery community is to make this sacred space visible to everyone.

Festivals of Religions and Religious Festivals: Heritigized Heterotopias

Alberta Giorgi
University of Bergamo

Maria Chiara Giorda
University of Roma Tre

In this chapter we explore the religious in the city from the perspective of festivals.[1] Religious festivals include activities ranging from traditional ritual celebrations to markets with religious gadgets. Unpacking the notion of religious festivals, we focus in particular on what we identify as "festivals of religions," by which we mean events during which religions are put on display. In what follows, we make a case for the relevance of this category in the study of contemporary forms of urban religion, in between the religious and the secular. Like many other forms of religion in the city, festivals of religions contribute to disseminating information about religions, and they are likely to enhance sensitivity toward religious diversity by promoting knowledge, discussions, and encounters. At the same time, we argue that they may have desacralizing and culturalizing effects.

Religious celebrations are powerful performances that bring sacredness to ritual gatherings. During religious festivals, the ritual power of celebrations increases, as the connection with the divine and the extraordinary is enacted in special times and places. On the other hand, festivals of religions encourage familiarization with otherness, seeking to downplay what may be perceived as extraordinary; instead of exceptional, religions in festivals of religions are interconnected with everyday life. In addition, while religious festivals focus on one religious tradition and are organized by religious institutions, festivals of religions are usually promoted by secular organizations.

Drawing on the case of Italy, we explore the different forms of festivals, illustrating possible classificatory dimensions. To account for different types of initiatives and events, our research involved an exploratory analysis. First, we inductively constructed a typology by drawing on a critical review of the literature on festivals and on exemplary and well-known cases. We circumscribed our research to one specific national case study, to reduce complexity and increase its completeness. We also explored the websites of well-known festivals of religions to check whether they mentioned other festivals or similar initiatives. Second, we selected the cases through theory-based purposeful sampling (Patton 2002). Finally, we fine-tuned the typology by adopting the twofold strategy of saturation and confirmation (or disconfirmation; Emmel 2014). More specifically, once we identified the possible classificatory dimensions and drafted the typology, we adopted a threefold strategy to test its validity: (1) we explored the national websites of religious traditions and interfaith associations; (2) we searched the archive of the nonpartisan newspaper *La Repubblica*, considering both national and local editions; and (3) we submitted our analysis to key witnesses and experts for confirmation.

The next section of this chapter situates our analysis in the literature on urban religions, while section three provides a brief overview of the literature on religious festivals and explores the conceptual meaning of "festivals of religions." The fourth section details the exploratory case study of Italy and proposes a framework for analysis, while in the last section we explore the implications for the analysis of religions and the city.

Religions and the City

The role of religion in cities is increasingly garnering attention. Enshrined in the Western narrative of entanglements between secularism and modernity (Wohlrab-Sahr and Burchardt 2012), the idea of the "secular city" has begun to lose ground. Research has indicated how religions thrive in urban environments in both the Global North and South, and how they shape—and are shaped by—urban dynamics, local and trans-local dynamics, culture, materiality, location, and mobility (Garbin and Strhan 2017). As Maria Chiara Giorda points out, "Scholars have begun to account for the ways religion is becoming an 'urban way of life' [...] Recent research in urban sociology and geography has also revealed the complicated coexistence of gods, religions, and beliefs in the city" (Giorda 2019, 12).

In other words, rather than looking at religion *in* the city, scholars have largely shifted their focus to religion *and* the city. Jörg Rüpke has explored the co-constitution of religion and urbanity by emphasizing their complex interlocking relationship (Rüpke 2020). Drawing on the definition advanced by anthropologist Stephan Lanz, Rüpke focuses on urban religion as "a specific element of urbanisation and urban everyday life … intertwined with … urban lifestyles and imaginaries, infrastructure and materialities, cultures, politics and economies, forms of living and working, community formation, festivals and celebrations […] a continual process in which the urban and the religious reciprocally interact, mutually interlace, producing, transforming and defining each other" (Lanz 2014, 25 quoted by Rüpke 2020, 3). Scholars working on this relationship mainly focus on the governance of religious diversity (Burchardt 2019; Griera et al. 2018; Martínez-Ariño 2017), space and the "spatialization of religion" (Becci et al. 2013; Hervieu-Léger 2002; Knott 2005), and religious visibility in the public sphere, particularly regarding minority and/or migrant religions (Burchardt et al. 2018; Garbin 2013; Giorgi 2019a; Göle 2011). Research focusing on places of worship shows the complex entanglements of visibility and spatialization (Brighenti 2010; Burchardt and Griera 2018). Tackling aesthetics, architecture, and infrastructure, "visibility" touches the socio-technical and material life of cities (Burchardt and Höhne 2015).

In Southern European cities, the visibility of non-Christian religions and the location of their places of worship are directly related to public and political recognition—the more accepted a religious group, the more central and visible its place of worship is. Prominent debates around purpose-built mosques in Europe are clear examples of this entanglement of visibility, reputation, and localization. To avoid polarized public debates, less accepted religious groups therefore have two options: either they locate their places of worship in the peripheries (or outskirts) of the city, or they can downplay their visibility.

In this context, public religious events concerning religion (such as public rituals, prayers, or festivals), generally being formal and institutionalized, offer minority groups visibility in urban spaces, ranging from publicly accessible indoor sites to outdoor locations to the entire city (see Garbin 2012b). Public religious performances have been interpreted as practices of temporary sacralization of urban spaces that blur the boundaries between secular, religious, and cultural spheres, in a Durkheimian perspective, between the secular and the sacred (Burchardt 2017), and between the local and the global (Saint-Blancat and Cancellieri 2014). Through public events, invisible religious minorities can make their voices heard, even if only at a specifically delimited place and time. They can temporarily transform their invisibility into visibility; in this sense, visibility refers to both the spatial and temporal dimensions.

Practices that increase religious visibility are politically significant. Generally speaking, the visibility of minority religions in European discourse has been paralleled by the visibility of Muslim migration in European cities (Bader 2009; Berger et al. 2008). What may be perceived as radical alterity (Modood 2013; Scott 2018; Selby and Beaman 2016) has prompted a broader debate about community, identity, and borders, in which religion "has been transformed into a dispositive of familiarity and otherness" (Giorgi 2019b, 15; see also Brubaker 2017; Marzouki et al. 2016). This mobilization of religion in terms of identity within political discourse is tied to the broader "cultural turn" of religion, according to which religious aspects related to community, values, and tradition are more relevant than faith, practices, and doctrine (for a discussion see Beaman 2013, 2020). Public religious performances are also intertwined with the dynamics of "eventization," branding, and, "heritagization" of the sacred (Astor et al. 2017; Pfadenhauer 2010). Kim Knott et al. (2016), for example, show how religious displays in the form of public celebrations and events contribute to cities' branding and consumer culture.

On the one hand, festivals of religions are a form of public expression for religions. Therefore, they make religions visible in and to the city, informally legitimizing their presence in the urban environment, which is especially important for religions that are usually invisible. On the other hand, the spatialization and temporality of festivals alter the temporality and spatiality of ordinary life, creating "a state of exception" (for an example using analysis of music festivals see Luckman 2014). Thus, festivals of religions can also be seen as having invisibilizing effects, making minority religions something fascinating but outside of everyday life.

Festivals and Religion

Sociological research has explored festivals with a focus on various dimensions. Research ranges from analyses of the economic and cultural impacts of festivals on host communities (Crespi-Vallbona and Richards 2007; Sassatelli 2015; Derrett 2003) to investigations into their role in consumer culture (Bennett et al. 2014). Two strands of literature are particularly relevant to our analysis, as they offer useful insights into conceptualizing contemporary festivals of religions.

One strand of research focuses on cosmopolitanism and analyzes festivals as events that enable encounters among various cultures (Sassatelli 2018) while also underlining the risks of domesticized representations of alterity and cultural appropriation (Goldstein-Gidoni 2003). From this perspective, events such as festivals of religions can be framed and analyzed as examples of the "culturalization" of religion (i.e., initiatives that showcase and domesticate religious differences). The second strand of literature focuses on festivals as heterotopias (Foucault 1998, 2000) or contexts that alter ordinary spatiality and temporality (Ciancimino 2018). Festivals are intrinsically ubiquitous experiences, situated at the same time here and elsewhere and connected to multiple temporalities (especially considering the role of technology in modern festivals). This character of liminality (Turner 1982a) appears to be particularly relevant in the case of those festivals involving religions, which are inherently otherworldly, connecting different realities and locations. Religious rituals enable time out of ordinary time and ritual time (Turner 1982b) as well as exceptional spaces (de-localization and re-localization), offering the experience of an encounter between human and other-than-human beings (Ciancimino 2018, 5; see also Gardiner 1993; Ingold 2000). In this sense, religious festivals amplify the collective experience generated by religious rituals through which the sacred is enacted and conveyed, in a Durkheimian perspective.

Indeed, analyses that observe the relationships between festivals and religion usually adopt a Durkheimian perspective, focusing on the ritual element. Catherine Bell, for example, identifies six categories of ritual actions: rites of passage ("life-crisis" or "life-cycle" rituals), calendrical and commemorative rites, rites of exchange and communion, rites of affliction, political rituals, and rites of feasting, fasting, and festivals (Bell 1997, 91). This last category includes public ceremonies aimed at building and enhancing a sense of community through the public expression of religiocultural elements and values (Bell 1997, 118–26). Bell references Ramadan, the ritual of potlatch, carnivals, and pilgrimages (on carnival see Testa 2014, 2020). In her discussion, the precise definition of festival is unclear. "Religious festival" is indeed a broad term that may include various types of public religious celebrations. In general, religious festivals are included in the larger category of "religious feasts"; complex and multilayered research and debate reveal the blurring borders between religious, traditional, and popular feasts. Natale Spineto, one of the main experts in the field, outlines the difficulties of classification (Spineto 2015, 15–44). He points out that all public festivities have religious and sacred historical roots and demonstrates the complex overlapping of categories. Religious feasts in Europe include festivities institutionalized in the secular calendar (bank holidays like Christmas, for example), feasts from the Christian liturgical calendar, and traditional local feasts, which often bear traces of pre-Christian spirituality and pagan rituals. These categories show significant overlap, and there is also overlap and intersection between traditional nonreligious feasts and nontraditional/nonreligious local feasts (Spineto 2015, 20). Spineto includes festivals in the broad category of secular feasts (Spineto 2015, 18). Secular feasts are public events that are usually open to everyone; most of them (such as sport events, Halloween, or Saint Valentine's Day) are not characterized by civic or community value, but, on the contrary, by consumer culture.

From its original meaning of musical and popular feasts dating back to the 1930s, the word "festival" typically indicates artistic exhibitions (such as music, theater, or movie festivals), sometimes involving competitions (Spineto 2015, 85). Over the years, the element of competition has lost its relevance as a classificatory dimension and festival themes have diversified, encompassing numerous initiatives and events all around the world (Ciancimino 2018). Contemporary festivals can be interpreted as public events populated by spectators ranging from insiders to curious people. From this perspective, festivals of religions can be framed as secular and cultural initiatives which are related to religions without being religious celebrations; the audience is not composed solely of religious insiders and there are no sacred ceremonies. In this sense, festivals of religions are different from both religious festivals and secular festivities. We argue that the analytical distinction is vital for conceptual clarity and a better understanding of the role of religion in modern cities.

Generally speaking, however, festivals of religions can be interpreted as both public and secular performances of the sacred—they put on display what is collectively recognized and acknowledged as "religion." In this context, festivals of religions contribute to the public and secular discourse of what religion is— and which forms of religion are commonly accepted—by producing discourses on how religion is lived and experienced, and selecting what is worth knowing (and displaying and promoting) about religions, religious diversity, and spirituality.

Festivals of Religions in Italy: A Typology

Combining Spineto's analysis with the literature on religion and cities, we can identify three types of festivals related to religion (festivals of religions) by considering the organizers, location, aim, and scope of initiatives as illustrated in Table 5.1. In reality, of course, lines may be blurred and categories may overlap; nonetheless, the typology we propose has proven extremely useful for the analysis of religions and the city because it sheds light on the complex and contradictory dynamics of sacralization and secularization that are at play.

The first type comprises public celebrations organized for religious festivities. This is the case, for example, for Easter public processions and Christmas Nativity scene competitions. These "festivals" are usually organized by institutionally recognized religious communities, often with the recognition and support of local and national institutions (Griera and Burchardt 2020, Burchardt and Griera, 2020). They are usually located in the city center and, while locally organized, are typically characterized by a large scope, addressing the entire community of believers beyond local particularism. Religious parades (*le processioni*) held to celebrate saints combine religious traditions with urban dimensions of life. From *Santa Rita* in Turin to *Madonna del Rosario* in Palermo, local Catholic institutions and communities officially organize, each year, marches through the streets, usually in the vicinity of the church, that are characterized by praying and singing. In recent years, the diverse identities of Italian cities have been marked by a growing number of parades and festivals organized by Catholics who are also ethnic minorities. This is the case, for example, of the parade for the *Madonna delle Rose,* which is organized by the Catholic Filipino community in Turin and takes place both inside and outside the church in the neighborhood of San Salvario, with cars set up with images, sacred objects, and prayers.

The second type involves community festivals, pagan, and spiritual events, and initiatives aimed at celebrating nature (Becci 2020; Palmisano and Pannofino 2020). Contemporary festivals in Italy are usually fairly small and local in scope. One of the most recent overviews about *"feste," "sagre"* feasts, and festivals related to religions in Italy is Ciancimino's *Food, Festival and Religion: Materiality and Place in Italy* (2018), which considers the role of food and nature in these events. In the introduction, the author asserts:

> There are hundreds of festivals in Italy each year, throughout the twenty regions along Italy's long peninsula and extending to the large islands of Sardinia and Sicily [...] in communities that maintain traditions, folklore and lived religion through intriguing forms of place-based materiality. (Ciancimino 2018, XI)

In her ethnographic exploration of local festivals in Piedmont and Lombardy (northern Italy), Ciancimino points out the performative and ritualistic role of community festivals that "celebrate place, lived religious tradition and home" (Ciancimino 2018, 57). These events take place in rural areas and their organizers are usually hybrid committees that include spiritual groups, officially recognized religious institutions, marginalized religious actors, local associations, and public actors. Examples include the festivals organized by Ossian d'Ambrosio and Maria

Feo, a couple leading the Druid community in northern Italy: the *Festa Celtica di Beltane* (held in May) and two smaller events at the Autumnal Equinox and Samhain (end of October). They have created an ecological and place-oriented tradition of Druidry and coordinate a school called *La Confraternita dell'Antica Quercia* (The Confraternity of the Ancient Oak). The supporting organization behind these events is the *Associazione Culturale Antica Quercia* (Cultural Association of the Ancient Oak; Ciancimino 2018, 102). Indeed, in the cities of Turin, Milan, Bologna, Rome, Naples, and Palermo, there is a vivid movement currently rediscovering and revitalizing Paganist traditions, such as Wicca, Druidry, and feminist divine spiritualities (Ciancimino 2018, 129).

The first two categories outlined above can be framed as opposite poles—on the one side, institutionally recognized religious groups publicly visible in the city; on the other, more informal and marginal groups are localized outside of urban areas. The third category includes hybrid initiatives organized by secular actors in the city, which often display marginalized groups to disseminate knowledge, thereby increasing dialogue among religious groups and enhancing multiculturalism and diversity.

This third category includes all initiatives that have been developing over the last decade aimed at promoting interreligious and intercultural dialogue and activities, during which religions are showcased and publicly performed (Griera, Giorda, and Fabretti 2018). Leaders of different religions cooperate with one

Table 5.1 Classification of festivals involving religion

	Organizers	Usual location	Aim	Scope	Examples
Religious festivities	Majority or recognized religions (often with the support of public institutions)	City center	Celebration of religion	Universal (community of faith)	Parades for local Saints
Community festivals	Local religious/ spiritual groups; associations	Rural areas	Celebration of community and spirituality	Local	Festa Celtica di Beltane
Festivals of religions	Secular actors	City center; specialized areas	Knowledge, dialogue	Translocal	Festival dell'Oriente; Torino Spiritualità

another, and often with local municipalities as well as cultural and academic institutions, with the goal of communicating, transmitting, and displaying (rather than embodying) the religious experience. These initiatives target a diverse audience with a translocal scope. Participation is voluntary, motivated by curiosity, entertainment, and the desire to engage with diversity (Ciancimino 2018; Spineto 2015).

One of the first Italian initiatives of this kind is the festival *Torino Spiritualità*. Since its origin in 2005, the festival has focused on enabling communication between secular and religious cultures by increasing religious literacy and showing how religious concepts can be "secularized" and mobilized in our daily spiritual and ethical considerations. Over the years, the festival's focal point has slightly changed, and it now mainly supports dialogue among various religious cultures (Giorgi 2015). As its website mentions, the festival involves "five days of meetings, dialogues, and lectures that will help us to grow together through debates between consciences and the crossing of faiths, cultures and religions from all over the world" (Torino Spiritualita). However, every year, the festival makes itself known beyond just the five days; many related initiatives are organized throughout the year with around 20,000 to 30,000 annual attendees. Moreover, the festival takes place in various locations throughout the city. The underlying idea is the capillary dissemination of initiatives, the engagement of the inhabitants, and the cross-fertilization between the festival and the city. Over the last decade, similar initiatives have popped up all over the country, often in tandem with the growth of international migration and the settlement of migrant communities.

We identified two dimensions of variation according to which the cases can be positioned: the type of organizers and the degree of interaction with what is on display. For the first dimension, cases range from public-institutional organizers, such as municipalities, to secular groups, interreligious associations, and religious communities. For the second dimension, cases range from minimum interactions, such as public debates and movies, to maximum interaction, as seen in the case of *Iftar Streets*, organized by local Muslim communities. We have explored and analyzed the self-descriptions put forward by festival organizers to understand how they perceive themselves, as illustrated in Figure 5.1.

At the lower level of interaction are initiatives showcasing religion and religious differences for primarily multicultural purposes. These initiatives are organized by local institutional actors or, more commonly, local secular associations interested in promoting sociocultural pluralism and encouraging dialogue. One example is the *Festival dell'Oriente* (the East Festival), which was

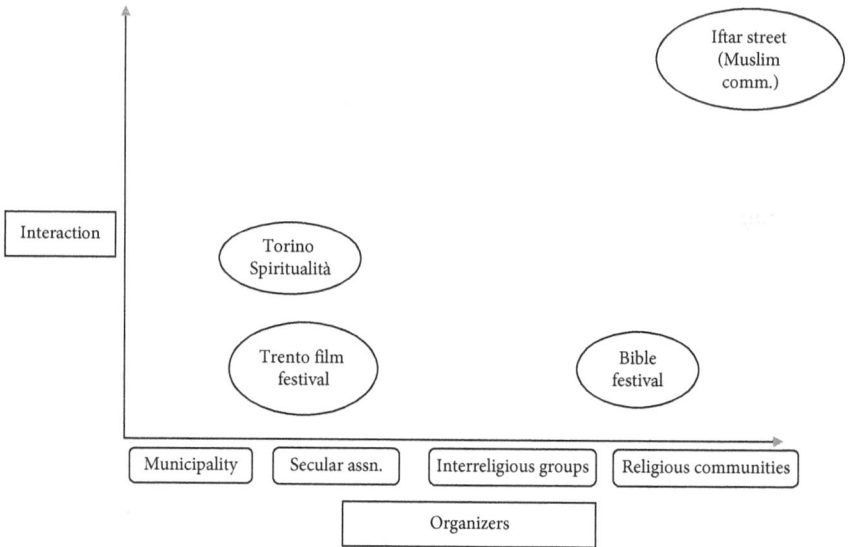

Figure 5.1 Festivals of Religion.

launched in 2011 as a spin-off of a martial arts competition to enrich the event with cultural initiatives. Over the last decade, the event has gained a great deal of economic and public importance; it takes place in twelve Italian cities and includes 200 stands featuring local products, conferences, performances, and spiritual encounters. The East Festival is promoted as a secular event and is usually located in dedicated areas separate from downtowns. According to the organizers, the festival attracts 1.8 million attendees each year.

The festival aims to showcase "the East and its huge artistic heritage […] faithfully represented by typical dances, traditional chants and folkloric exhibitions." This description brings to mind a stereotypical vision of "the East" based on the Orientalism framework explored and exposed by many scholars (e.g., Said 1978). From this perspective, the festival contributes to the popular imaginary without including scholars or conscious insiders and, in so doing, perpetuates the Orientalist risk (the most famous outcome of which is the "gymnastization" and "spectacularization" of yoga; Mori Squarcini 2019). The gap in this festival between biased experience and critical knowledge is therefore evident.

Other examples are more directly related to religion, such as the numerous film festivals organized by Catholic associations and institutions around the country. The oldest one is *Religion Today*, launched in 1997 in Trento. Other examples are the *Film Festival in Terni*, organized by the local Catholic Diocese,[2] and the festival *Molte Fedi* (Many Faiths),[3] organized in Bergamo by the local branch of the National Association of Catholic Workers. In their early days, these initiatives started with stands of food, conferences, and workshops, with the general aim of increasing knowledge about religious differences and, more broadly, about "the others." Catholicism in Italy is particularly active in promoting dialogue and controlling interactions among different religions. Another example is the *Festival Biblico*,[4] promoted by several dioceses in the northeast region of Veneto, which is aimed at enhancing public knowledge of the Bible. This festival features an abundance of voices and approaches, involving scholars, artists, actors, and musicians. It takes place in various venues (outdoors and in theaters, churches, and gardens) and various cities (Vicenza, Verona, Padova, Rovigo, Vittorio Veneto, Treviso, and Alba).

Other initiatives aimed at directly engaging with religious diversity are usually organized by secular associations and may feature slightly higher levels of interaction. One example is the *Festival of Religions* in Florence, the first of its kind, launched in 2014 by the secular association *Luogo di Incontro* (The Place of Encounter) and supported by the municipality (and, later on, by the University of Florence and the Ministry of Tourism and Cultural Heritage). Festival activities include public conferences on religious topics and collective rituals. It takes place in various secular and religious environments in urban (and peri-urban) areas. The festival aims to propose moments of dialogue and reflection on topics of pressing cultural, religious, and social importance. Its name was chosen to evoke the idea of a cultural laboratory, a proper "place" for ideas, people, and thoughts to genuinely "meet" with each other.[5] Another example is the *Festival Mondo Religioni. Incontriamo le religioni del mondo* (World Religions. Meet the religions of the world),[6] held since 2018 by the Italian Association of Sociology of Religion with the support of the Lazio region at the Istituto S. Gallicano in the center of Rome. The festival aims to promote dialogue among scholars, journalists, leaders, and members of all religions. It features conferences, documentaries, workshops, and round tables that address the complex role of religions in contemporary societies. It also includes side events like concerts and collective prayers.

The highest level of interaction is found at festivals that put religious communities themselves on display to build bridges with the local population. Particularly relevant from this perspective are events promoted by Muslim communities—with the support of municipalities—which open mosques to everyone (e.g., *Moschee aperte*/Open Mosques). *Iftar Streets*, for example, celebrates the daily end of the Ramadan fast with an evening meal open to the neighborhood. We have included these events among the festivals of religions on account of their explicit aim of fostering dialogue, increasing familiarity, and deconstructing fears and stereotypes. Giorda and Hejazi argue that these events can be seen as Muslim communities' attempts to repurpose the traditional formula of street festivals and feasts to suit the needs of religious dialogue. Launched in 2014 in Turin, Iftar Streets has over time become a "brand" for similar events in many Italian cities, attracting many people. Maintaining their crucial role for the religious community, they also offer the general audience a domesticated experience of diversity within the familiar symbolic boundaries of local and community feasts (Giorda and Hejazi 2019). The increasing popularity of these public rituals illustrates the new symbolic language mediating communication between the religious and secular public spheres.

These examples illustrate the internal diversity of the events contained within the category of festivals of religions, which include local as well as national events, ranging from institutionalized initiatives promoted with the support of the municipalities to self-organized meetings and ceremonies. Despite their diversity, these festivals share an aim of dialogue—be it between religions or between one religious community and the general audience—which is in fact the primary target of these events. The relevance of these public performances of rites and prayers lies in the possibility they create for an encounter of differences; in this sense, the secular aspect of festivals of religions usually prevails over their religious significance.

Religion and the City: What Is Worth Showing

The analysis presented in this chapter contributes to the literature on festivals, proposing a typology for different forms of festivalization of religion. Mostly, however, it contributes to—and communicates with—the growing literature on urban religions by exploring the case of festivals of religions as a laboratory for complex intersections and entanglements of religion and the secular. In this study, as we have already mentioned, we argue for the importance of analytically separating festivals of religions from other forms of religious expression in cities. Festivals of religions are distinct from both religious feasts and secular events. While they are about religions, they also bear secular significance. The main differences lie in the aim and effects of these initiatives. Festivals describe themselves as places of encounter with the purpose of disseminating knowledge about religion and enabling dialogue and exchanges. Even in cases that include religious and spiritual celebrations, their primary goal is to build a bridge through diversity to connect secular and religious cultures, fitting perfectly into the "multiple" secular panorama of urban contexts where opposite tensions play a social and cultural function. At the same time, they reinforce the identities on display with culturalizing and folklorizing effects, as they have the power to enlarge the boundaries of (religious) communities. Rather than blurring the boundaries between the religious and the secular, or between religions, festivals of religions have the effect of standardizing the language of different religions by offering similar platforms for displaying different religious "contents," such as rites, theology, celebrations, or leaders and exemplary figures. In festivals of religions, differences are domesticated and made easily understandable through translation into one common language, thus enabling dialogue and discussion.

At the same time—and this is the second element we would like to point out— festivals of religions offer public legitimacy to different religious traditions and to religious diversity. Many Southern European countries have layered regimes for the relationships between the state and religions. Aside from direct regulatory effects, these regimes also have indirect effects on the public reputation and legitimacy of different religions; depending on the type of relationship established with the state administration, religions hold different public statuses. However, festivals of religions may influence the reputation of religions regardless of their public status, with bottom-up mechanisms that enhance their visibility and, as a result, the familiarization and the domestication of difference, which becomes part of everyday life. Among the mechanisms which enable the process of visibilization of religions and religious diversity is the complex and mostly invisible coordination of different actors needed for the organization of festivals, in terms of both logistics and communication. Secular and religious actors are strictly interconnected in this organizational process. As a consequence, the more these festivals of religions go beyond the "first/zero edition," the more they become consolidated from an institutional and organizational point of view. In recent years, the culturalized version of religious diversity has expanded from urban areas to local towns, demonstrating the impact of such initiatives on society beyond cities.

Public visibility and improved reputations, however, come with strings attached; while religious festivals may be interpreted as "mobile heterotopias" which sacralize otherwise-secular places for limited periods of time, festivals of religions are in fact forms of what we may define as "heritagized heterotopias" which secularize otherwise religious actors and events for limited times in special places. If, in a Durkheimian perspective, secular and religious events may have similar effects of creating collective experiences that enact the sacred, festivals of religions may be seen as having the opposite effect, decoupling the sacred from religious events. Festivals of religions select those aspects of religions that are appropriate for displaying, thus at the same time defining the contents and characters of "festivalized" religions. In this sense, festivals of religions act as living heritages for which the cultural and traditional aspects of religions play a symbolic role, transcending the specifics of the faith. The temporality and spatiality of these festivals of religions are firmly situated in the here and now; they do not break the ordinary routine of urban environments. Nonetheless, they have an "othering" effect through the mere act of displaying for dialogue. As many scholars have pointed out, diversity and otherness are categories that identify what "sticks out"; to a certain extent, then, they have the effect of reaffirming the hegemony of the majority, which is the norm against which diversity is measured and defined. In this sense, festivals of religions, aimed at enabling encounters with diversity, may in fact have the paradoxical effect of reaffirming that diversity while simultaneously evading the issue of power relationships among those religions. Showcased religions enter the urban environment as something different, something exotic, and require the mediation of public events to be properly integrated into the social fabric. In this sense, festivals of religions legitimize religions in cities while at the same time reaffirming the secular nature of the urban arena.

Part Two

The Politics of Religion in Urban Spaces: Power and Symbolism in the City

A Bridge Too Far: Yoga, Spirituality, and Contested Space in the Pacific Northwest

Paul Bramadat

Centre for Studies in Religion and Society, University of Victoria, Canada

In the summer of 2015, a seemingly harmless plan to celebrate the inaugural International Day of Yoga (hereafter, IDY) in Vancouver, British Columbia, generated a powerful backlash.[1] What might have been for some a public expression of their interest in a trendy wellness activity, and for others a meaningful demonstration of an important spiritual practice, was cancelled just a week after it was announced. The fact that this acrimonious debate occurred in the Greater Vancouver Area (population 2.4M) might surprise some readers. After all, the city is often caricatured as "Vansterdam," the heart of "British California," "lotus land," the "left coast," and "the Best Place on Earth" (according to one of British Columbia's official license plate slogans); moreover, it is nested within a country still closely tied to and generally accepting of liberal multicultural policies. Not only is this cosmopolitan city famously "super-diverse" (Vertovec 2007), it is arguably also "religiously super-diverse" (cf. Amin and Thrift 2017; Becci, Burchardt and Giorda 2016, 74; Griera 2012). As such, one might generally expect the city to welcome the coexistence of multiple visions of the good life, rationality, wellness, identity, and secularism.[2]

In this brief but revealing controversy, most interlocutors focused on local political considerations, paying somewhat less explicit attention to the now common critique that postural yoga is elitist and vapid, and virtually none to claims and metaphors related to spirituality that circulated widely among practitioners and promoters. How did this single postural yoga class so quickly and definitively galvanize public opinion, and what can this teach us about the machinations of public discourse? As I argue below, this controversy reminds us that yoga is a polysemic signifier (Foxen 2020; Jain 2014; Lucia 2020; White 2012) that gets deployed in pursuit of a wide variety of objectives. For the insiders and promoters cited below, emphasis is typically placed on the "spiritual" nature and benefits of postural yoga. In contrast, as we will see, the critics of the Om the Bridge event focus on the more obviously political dimensions of the event, but in ways that are nonetheless connected to broadly circulating critical perspectives on yoga.

Postural yoga is growing rapidly in the West as part of a multibillion dollar global wellness industry (Ivtzan and Jegatheeswaran 2015; Jain 2014 and 2020; Park, Braun, and Siegel 2015; Syman 2011); it is commonly marketed as an escape from or antidote to some of the ills of modern society (Lucia 2020; Syman 2011); it is often described by insiders as rooted in an ancient practice (that actually takes its current shape in about the last 100 years) (Foxen 2020; Mallinson and Singleton 2017; Singleton 2010); and it is explicitly tied to particular ways of imagining India (De Michelis 2005). So, postural yoga is inherently political in that there is no simple, stable, apolitical entity called yoga that is subsequently politicized for some extraneous or instrumental purpose. Although yoga is political in this broad sense, this fact is often obfuscated by the religious or spiritual rhetoric that accompanies claims and assumptions about the origins, essence, and benefits of yoga. Indeed, in this case even the principal interlocutors in the public realm—especially British Columbia's Premier Christy Clark—appear to have been shocked by the vitriolic response of many people in the broader community. Given the obvious benefits the premier would have received if she had aligned herself with one of the province's most common wellness practices, her response to the harsh public reaction may seem naïve or even disingenuous. In this piece, I am not interested in her actual intentions but rather the way the controversy allows us to think about the different registers in which IDY promoters and protesters articulated their perspectives.

To understand why one sees the ubiquitous use of religious or (more often) spiritual rhetoric in the launch and promotion of the IDY, but then the virtual disappearance of these concerns in the critical discourses that comprised the controversy, one needs to move beyond (or through) emic accounts that may frame the practice as an uncomplicated, apolitical sui generis spiritual activity (McCutcheon 1997; see also Altglas 2014). A more disinterested approach allows us a better perspective from which to comprehend both the particularities and broader implications of this event. In this debate, the near silence about the spiritual or religious dimensions of yoga is peculiar, not just because this rhetoric is central to the way the event was promoted, but also because Vancouver is widely considered to be a safe haven for all manner of spiritual and cultural experimentation. For example, the city is the home of the famous "Highway to

Heaven" (Dwyer, Tse and Ley 2016) in Richmond, a suburb of Vancouver that is zoned in such a way that over twenty places of worship exist side by side on the same street (with virtually no conflict); it is part of a province that is seeing a renaissance of Indigenous culture and spirituality (Asch, Borrows and Tully 2018); it is at the very heart of the Cascadia bioregion in which what I have called "reverential naturalism" seems, for many, to be the default orientation toward the physical environment.[3] Moreover, although Canada is no political paradise (with the state seeking during the past two decades to atone for the historical mistreatment of Indigenous peoples as well as Asian newcomers), residents consistently express their support for multiculturalism and diversity both as de facto realities and de jure features of Canadian politics and law (Environics 2015). In short, there was every reason to think that the premier could realize her ambition for Om the Bridge to be the largest IDY event outside of India.[4] While Clark finally complained that politics "[got] in the way" of the IDY, in fact this controversy helps us understand better the broader social and political backdrop against which critics and practitioners make claims about postural yoga.

A Timeline

March 11, 2011: Christy Clark and the provincial BC Liberal Party assume leadership of British Columbia; she holds power until July 2017.

December 11, 2014: The United Nations unanimously proclaims June 21 as the International Day of Yoga through resolution 69/131.

April 16, 2015: Indian Prime Minister Narendra Modi, of the Hindu nationalist Bharatiya Janata Party, visits the lower mainland of British Columbia, making stops at a Sikh *gurdwara* and Hindu temple; this is the first visit to Canada by an Indian PM in forty-two years.

June 5, 2015: Premier Christy Clark formally announces that on June 21, 2015, the province will host its IDY event on the Burrard Street Bridge; the bridge will be closed from 4:00 a.m. to 11:00 a.m., and the IDY yoga class is scheduled from 8:30 a.m. to 9:30 a.m.; the total cost to the province will be $150,000; public responses to this proposal on both conventional and social media for the next week are almost entirely critical.

June 11, 2015: Clark tweets a picture of herself in front of a Taoist Tai Chi centre with the caption: "Hey Yoga Haters—bet you can't wait for international Tai Chi day!"; Vancouver Mayor Gregor Robertson immediately announces he will attend National Aboriginal Day instead of IDY (as quoted in City News 1130).

June 12, 2015 (10:00 a.m.) Clark tweets: "Yoga Day is a great opportunity to celebrate peace and harmony—it's not about politics. I don't intend to participate."

June 12, 2015 (11:00 a.m.): The Om the Bridge corporate sponsors, Lululemon, YYoga, and Altagas announce their withdrawal from the event.

June 12, 2015 (12:30 p.m.): Clark officially cancels the event with a statement on Twitter that reads, in part:

> Yoga is about attaining inner peace and harmony [...]. Unfortunately, the focus of the proposed Burrard Street Bridge event has *drifted towards politics*—getting in the way of the spirit of community and inner reflection [...]. I want to thank our sponsors for organizing an inclusive event with the very best of intentions. Though we are forced to cancel the Burrard Street Bridge event, I hope British Columbians will still feel encouraged to participate in their [IDY] events elsewhere. (as quoted in Ian Bailey's 2015 *Globe and Mail* article, emphasis mine)

Background

Space does not permit an account of the history of yoga in general or the growing popularity of postural yoga in the West (see Alter 2004; Altglas 2014; De Michelis 2005; Jain 2014; Mallinson and Singleton 2017; Singleton 2010; Syman 2011; White 2012). Suffice it to say that in the past two or three decades it has become a major feature of the wellness and spiritual subcultures of North America. We can, nevertheless, observe that many students are attracted to *asana* practice for its mental health and relaxation benefits; some are attracted exclusively to its capacity to improve strength and flexibility; some come to yoga as a form of physiotherapy after an injury or the onset of a disease; some are drawn to postural yoga to parade or enhance their beauty; some students are interested in yoga communities for a sense of social belonging; other students use *asanas* as means of achieving sufficient mastery over their mental and physical states that they might one day achieve liberation from suffering, illusion, and the cycle of birth and rebirth. As one might expect, many students would identify with several of the approaches I have listed; sometimes simultaneously, and sometimes sequentially.

While postural yoga practices may not be commonly understood or described as explicitly religious activities in Western liberal democracies (cf., Gunther Brown 2019), practitioners often regard them as important parts of their spiritual lives (Altglas 2014; De Michelis 2005; Lucia 2020), and IDY promoters certainly used this rhetoric. In particular, the official stakeholders in the IDY debate emphasized IDY's connection to spirituality, understood to connote the variety of practices and perspectives usually framed as alternatives to institutional religion and usually associated with an individual's pursuit of wholeness and healing. For example, the UN declaration of IDY on its general website was itself rather pro forma, but the UN's public-facing website used evocative language. On the latter site, we learn that "yoga is an ancient physical, *mental and spiritual practice* that originated in India. The word 'yoga' derives from Sanskrit and means to join or to unite, symbolizing the *union of body and consciousness*" (United Nations n.d.; emphasis mine).[5] AYUSH (the Indian government ministry intended to promote Ayurveda, Yoga, Unani, Siddha, and Homoeopathy) as well as the Indian Ministry of External Affairs (MEA) unveiled this IDY logo in April 2015 (Figure 6.1 from original slide presentation).[6]

In addition to the official explanations provided by the MEA and AYUSH on the slide itself, it is worth noting that the yogi's head in this logo is positioned directly over the Indian subcontinent.

The IDY "Common Yoga Protocol" document produced by AYUSH and published on the MEA's website in May 2015 explains that "yoga is essentially *a spiritual discipline* based on an extremely subtle science which focuses on bringing harmony between mind and body" (MEA 2016; emphasis mine).

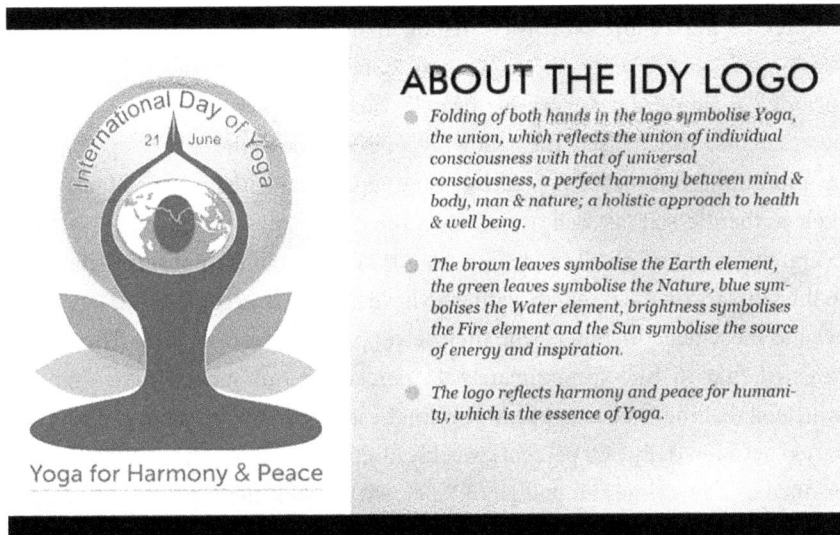

Figure 6.1 International Yoga Day presentation. Reproduced with permission of Vikas Swarup.

Moreover, in September of the year prior to the adoption of the resolution at the UN, Prime Minister Modi addressed the UN and said, "Yoga is an invaluable gift of India's ancient tradition. It embodies *unity of mind and body*; thought and action; restraint and fulfilment; harmony between man and nature; a holistic approach to health and well-being. It is not about exercise but to *discover the sense of oneness with yourself, the world and the nature*"[7] (emphasis mine).

Even the premier of BC employed the rhetoric of spirituality and its cognates in her June 5, 2015 announcement of the IDY, cited on the government of BC website. Christy Clark said:

> India has given the world a great gift in yoga, with *dedicated followers* around the world. It's become part of the cultural fabric in B.C., and particularly so in the Lower Mainland [i.e., the Greater Vancouver Area]. That's why we're inviting beginners and yogi masters alike from across the province to Vancouver—to come together to celebrate yoga in record numbers, and most importantly, have fun.

Nonetheless, a week later in the wake of strong opposition, she announced via the same government website: "Yoga is about attaining *inner peace and harmony*. [...] Unfortunately, the focus of the proposed Burrard Street Bridge event has *drifted towards politics—getting in the way* of the spirit of community and *inner reflection*"[8] (emphasis mine).

Furthermore, it is important to note that residents of the Pacific Northwest commonly attribute "spiritual" meanings to their postural yoga practices. An international research project I lead on the religious, spiritual, and irreligious features of the Pacific Northwest region of North America (BC in Canada, Washington and Oregon in the United States; sometimes called "Cascadia") included a significant survey of the religious and spiritual practices favored by residents, which used the following operational definition of spirituality: "a profound and usually positive experience that helps individuals find their authentic self, as well as connects them to a mysterious, universal, and overarching reality" (Wilkins-Laflamme 2018). The results were surprising both to the scholars on the research team who have lived in the region for decades and even to those team members who themselves practice postural yoga. The survey revealed that in BC, approximately 41 percent of our representative sample indicated that they had engaged in yoga in the last year; the frequency of practice varied between daily (4.8 percent), weekly (14.5 percent), monthly (8.1 percent), or once or a few times annually (13.3 percent). When these practitioners were asked if they experienced their practice as spiritual, 55 percent of them said definitely yes (13 percent) or probably yes (42 percent).

Cost, Convenience, Contrition

According to the promoters and insiders of IDY, postural yoga is a spiritual discipline that is about inner peace and harmony, a sense of oneness, a unity of mind and body, a spiritual practice, and a union of body and consciousness. Anyone who has spent any time in North American yoga subcultures or who is familiar with the scholarly and popular discourses about yoga (Jain 2014) will recognize these claims. As I noted, the event was cancelled when the premier felt it had veered away from the noble attributes I have just enumerated.

There is a rich literature that illuminates the ways in which claims about yoga's spiritual essence (or impacts) might, on the one hand, enable practitioners to pursue their personal interests in health and well-being, but also might, on the other hand, normalize neoliberalism, conventional aesthetic norms, orientalism, nationalism, therapeutic individualism, and even narcissism (Antony 2018; Bost 2016; Jain 2014, 2020; White 2012). While a thorough consideration of these critiques is beyond the scope of this contribution, some of them will be engaged later as I try to explain the forces behind this event's cancellation.

I have read all available official government statements about and media coverage of this event, and as it was unfolding I paid close attention to call-in shows and other sites of social discourse (Facebook, cafes, yoga studios, blogs, comments sections of news articles, gatherings of friends and family, university environments, etc.). Since I want to reflect on some deeper forces at work behind the consensus that developed in this debate, I need to describe and assess the three main and arguably specious claims evident in a discourse analysis of this debate.

First, critics claimed the event cost too much money. However, the province of BC and the city of Vancouver provide material and logistical support for many other major events in the Greater Vancouver Area (GVA), such as the Vancouver Marathon, Diwali, the International Jazz Festival, and Vaisakhi. The province's guidelines published on the Destination British Columbia website (for just one potential funding program) indicate that for a "large event," organizers are eligible to apply for up to $175,000. Of course, the downstream economic benefit of IDY to the yoga community (studios, merchandisers, teachers) and to the relationship between India as a trading partner and major source of immigration is unknown. Nevertheless, not only did IDY not represent the first time the province or city had provided support for special events; indeed, the cost of this event was within the normal range.

Second, many people protested that the closure was inconvenient. Closing the bridge from 4:00 a.m. to 11:00 a.m. would have been irritating for some Sunday morning travelers. A number of commentators observed that 37,000 motorists use that bridge each Sunday, without noting that traffic would be disrupted during the lightest period of the day (Smyth 2015). In addition to the Burrard Street Bridge, drivers can also use the Granville and Cambie Bridges as well as a light rail service and pedestrian ferries. Moreover, road closures for other events are far longer and more complicated. For example, for the BMO Marathon, key public spaces are closed for parts or the whole of a fourteen-hour period between 5:00 a.m. and 7:00 p.m. In the case of Vaisakhi, the festivities take place in two different neighborhoods, on different days; the street closures and traffic disruptions last for most of the days in question. Notably, these annual events have not led to the vitriolic response we saw in the IDY debate.

Third, critics observed that the timing of the event displayed an inadequate amount of contrition. Coincidentally, June 21, 2015, was also Canada's National Aboriginal Day (now named National Indigenous Peoples Day), an official opportunity to recognize and honor these communities. This coincidence would not have created logistical challenges for participants, since the National Aboriginal Day celebrations were scheduled to begin two and a half hours *after* the yoga class, at Trout Lake, which is eight kilometers east of the Burrard Street Bridge. It is useful to observe that other major special events scheduled throughout the same day included: the Vancouver International Jazz Festival, the FIFA Women's World Cup, the Goodlife Fitness Urban Adventure Race, and Bard on the Beach (a major Shakespearean festival). Some of these events were several days in duration; all of them involved traffic disruptions and direct or indirect support from the federal, provincial, or municipal governments; none of them generated public outcry.

So, other events were equally or more expensive, equally or more disruptive of traffic, and actually overlapping with (rather than simply occurring on the same day as) National Aboriginal Day. To put it playfully, a person could easily have attended the IDY event, National Aboriginal Day, *and* still have enough time for *Macbeth* or a show at the Jazz Festival, should they be so inclined. Moreover, as I mentioned, there was a curious silence with regard to the spiritual rhetoric at the heart of the proponents' claims about the meaning and value of postural yoga and IDY. As such, in search of other ways to explain the robust opposition to IDY, we need to reflect upon five additional factors.

Political Opportunism

Strictly speaking, the religious or spiritual aspects of yoga that were so central to proponents' claims were not ignored by everyone. John Horgan, the leader of the official opposition actually commented on the IDY in a manner that— were it to have been aimed at a conventional religious practice or group—would certainly have been considered far more problematic than Clark's Tai Chi tweet. In the summer of 2015, Horgan was leader of the BC New Democratic Party (a large social democratic party that won the 2017 provincial election). During the debate the following photograph of Horgan (Figure 6.2) was sent out on Twitter by a Vancouver reporter, Sonia Aslam, with the caption, "The NDP leader adds ppl don't hate yoga, but the event itself which'll temporarily close a bridge. His response ... "[9]

Horgan posed for this picture on June 11, by which point it seemed clear that the negative consensus around Om the Bridge had crystallized. Presumably that was why he intuited that his glib expression would not create a backlash from yoga practitioners (not to mention Hindu or Buddhist meditators). This was a shrewd assessment, as I could find no evidence of negative response to this image.

Figure 6.2 John Horgan on Yoga Day. Reproduced with permission of Sonia Aslam.

In Aslam's discussion with Horgan about his response to this controversy, he explained: "I think [IDY and Clark's 'Tai Chi Day' tweet] are offensive to people, particularly people who are struggling. People are trying to make ends meet and they see the highest priority of the leader of the government is to roll down mats, close a roadway on Father's Day, on National Aboriginal Day—she's going to say 'Come and look at me. I like to do yoga'"[10] (as quoted in City News 1130).

In this comment yoga is framed as both a risible elitist activity at odds with the basic pursuits of ordinary British Columbians and an opportunity for Clark and others to self-aggrandise. The undertone of "Come and look at me. I like to do yoga" is hard to miss, especially when it is read alongside of the (above) image associated with this story and Horgan's claim that the hastily organized IDY represented Clark's "highest priority." With this image and these comments, Horgan signals that he is not himself a member of the ruling elite but a regular British Columbian who understands the frivolity of yoga, the "real needs" of the people, and the hubris of the scheduling of the IDY. His interview strikes a blow against what one Indigenous leader described as Christy Clark's "blatant opportunism" for promoting this "completely flakey" event (as quoted in Crawford 2015).

One might expect commentators to link Clark's opportunism with Indian Prime Minister Modi's interest in using IDY to brand yoga as essentially Indian, and implicitly Hindu (Jain 2014; cf. Miller 2018). Although various kinds of yoga have been present in North America for over a century (Foxen 2020; Syman 2011), the exponential growth of postural yoga in recent years in the West cannot be extricated from either the burgeoning wellness industry or the political interests of the Indian government. However, critics of Om the Bridge rarely mentioned the way Modi instrumentalizes yoga in pursuit of political objectives, and generally referred to him simply to note that he was behind the establishment of IDY.

Housing

Architects, urban planners, and other commentators coined the term "Vancouverism" a few decades ago to refer to the city's distinctive blend of high density, mixed-use buildings, abundance of green space, and relatively unfettered access to and views of the surrounding ocean, islands, and mountains.[11] One of the key characteristics of the city's brand is its large South Asian and East Asian communities. It is worth noting that in the Greater Vancouver region, 67 percent of residents identify as "visible minorities" (non-white and non-Indigenous), and in Richmond, one of the region's largest areas (and the location of the "Highway to Heaven"), that figure is 76 percent.[12] In roughly the last twenty-five years, many Chinese Canadian immigrants—along with a significant number of Chinese nationals—have invested heavily in Vancouver's housing market. This additional demand has increased housing prices in Vancouver to the point that it has become one of the most expensive housing markets in North America. The city remains an attractive place to live and visit, but the cost of housing has become nearly prohibitive for anyone other than very wealthy people (Todd 2018). Moreover, many of the overseas investors purchase their Vancouver properties as investment vehicles, and as such, many of the condominiums and townhouses that are such an important feature of Vancouverism remain empty. This, predictably, makes it difficult for Vancouver to fulfil the dreams of Jane Jacobs and others interested in progressive face-to-face forms of conviviality.

Precarity and the high cost of housing might seem unconnected to the Om the Bridge controversy, but I would argue that these material conditions have contributed to a suspicious mood among some residents with regard to emblematic elite practices and subcultures. By 2015, Clark's government had become associated with many of the challenges facing British Columbia, including the crisis in Vancouver's housing market.[13] Arguably, Clark's Om the Bridge idea seemed to exemplify—for some—her lack of compassion for those Horgan referred to as "struggling." In another intervention, Horgan commented: "Millionaires get tax breaks and the premier shuts down a road so she can have a yoga class. I think that offended people" (Crawford 2015). This sentiment is echoed by one of the only other somewhat appreciative public responses I could find in the debate, in which transgender activist Tami Starlight and the leader of the Anti-Oppression Network noted that she is "supportive of the spiritual and cultural celebration behind International Yoga Day but [...] Clark's approach to the event was 'ill-conceived' and 'a bit distasteful'" (Eagland 2015).

Indigeneity

The most formal protests against the IDY were proposed by the Anti-Oppression Network, which created a Facebook page entitled "Decolonize Burrard Bridge on National Aboriginal Day." The Network sent out a call to "Be an ally on National Aboriginal Day," encouraging a rally at the bridge and asking members of the public to "hold space for Indigenous people, who continue to be systematically ignored, by crashing Christy Clark's yoga party." Burton Amos, an Indigenous man, took to Twitter to laud the fact that a "Flash Mob" had been planned: "I am now asking every creative person I know to come to that bridge at 8:00 a.m and support us to show Christy Clark we mean business! Aboriginal Day is our day and we will not be disrespected! [....] This time it's really important" (Eagland 2015). Why a relatively brief bridge closure and a one-hour public yoga class should lead to complaints from a group called the Anti-Oppression Network might seem puzzling, but the reference to Clark's "yoga party" makes it clear that the group juxtaposes the (frivolous and elite) IDY event against the (important) efforts to ameliorate the significant challenges facing Indigenous people.

Since contemporary Western postural yoga culture is closely associated not just with economic elitism, but with a cohort of often-white, relatively affluent, thin, young, female students and teachers, one might have expected IDY critics to emphasize the "cultural appropriation" of yoga by non-Indian students and teachers. After all, this was, and still is, a major component of broader public and academic debates around yoga in North America (Antony 2018), and it is also part of the conversation related to Modi's efforts to brand yoga and remind the world of its roots in Hindu philosophy (Gowan 2014).[14] However, this did not become a major theme in the debates, perhaps because Indigenous issues were already foregrounded by the coincidence of the IDY and National Aboriginal Day scheduling, which could make concerns around appropriation less salient in this context. It is also important to observe that the federal government's landmark Truth and Reconciliation report, which documented in gruesome detail the ways Indigenous people had been abused and alienated from Canadian life, had been released just days before Clark announced her IDY event. As such, one can at least speculate that there might not have been enough space (or need) in the discussion to highlight the mistreatment or misrepresentation of (other) subaltern communities.

Decentralization

Unlike many conventional religious denominations, the broader wellness and yoga subcultures are inherently decentralized. In the IDY event, it was difficult to identify any proponents for the event beyond the government itself and its problematic corporate partners (see below). There are large studios and popular teachers (and obviously a great many students) in the GVA, but few publicly championed Clark's event—perhaps because they were also aware of the almost immediate hardening of public opinion around the event. So, as the widespread opposition to the IDY event began to consolidate, the lack of a meaningful or broad-based community of support meant the opposition movement gained momentum quickly. Given the absence of anyone who might be legible as a social carrier, in a Weberian sense, of values sympathetic to the bridge closure, there was virtually no one to challenge the acceleration of the IDY criticism.

IDY's Corporate Proponents

When Clark announced the Om the Bridge event, she did not involve any representatives from the ethnoreligious communities for which postural (and other forms of) yoga are integral practices. Instead, it appeared that the event was her idea (presumably inspired by her recent interactions with Modi), and her nongovernmental collaborators were in fact three corporations: Lululemon, YYoga, and Altagas. YYoga operates a major chain of large studios in the GVA and drew virtually no criticism during the debate. Altagas seems like a counterintuitive partner since they are located in the neighboring conservative, oil-rich province of Alberta. Although few BC residents would be familiar with this natural gas company, journalists reported that Altagas had contributed to Clark's previous electoral campaign (Smyth 2015).

However, arguably much more damaging to Om the Bridge was the fact that in the spring of 2015, many people would still remember how the Vancouver-based brand, Lululemon's founder and billionaire CEO, Chip Wilson, attracted attention when women complained both that the company's yoga pants were too sheer and that they often pilled. In a television interview posted on CBC News website November 7, 2013, Wilson responded that "quite frankly, some women's bodies just don't actually work [for the yoga pants]. … It's really about the rubbing through the thighs, [the pilling is caused by] how much pressure is there." There was a massive and immediate backlash against Wilson's "fat-shaming," which led him to post a tepid YouTube apology video on December 10, 2013. He soon left the leadership of the company, but maintains an active corporate and public profile in real estate and apparel. Wilson owns the largest and most expensive residence in the province (valued at $75M in 2015), a massive 30,000sq. ft. home in Vancouver's Point Grey neighborhood, the riding once represented by Christy Clark. The negative press around Wilson and the involvement of Altagas and a large and lucrative chain of yoga studios created the impression that IDY was the brainchild of people and corporations without a strong sense of loyalty to ordinary residents. It may therefore be the case that, for some people, the IDY was an opportunity to protest neoliberalism and the province's Liberal government that had embraced it.[15]

Conclusion

Clearly, postural yoga is an integral part of Vancouver's "holistic milieu" (Heelas and Woodhead 2005), along with Reiki, meditation, acupuncture, Ayurveda, and Traditional Chinese medicine. Yoga studios, teachers, students, workshops, festivals, and distinctive clothing styles are ubiquitous in this cosmopolitan and multicultural city. Two widely circulated tweets from June 5 capture perfectly the fact that commentators understood this controversy to reflect Vancouver's unique civic personality. One person tweeted: "Burrard Bridge to be closed for a giant yoga event. Only in #vancouver." Another wrote: "They are closing the burrard bridge down so people can do yoga? That's possibly the most Vancouver Vancouver can get." As one journalist put it in the June 5 CBC News article that posted these tweets, this debate is "a peak Vancouver moment."

The city's openness to virtually all cultures and subcultures is part of its brand (cf. Becci, Burchardt and Giorda 2016, 87). Although Vancouver regularly accommodates a wide variety of activities associated with groups organized around religious, spiritual, commercial, athletic, artistic, and philanthropic endeavors, key political figures along with a large number of Vancouverites seem to have concluded that this public yoga class represented a "bridge too far." Initially, it is puzzling that an event conceived and marketed as a relatively inexpensive celebration of a phenomenon that is simultaneously spiritual, physical, social, commercial, ancient, modern, global, and local would fail to be embraced—or even tolerated—by this particular public. It bears repeating that approximately 20 percent of all British Columbians frame their own postural yoga practice as a means of increasing their "spiritual" wellness, wholeness, and awareness. To put the size of this cohort in perspective, it is the equivalent of *all* self-identified Anglicans and United Church Christians, *plus all* Buddhists, Hindus, Muslims, Jews, and Sikhs in the province. While the practice is also certainly implicated in social forces such as neoliberalism, nationalism, and therapeutic individualism (Jain 2020), such associations coexist (awkwardly) with the spiritual values to which the promoters and practitioners have referred.

In this case, the spiritual rhetoric that surrounded Om the Bridge could not protect the proposed event, which collapsed within a week of being announced.

Not only were critics evidently uninterested in the spiritual claims and metaphors used by promoters and practitioners to describe the significance of yoga; they offered three prima facie untenable reasons for their opposition. As the five additional explanations I have offered suggest, however, the city's deeply entrenched expansive form of pluralism retracted in this instance due to strong pressures from both what we might consider very conventional party politics and nascent (anti-elitist and pro-Indigenous) identity politics. Although some of the more sophisticated arguments one hears against the burgeoning postural yoga industry in North America (e.g., regarding cultural appropriation and Indian nationalism) were not fully articulated in this debate, the controversy lasted only a week and ended abruptly. It is quite possible that had the imbroglio lasted longer a more fulsome debate might have occurred.

In an urban context in which maximum deference is usually extended to articulations of spiritual and religious values and practices, there was no backlash against the critics—even from residents who might resent the tone and conclusion of the debate—arguably because as a cultural practice, postural yoga is deeply ambiguous: it is neither simply the product of a religion nor a relatively (or putatively) unproblematic personal practice such as meditation (cf. Griera and Clot-Garrell 2015a). The Om the Bridge controversy may remind us that religious and spiritual claims are not sui generis but always part of larger social discourses that reveal a great deal about quite this-worldly concerns, interests, and values. In 2015 the most relevant factors included Clark's political vulnerability, her choice to collaborate with a CEO whose public persona had become quite problematic, the growing crisis of affordability, and the fact that the event coincided with the beginning of a sea change in the public interest in reconciliation with Indigenous peoples. Vancouver's International Day of Yoga thus demonstrated the deep and unresolved tensions below the surface of one of the world's most diverse and accommodating cities.

"It's the First *Sukkah* since the Inquisition!": Jewish Celebrations in Public Spaces in Barcelona

Julia Martínez-Ariño
University of Groningen

On September 25, 2018, "the first public *sukkah* since the Inquisition," as a local politician presented it on her Facebook page, was built in a public square in Barcelona's city center, close to the medieval Jewish neighborhood. The *sukkah*, a Jewish architectural element erected for the celebration of *Sukkot*—or Festival of Tabernacles—to commemorate the forty-year journey through the dessert, was built in a rather discreet fashion on the edge of the square. The opening event was attended and celebrated not only by members of local Jewish communities (mostly members and affiliates of the international Hassidic movement, Chabad Lubavitch), but also by municipal authorities. The hut remained open to the public for five days, allowing those who wished it to have a first-hand experience of the Jewish celebration.

Similarly, for several years now, a large *hanukkiah* has been lit for one evening to celebrate the Jewish festival of *Hanukkah* in the square where the Barcelona City Hall and the seat of the Catalan government are located. For a few hours that night, the lights of the *hanukkiah* exist alongside the Christmas lights that illuminate the streets. The nine-branched, 5-meter-tall candelabrum is located in a prominent position in this central square, flanked by a big banner with an image of a candelabrum with the dates of the festivities. On a stage next to the screen, biblical stories are read aloud, music is played, and men dance in circles in front of a few rows of chairs, thereby giving a festive character to the celebration.

What does the performance and staging of these two Jewish religious celebrations tell us about religion in urban spaces? What can we learn about the "eventization" of religion, as a process whereby religious practices, rituals, and celebrations are transformed into performances and experiences that appeal to the senses, with the support of technology and new social media, a particular dramaturgy, and bodily dispositions? How does the transformation of urban religious landscapes, which are becoming increasingly diverse, impact the visibility of minority religious groups and religion more broadly? And what is the effect of the eventization of religion on public spaces, their uses, and their meanings? Finally, what factors might explain why these two public events take place in urban spaces in the center of Barcelona?

In this chapter, I will show how the practices of lighting the *hanukkiah* and constructing the *sukkah* in Barcelona's public spaces temporarily mark a part of the urban territory as Jewish, thereby blurring the boundaries between secular and religious spaces. In the particular case of the *Hanukkah* celebration, which coincides with the Christmas period, the overlap of two religious street lightings shows the simultaneous presence of different identities in one space. Moreover, these two Jewish public celebrations draw our attention to issues of visibility, authenticity, and the temporary appropriation of urban space. I will further examine how a conjunction of legal and policy frameworks, transformations within the religious field and political constellations of the city, and the discursive framing of the events have favored their public performance. This last element is, as I argue, of particular significance in the case of Jews in Spain; framing the two events as a form of historical reparation for past wrongdoing against Jews gives them a special aura of celebration as well as heightened political and historical significance.

Religious Celebrations in Urban Public Space and the "Eventization" of Religion

Contrary to what secularization theory had once predicted, cities are spaces of religious innovation and vitality (Burchardt and Becci 2013). Public religious celebrations in the form of parades, music festivals, and rituals take place in urban spaces, transforming both religion and cities (Orsi 1999). While scholars have attended to places of worship and the sociopolitical dynamics around them (Ahmed et al. 2016; Brenneman and Miller 2016; Gale 2005; Kong 1993; Kuppinger 2014; Miller 2018; Zwilling 2015), interest in religious festivities and celebrations in public spaces has also grown (Kong 2005). A variety of urban and religious processes converge in these celebrations. As Saint-Blancat and Cancellieri (2014, 646) argue, "[e]xamining religious public performance, some long standing, some ephemeral, helps us to understand two types of processes: how religious practices adapt themselves to urban environments (Peña 2011) and the dynamics of the socio-spatial dialectic between religion and contemporary urban spaces." Moreover, as Lily Kong shows in her study of religious processions, focusing on these types of celebrations allows us to study "the micro-politics of urban life and its conflicts" (Kong 2005, 227). That is, studying events allows us to capture how meanings and priorities are negotiated between state actors, religious leaders, and individuals (participants in the events or not) at the level of everyday local interactions. This approach focuses on the negotiating of public space "less so as a juridical and normative concept and more as a regime of social interactions and an arena of visibility" (Saint-Blancat and Cancellieri 2014, 647). These negotiations refer primarily to place-making practices—whereby diasporic groups appropriate certain spaces and make them places of belonging—as well as negotiations of secular–religious boundaries (Garbin 2012b). Moreover, the study of urban public religious events has shown that boundary-making processes take place both between religious groups and the rest of society, and within religious groups themselves (Kong 2005).

Closely connected to these scholarly concerns is literature on the ways these urban religious parades and processions become, as it were, "eventized." The eventization of life, including leisure activities, culture, and faith, is a characteristic process of urban life, in addition to pluralization, individualization, and commercialization (Betz, Hitzler, and Pfadenhauer 2011). Eventization implies the transformation of a cultural product or a leisure activity into a "spectacle that appeals to all the senses and stages it in a 'cultural world of experience'" (Hitzler 2002, 202, cited in Pfadenhauer 2010, 382). Events can be defined as "the deliberate organization of a heightened emotional and aesthetic experience at a designated time and space" (Jakob 2013, 448). This definition, then, implies a distinction between mundane everyday life events and those that are framed in a way that encourages participants and observers to pay attention to their sensory experiences, the latter of which I approach as an entry point for understanding typically urban religious innovations. In other words, events emphasize "a clearly recognizable dramaturgy comprising a lead-in, a climax, and a finale; emotionalization via choreographed visual stimuli and technically perfect musical performances that appeal to all senses; and an intensive media relations campaign to ensure maximum coverage in the various media channels prior to, during, and after the event" (Pfadenhauer 2010, 388). Events are characterized by "the promise of a total experience" (Gebhardt, Hitzler, and Pfadenhauer 2013, 10) which speaks not only to the intellect, but also to all the senses. Events can also be seen as forms of re-enchantment that allow the creation of a sense of unity or collective existence in late modern societies (Betz, Hitzler, and Pfadenhauer 2011; Gebhardt et al. 2013).

In the study of religious rituals and celebrations, the concept of urban religious "events" or "festivals" has also become relevant. "Faith events are characterized by a combination of traditional elements of church liturgy and pastoral care and eclectic borrowings from youth subcultures, the entertainment industry, and other experientially oriented components of contemporary event culture" (Pfadenhauer 2010, 392). From this perspective, there is an emphasis on sensations and emotions, including the bodily, visual, acoustic, taste, and emotional dimensions, without disregarding the theological aspects involved, including dogma and piety (Ingalls 2012). These elements all contribute to making public rituals spectacular, which enables them to attract the attention of participants (Marshall 2002). Religious events are spaces for the making of religious individuals because they are often framed as opportunities to encounter the divine (Pfadenhauer 2010) as well as occasions for the production, reinforcement, and representation of community feelings and boundaries that are achieved through the co-presence of various individuals and ritual practices (Garbin 2012b; Ingalls 2012; Marshall 2002). Moreover, as other authors have shown, social media play a crucial role in transcending the local temporal and spatial boundaries of these religious events (Endelstein 2017; Garbin 2012b). They do so by allowing people located in different places to participate remotely in, or be witnesses of, the events. Moreover, social media can produce long-lasting records of the events, allowing for asynchronous engagement with them.

In what follows, I will analyze the ritual of the lighting of the *hanukkiah* and the celebration of *sukkah* in public spaces in Barcelona as religious events that create "enacted [Jewish] spaces" (Lipphardt, Brauch, and Nocke 2016, 19). While not comparable in scope and impact to larger religious events, such as the Catholic World Youth Day (Pfadenhauer 2010) or the *Ashura* processions of Shia Muslims (Astor et al. 2018), I argue that these two religious events provide a privileged vantage point for analyzing larger social changes related to the religious diversification of urban populations and understanding the sociospatial dynamics that play out in the use, appropriation, and re-signification of urban public spaces. Moreover, unlike some of the previously mentioned studies, which focus mostly on ritual characteristics and how they influence individual identifications (what Kong (2005) calls the *poetics* of processions), in this chapter I pay more attention to the discourses that surround these events and their wider sociopolitical implications—the *politics* of processions, in Kong's terms. For this, an understanding of the social, historical, and political context will be necessary.

Jewish Celebrations in Public Spaces in Barcelona

Contemporary Jewish life in Barcelona and in Spain more broadly is rather discreet; only rarely are expressions of Jewish cultural and religious identity publicly visible (Martínez-Ariño 2016). The Jewish population of Catalonia (including the capital city of Barcelona) is estimated at around 8,000 (Rozenberg 2010), but this number fluctuates. Moreover, of these inhabitants, about half are affiliated with one of five Jewish communities (one ultra-Orthodox, two Orthodox, one Masorti, and one Reform/Progressive). Jews in Barcelona come from both Sephardic and Ashkenazi origins and are, like the rest of the society, an aging group. Formed of mostly highly educated people, the Jewish population is made up of second-, third-, and fourth-generation citizens (of Turkish, Greek, and Moroccan origin), more recently arrived immigrants, especially from Latin America (in the 1970s, 1980s, and 2000s) and Israel (in the 2000s), and local converts (Martínez-Ariño 2012, 2016). Among the latter, some refer to reminiscences of Jewish traditions in their families as the trigger for their conversion or "return" to Judaism.

The small size of the communities, next to an attitude of caution and the widespread presence of anti-Semitic stereotypes and attitudes[1] among the Spanish population (Baer and López 2012; Beyer 2019) have made it quite rare to encounter public expressions of contemporary Jewish life in Spanish cities. This invisible presence contrasts with other, more visible religious groups, mostly Catholicism, for obvious reasons in Spain. Minority groups including Muslims, Sikhs, and those attached to forms of holistic spirituality are also visibly present in urban public spaces (Clot-Garrell and Griera 2019; Griera and Burchardt, 2020; see also Griera and Clot-Garrell in this volume). However, there are a few exceptional occasions when Jewish life brings religious rituals to the streets and squares of big cities, mostly Madrid and Barcelona. The lighting of the candelabrum for *Hanukkah* in public spaces has taken place in these two cities for about fifteen years now. More recently, in 2018 and 2019, the festival of *Sukkot* was also celebrated in a public square in Barcelona.

Lighting the Hanukkiah

Hanukkah is one of the most well-known celebrations in the Jewish calendar. To commemorate the victory of the Maccabees over the Greeks and the re-inauguration of the Second Temple, a new candle is lit every day for eight days, usually in private homes or synagogues, but also increasingly in public squares and parks. The celebration has acquired a missionary character since the international ultra-Orthodox Hassidic movement Chabad Lubavitch has brought this event to the streets. By reminding nonpracticing Jews of the importance of the ritual and establishing norms of conduct around the celebration, this ultra-Orthodox movement is attempting to bring them back to Judaism. In so doing, they reinforce moral constraints that limit the scope of possible (Jewish) subjectivities (Orsi 1999).

This celebration is not exclusive to the city of Barcelona. Increasingly, Jewish communities and philosemitic organizations in other Spanish cities, including Madrid, Girona, Melilla, and Oviedo, celebrate *Hanukkah* in public spaces. Interestingly, the celebration often counts not only on the formal approval but also on the presence and active participation (e.g., lighting candles) of political and administrative municipal authorities, which gives the celebration a more official character. Other European cities are also witnessing the spread of this event, with the whole celebration following a rather standardized pattern across cities—the result of homogenizing processes linked to globalization and the expansion of transnational religious movements (Endelstein 2017).

In Barcelona, *Hanukkah* has been celebrated in public for over a decade now. The event, promoted by Chabad Barcelona with the support of the small business association of the city's medieval Jewish neighborhood (which currently has almost no Jewish residents and hosts only one or two Jewish-themed businesses run by Jews), takes place with the formal permission of the municipality. It consists of the staging of the lighting of the candelabrum in the City Hall and Catalan Government Square. While the number of people who attend the event in Barcelona does not exceed two to three hundred people, the celebration is quite visible for passers-by, tourists who visit the square, and local businesses. Moreover, the celebration is often covered by local media outlets, which superficially introduce the tradition to the non-Jewish majority. Many aspects contribute to this visibility, including the recitation of prayers and blessings amplified with microphones in a secular space, the stage and rows of chairs set up in the central square (partially disrupting the normal free movement of pedestrians), the size of the candelabrum and the banner attached to it, the music that is played, the dancing, the garments of some of the participants, and the distribution of *sufganiot*, the traditional sweets of this celebration. One particularity of Chabad Lubavitch that makes its members so visible in comparison to other Jews is the attire that they use; men usually wear black suits and hats and have long beards, while women often wear long skirts and dark colors, hiding their hair for modesty's sake. Many Chabad women wear wigs for this reason.

Every year, this celebration relies on the presence of at least one municipal politician as well as (occasionally) a civil servant from the municipal administration. The presence of these municipal actors is not merely ornamental; they are invited to light one of the candles of the candelabrum and give a short speech to those present. In recent years, it has been the deputy mayor for Citizenship Rights, Culture, Participation and Transparency, often together with the commissioner for Intercultural Dialogue and Religious Pluralism of the Barcelona Municipality, who have attended and participated in the event. On previous occasions, the director of the Barcelona Religious Affairs Office was present.

Constructing the Sukkah

Between September 25 and 30, 2018, a *sukkah* was built in a public square in the Barcelona city center, close to where the eventization of *Hanukkah* takes place every year. The *sukkah*, a temporary hut intentionally built with precarious materials, commemorates the difficulties that the people of Israel went through in their forty-year passage through the desert during the Exodus from slavery in Egypt. The hut represents "a place-making tool that creates a symbiotic place of belonging" (Lipis 2016, 28). It is a temporary ritual architectural structure that creates a unique environment where Jews can celebrate the rituals related to the festival of *Sukkot*. While the materials with which *sukkot* are built can vary, the roof must be totally or partially open to the sky. On the day of the inaugural celebration in Barcelona, an open talk with neighbors was scheduled to allow them to get to know more about the celebration and experience the event first-hand. Even though Chabad Lubavitch Barcelona was the key organizer, a member of a Reform Jewish community communicated their intentions to a local politician informally in advance. Members of other local Jewish communities also participated in the inauguration. Food and drinks were distributed to members of Jewish communities, neighbors, politicians, and bystanders. Before that year, a small *sukkah* built in the backyard of one of the Chabad facilities had been used for the community's celebrations.

Although the building of the *sukkah* in central Barcelona was possible, it could not take place in the location originally proposed by the organizers. They had wanted to build it in the square next to Barcelona Cathedral, a location with much more foot traffic than the square where it was finally built. The organizers preferred the cathedral square mainly because they assumed that it would be more accessible and visible for Jewish tourists wishing to celebrate *Sukkot* while on vacation. As one of the Chabad members put it, the idea of building the *sukkah* emerged from "a need that we had to have a *sukkah* like other big cities in the world, especially because of the large number of tourists as well as locals. And we wanted to place it in as strategic an area as possible, from the perspective of both tourist attendance and proximity to *kosher* restaurants." Moreover, the cathedral square is a much larger space—one which represents the power of the Catholic Church. Building the *sukkah* there would have not only granted more visibility and prominence to the *sukkah*, but also would have questioned the Church's hegemonic dominance of that space. The municipality, however, refused this request, noting that at that time of year the city was also celebrating the Patron Saint Festival—a four-day festival that transforms many city spaces into locations for concerts, theater plays, and other street art performances. The Jewish stakeholders requesting permission for the *sukkah* had no option but to adjust to the space for which official permission was granted. This adjustment to, and acceptance of, a different space for a minority religious celebration has also been reported for the local celebration of other minority religious festivities, such as the Islamic procession of *Ashura*, "highlighting how majority traditions in the city take priority over minority traditions when the two enter into conflict" (Astor et al. 2018).

During the inauguration of the *sukkah*, various members of the Jewish community in Barcelona explained the meaning of the event in practice to the municipal authorities. They emphasized the idea of hospitality, offered them special sweets, and shared recipes with them, all in an atmosphere of joy and celebration. As one of the Jewish persons initiating the request to the municipality told me, the organizers wanted to make it clear to the authorities that this was a very special occasion. They praised the decision of the municipality to allow and support the celebration: "I told her [the municipal politician representing the district where the *sukkah* was built]: 'Look, you have made it possible for there to be a *sukkah* for the first time in history. This is a historic event! We are deeply grateful. These last years, we had to do it clandestinely. Now we have moved into visibility.'" A member of another Jewish community explained that this public *sukkah* put Barcelona on the same plane as other big world cities which have hosted public *sukkot* for years.

The Multidimensional Nature of Religious Events

Public religious events have implications for both the religious group involved and the wider environment surrounding them (Baumann 2002). According to Garbin (2012b, 429), "diasporic religious processions are occasions for the dramatization of concerns internal to a group" while, at the same time, "they also involve an engagement with the outside world through the visible and audible staging and performance of a range of collective identities." The two religious celebrations that I have presented above can also be considered what Endelstein (2017, 57) calls "polysemic events" in that they have different meanings and communicate different things for both insiders and outsiders of the Chabad movement and the Jewish population more broadly.

First, from the perspective of Jewish communities, these two celebrations can be understood as "place-making" and "place-marking" tools. By placing architectural and material objects and performing religious rituals in specific public spaces, these two celebrations produce "places of belonging" (Lipis 2016, 31) where the diasporic Jewish community and a feeling of belonging within it are created and reinforced. In other words, these events create Jewishness and are therefore constitutive of Barcelona's Jewish communities. Moreover, the performances of these two Jewish religious celebrations in the city's public squares temporarily mark parts of the urban territory as Jewish. Place-marking practices are of particular importance for minority and diasporic groups, as they allow the appropriation of certain spaces that are otherwise dominated by symbols and meanings belonging to the majority group. Access to and temporary appropriation of urban space by Jewish actors in the context of these two celebrations "implies trespassing physical and symbolic as well as institutional and informal thresholds which question the usual spatial order of urban territory" (Saint-Blancat and Cancellieri 2014, 652). For a couple of hours (in the case of the *Hanukkah* celebration) or five days (in the case of the *sukkah*), spaces used for secular purposes are temporarily sacralized. This is provisional, and it is precisely because of this temporary character that the events disrupt the normal social order of interaction in public spaces (Goffman 1963a). Both the public celebration of these events and the presence of architectural elements that block certain spaces to passers-by help create a "microcosmos," drawing a boundary between insiders and outsiders (Umashankar 2015), a "temporary status reversal in [*sic*] which transforms parade participants into 'owners of the streets'" (Ingalls 2012, 343). Through making and marking places as Jewish, these celebrations ultimately contribute to the vitality of the diverse religious landscape of the city.

Second, by temporarily reversing the status of those spaces, these celebrations blur the boundaries between secular and religious spaces. In public religious celebrations, such as street parades or the two examples outlined in this chapter, there is a temporary sacralization of space (Garbin 2012b). In this process, material and symbolic boundaries are drawn to make normative distinctions between the space of everyday social life and the space that, for insiders, requires certain norms of behavior in relation to what some consider the divine (for Jewish people or for society at large). In this sense, sacred space is built as "the location for ritual communication" (Anttonen 2005, 198). This process of sacralization happens through the use of religious symbolism, the performance of religious rituals, and the collective emotional experiences often attached to them (Finlayson 2017). In the two cases examined here, sacralization happens through the use of Jewish symbolism (the *sukkah* and the candelabrum), the performance of a religious ritual (the building and opening of the *sukkah*, the lighting of the candles), the embodied performance of celebrations (be it performing rituals and prayers and eating inside the *sukkah* or singing and dancing to celebrate *Hanukkah*), and the emotional experiences attached to them. All these elements temporarily suspend the secular social structure and rhythm of urban life (Kong 2005), which are reestablished once the events are over. The fragility of both the secular and the religious order of these spaces thus becomes apparent.

Third, these two events also represent a sort of "coming out" of the closet of discretion, a quest for public visibility and recognition. By organizing such religious celebrations in public, the Jewish communities of Barcelona "have crossed an ontological barrier" (Werbner 1996, 332), thereby challenging the dichotomy between public and private and claiming their right to be in public. These public events can be considered what I have called elsewhere "place-recovering practices" (Martínez-Ariño, 2020) in a context where traces of the medieval Jewish past are almost totally erased. These celebrations, then, do not only entail processes of individual and collective identity building, but are also an attempt to achieve public visibility. This "request for visibility implies a demand for social recognition[,] which entails becoming full actors who can display their own identity and specificity in public space" (Saint-Blancat and Cancellieri 2014, 646). In the case of Barcelona, as stated by a Jewish representative in an interview with me, "What we want to show is that even if Jews are not living in the medieval Jewish neighborhood anymore, there is a Jewish life." By displaying their festivals publicly, there is a clear claim of a part of the Jewish population to being seen and recognized in their specificity as part of the urban community.

The fact that many of these celebrations have a festive character and are seen as folkloric cultural celebrations rather than religious rituals facilitates the portrayal of a positive image of these groups, which may ultimately increase their acceptance and recognition by authorities and the wider public. In the concrete case of the two Jewish events in Barcelona, the festive atmosphere, together with the hospitality shown and the involvement of politicians, serves to project a positive image of Chabad—both to Jewish communities, who often see them as "too strict" or "too orthodox," and to politicians and the general public, who often view them as "exotic" and as supporters of Israel.

Moreover, the fact that the celebration of *Hanukkah* occurs at the same time and place as the Christmas lights and crèche is, according to one of my Jewish interlocutors, a very powerful cultural symbol. For him, having the two religious traditions represented in a space where the medieval Jewish community once lived is symbolically very meaningful. As such, the celebration of *Hanukkah* not only makes time sacred for its Jewish participants, but also de-monopolizes and diversifies sacred time. In other words, sacred time is no longer reserved exclusively for Christmas celebrations but is expanded to include the sacred time of the Jewish minority. Orsi argues that it is precisely through public displays of religion that inhabitants of cities "[announce] in their own voices the heterogeneity of cities" (1999, 48). Moreover, the quest for visibility for these events must be considered against the broader historical, religious, and political conditions within the city. In the context of the celebration of Christmas festivities, which dominate all public spaces and the media in Spain during that period of the year, the lighting of the *hanukkiah* does not overshadow the overwhelming presence of Christmas lights. The installation of the *sukkah*, which was first built during a period of strong political upheaval in Barcelona (i.e., demonstrations in favor of Catalan independence) as well as during the city's patron saint festivals, also went unnoticed for most of the city's population. However, due to the limited presence of Jewish religious references in Spanish public life, the possibility of encountering what Endelstein (2017, 65) calls "the curious protagonists of the event"—the Lubavitch men, but also the whole visual, acoustic, and culinary experience—grants these celebrations a somewhat spectacular character.

This visibility is not restricted to the immediacy of the celebration. The use of audiovisual aids and media, characteristic of Chabad Lubavitch (Katz 2010), has an impact on the event itself as well as beyond the specific time and space where it is held. The music and dancing involved in the Hanukkah event help create a more extravagant atmosphere, which is then projected to broader audiences through YouTube videos and Facebook posts published thereafter. This, together with the distribution of pictures in the Chabad Lubavitch movement's official media channels (Golan and Stadler 2016)—where it is possible to find a picture of a *menorah* or candelabrum from each city where a celebration has taken place—contributes to its perpetuation over time (Endelstein 2017). Other authors analyzing public expressions of religion have also reported this increased impact of religious celebrations in wider publics through social media (Astor et al. 2018). In this sense, it is important to understand that these urban religious events are not only local phenomena but also practices that connect the local with the global (Orsi 1999).

Finally, these celebrations are also an internal claim for authenticity and community representation. While these events reinforce the external boundary between Jewish communities and the rest of the population, they also make internal boundaries evident. These celebrations serve as a platform for Chabad to position themselves as the "authentic" representatives of Jewish communities. This struggle for authenticity has been heightened since the arrival of the movement in the city in the early 2000s. Moreover, by inviting other Jewish representatives while remaining the masters of ceremony, Chabad leaders present themselves as the religious authority over the other Jewish communities, not just over their "followers." This attempt to present themselves as the "true" representatives of Judaism, vis-à-vis both the Jewish population and municipal authorities, is criticized from within the Jewish communities. For Jewish representatives whose beliefs and ideological stance are distant from the ultra-Orthodox position of Chabad Lubavitch, the image that these public celebrations portray is not one with which they feel at ease. For some Jews, Chabad represents a conservative interpretation of Judaism that does not conform to their personal experiences. One of my interviewees, a Jew from a cultural association unaffiliated with the Chabad milieu, indicated his concerns about the spread of these public events led by Chabad: "We do not interpret this as something positive because it is projecting an image of Judaism which may be very respectable, but which I think that, first, is not representative of the Jewish community of Barcelona; and, second, ideologically, we do not share their understanding of Judaism as proselytizing and messianic." Therefore, members from other branches of Judaism in Barcelona do not take part in these events because they do not want to be associated with representatives and activities from the Chabad movement. This conveys the multivocal and contested character of these urban religious celebrations.

What Makes These Celebrations Possible?

While the celebrations that I have analyzed above are not exclusive to Barcelona, reflecting instead a transnational trend toward the eventization of certain Jewish festivities (Buckser 2005; Katz 2009, 2010), there are local factors that make them possible. In what follows, I present a conjunction of four factors that are relevant to the success of the events: (1) a favorable legal framework, (2) a transformation of the urban religious landscape, (3) a discursive shift in local politics, and (4) a framing of the events as a "return to normality." While all four have played a role in enabling these events, I argue that the fourth factor is most significant in explaining their success.

First, the legal framework in Spain is favorable to the celebration of religious events in public spaces. At the most fundamental level, the right to assemble and the right to religious freedom protect the possibility to organize these events. In particular, the Spanish Constitution of 1978, the 1980 Spanish Law of Religious Freedom, the 2009 Catalan Law on Places of Worship, and policy guidelines—such as the 2015 *Guidelines for the respect of diversity of beliefs in public spaces* from the Catalan government, inspired by the 2013 national guide, *Public space and religious freedom*—establish a legal and political framework that allows for the organization of public religious events. Moreover, recently created administrative procedures at the municipal level ensure that these regulations are put into practice on the ground. Of particular relevance here is the Barcelona city government's 2016 *Policy measure on the guarantee of equal treatment of religious organizations in relation to the celebration of one-time activities in public spaces*. It aims to ensure the exercise of the right to religious freedom and equal treatment, normalize the presence of religious diversity, and facilitate access to public space for religious organizations which are in a more precarious economic, legal, or organizational situation. All in all, this normative framework is permissive and can only be used to restrict public religious celebrations under very specific circumstances.[2]

Second, the transformation of the urban religious landscape, and in particular its diversification and revitalization, has also contributed to the possibility of celebrating these festivities. On the one hand, the growing number of religious minorities present in the city (Martínez-Ariño 2018) has made the celebration of religious rituals and festivities in public spaces more common for both urban inhabitants and public authorities. Examples beyond Jewish celebrations are the *Ashura* procession of Shia Muslims (Astor et al. 2018) and more newly arrived Catholic processions performed by immigrant groups (Fernández-Mostaza and Muñoz Henríquez 2018), all of which normalize the diversity of religious celebrations in the streets. On the other hand, a process of internal diversification and revitalization of certain religious groups—including, with the arrival of "orthodox and missionary" groups, Judaism—produces a reconfiguration of actor constellations that encourages more visible expressions of religiosity in public. As Endelstein (2017) has shown for the cases of France and England, it is the growth of this ultra-Orthodox movement that underpins the expansion of Jewish religious celebrations in public spaces. This, however, as I have shown above, does lead to some discomfort among those who adopt a more cultural approach to Judaism and who reject what one might call the religionization—a process whereby spaces, practices, and narratives are signified as religious (Dressler 2019)—of Judaism that Chabad Lubavitch has undertaken.

Third (although not completely new), since the new municipal government took office in 2015, an important discursive shift has taken place that emphasizes promoting the city as cosmopolitan and open, treating diversity as an urban asset. In the words of the municipality for the 2018 celebration of *Sukkot*, "The cultural and religious diversity of Barcelona builds a rich and strong city, and the normalization of this spiritual diversity in public spaces contributes to increasing the human richness of Barcelona" (Ajuntament de Barcelona n.d.). It is interesting that the municipal government's website gives a detailed explanation of the meaning and origin of the two festivals under investigation in this chapter as well as provides practical information about the dates and their locations in the city. Moreover, the website indicates that this information has been edited and published in a series of leaflets, entitled "Religious Festivals in Ciutat Vella," to explain to the district residents the various cultural and religious manifestations that take place in the streets. Public religious events are considered good opportunities to increase knowledge and promote the diversity of the city.

Fourth, I would argue that the framing of these religious events within a discourse of a "return to normality," a recuperation of memory, and the recognition of a religious minority has facilitated their celebration in public spaces. While the previous three factors may also explain the spread of public religious celebrations from other minorities, this fourth factor, I argue, is specifically relevant to these Jewish events. This discursive framing is particularly effective in the Spanish case due to the tragic history of the medieval Jewish communities who were persecuted, forced to convert, and ultimately expelled from the Iberian Peninsula by Spain's Catholic monarchs in 1492 (Pérez 2007; Ray 2013), and the long silence that followed. It is clear that community leaders are aware of the weight and effectiveness of this narrative. One of the Jewish representatives behind the organization of the two celebrations indicated to me in an interview that with these events, "there is a kind of reconciliation with the past, with the trouble that happened during the period of the Inquisition."

This discourse on "returning to normality" has served as a powerful motivator for the municipal politicians who have facilitated these two eventizations. The municipal councilor representing the concerned district reflected on the meaning of the celebration of *Sukkot* in a Facebook post a few days after the opening event. She narrated her experience of the inauguration of the *sukkah*, surprised by what she thought was the "excessive gratitude" she received from community members for having allowed its construction. She indicated that she eventually understood the reasons for this gratitude when community members repeatedly said, "This is the first *sukkah* since the Inquisition!" The historical relevance of the event, which the Jewish leaders had referred to in their request to build the *sukkah*, was reinforced at the moment of its opening. Moreover, the leaflet produced by the municipality to inform citizens about the festival took pride in the fact that this was going to be the first public *sukkah* in Spain: "The 2018 festivity of *Sukkot* in Barcelona will install the first public *sukkah* in the whole country." For this member of the municipal government, having succeeded in reversing this historical injustice was a reason to be proud, and she confessed in her Facebook post that she and her administrative collaborators could not hold back their tears while listening to the members of the Jewish communities present there. This emphasis on the recuperation of memory is not limited to these two cases, however. In 2018, a commitment by the municipal government to repair the memory of the city's medieval Jewish community led it to accept the Jewish communities' request to remove a street name that was considered derogatory toward Jews, and instead recognize their suffering by commemorating the contribution of the medieval Jewish communities and renaming a street after a medieval Barcelona-based rabbi. The then deputy mayor in charge of this decision stated in a newspaper article that "Barcelona can neither forget nor minimize the legacy [of its medieval Jewish community], and even less allow its stigmatization."[3] These developments should be understood in the larger context of an increasing interest in the recovery of Jewish heritage in Europe (Gruber 2002).

Conclusion

Through an analysis of two Jewish religious festivals, *Hanukkah* and *Sukkot*, in Barcelona's public spaces, I have argued in this chapter that urban religious events serve as entry points for analyzing larger social changes related to the religious diversification of urban populations and understanding the sociospatial dynamics that play out in the use, appropriation, and re-signification of urban public spaces. These events have multiple meanings and implications. For the Jewish communities involved in the celebrations, they serve many purposes, including the fulfillment of religious prescriptions and the practice of religious rituals, the making and "recovering" of a place in the city and the temporary marking of secular spaces as Jewish, the normalization of Jewish life, and the claiming of the right to express one's difference in a visible way. Moreover, with these two events generating simultaneity of religious identities, the Catholic hegemony over public space in Spain is temporarily challenged.

In this chapter, I have also disentangled a variety of factors that facilitate the celebration of religious events in public spaces. In addition to favorable legal, religious, and political factors, a particularly place-specific discourse and framing of the two Jewish celebrations as favoring a "return to normality" after the disruption of the Expulsion in the fourteenth and fifteenth centuries has been central in enabling the organization and celebration of these events. This discursive framing, which is specific to the Spanish context and its Jewish past, has played a crucial role in publicizing the urgency of the events. The analysis of the public celebrations of *Hanukkah* and *Sukkot* in this chapter has shown how the politics of memory, recognition, and reparation/restoration for an injustice which lasted for centuries has played a crucial role in favoring the public celebration and official recognition of the two Jewish religious celebrations. This highlights the political nature of urban religious events and suggests a need for thorough investigation of their intricate connections to particular times, spaces, and discourses.

Finally, the analysis of these two examples shows how religious rituals commonly performed in private spaces are eventized through the creation of appealing experiences that involve participants and spectators. This is particularly evident in the case of the *Hanukkah* event, where a well-designed choreography engages all of the senses. The jovial atmosphere produced by the music, dancing, distribution of food, and social interactions makes of these events a new cultural product that can easily be "consumed" and enjoyed by Jews and non-Jews alike. This eventization of religion transforms not only the public spaces where it takes place, but also the religious rituals performed as well as the urban dwellers. On the one hand, events transform public spaces into stages. Such stages become a point of attraction for people who want to admire the spectacle of what becomes almost a concert (in the case of *Hanukkah*) or a rather uncommon construction in the middle of the street (in the case of the *sukkah*). On the other hand, the eventization of religion exposes these celebrations to the general public, thereby becoming something of interest not only to those who participate but also to those who observe from the outside. Thus religious rituals may be turned into a performance. Finally, as this last observation suggests, ordinary citizens are also transformed through these events: participants become performers, and passers-by become spectators.

Spatial Discourses of Sanctity as a Means of Struggle and Empowerment in a Contested City

Nimrod Luz
Kinneret College on the Sea of Galilee

At the beginning of the third millennium, three major phenomena are relevant to any urban theory of conflicted or contested cities. The first is that an ever-increasing majority of humans are now residing in cities; the second is that, due to several globalization-related processes (immigration and mobility, growing disparities, hypercapitalism, etc.), cities are gradually becoming more vulnerable to external forces of a multi-scalar nature in tandem with growing social and political unrest; and the third relates to the burgeoning influence and presence of religious components in urban conflicts. Arguably, the urban sphere is increasingly experiencing the influence of religious politicization at various scales—especially in cities such as Acre, Talinn, or Istanbul, which are swept up in ethnonational urban struggles—but also in seemingly peaceful cities worldwide (AlSayyad and Massoumi 2010; Beaumont and Barker 2011; Garbin 2012a; Gökariksel and Secor 2015; Luz 2015; Tong and Kong 2000). The reemergence of religion as a component in urban conflicts and a key instigator of urban strife, most particularly in cities that feature a highly heterogeneous and multiethnic population, need not surprise us. In recent years and under various names, religion and religiosity are moving (some might say reentering, while others, including this author, would assert they never left) center stage to become powerful players in the public arena (Berger 1999; Casanova 1994; Latour 1993). Ongoing controversies in the United States surrounding gay marriage, abortion, and creationist–evolutionist debates serve as reminders that, far from the Weberian lamentation regarding the "disenchantment of the world" in the age of modernity, we are as fanatically religious as we ever were (Weber 1946). Religion-based struggles are becoming part of everyday life and everyday parlance in cities worldwide. Once again it would seem that "God walks among us," and current historical debates and processes cannot seriously be dealt with using binaries such as religion and nation, religion and secularization, or religion and the urban. This probably explains why scholarly works in recent years show a renewed interest in uncovering connections between religion and politics (Asad 1999; Kong 2010; Pullan et al. 2013). This interest stems from the realization that previous scholarly positions regarding the role of religion in our (post)modern daily life merit further reflection and fail to explain the contemporary surge of religiosity and religion in cities worldwide (Bakshi 2011; Komarova and O'Dowd 2013; Larkin 2010).

Cities have always been the place of our meeting with the "other" and "otherness" (Barthes 1981; Simmel [1903] 1971). They are spaces where different cultural perceptions are negotiated and contested among various groups who share the urban landscape and compete over tangible and intangible resources. Starting with Robert Park and the Chicago School, scholars of urban studies have long paid attention to how certain social groups come to experience and represent the city in distinct ways (Dear 2002). These very representations in public discourse are shown to be entwined with the production and reproduction of the material needs as well as signs and symbols sustaining group identity. While the urban landscape has a material reality as a tangible landscape, it is also experienced and conceptualized through the organization of social life (Massey 1992). Religion is becoming more and more relevant in the urban landscape and urban conflicts, mostly through rituals and spatialization and contestations over sacred sites (Garbin 2012b; Stadler 2015). This chapter sets out to explore these representations, discourses, and tangible manifestations of the sacred within the urban sphere, investigating the way they inform and sustain group identity within a highly contested urban landscape. I argue that these representations and discourses should serve as lenses for viewing urban (and national) politics, since they provide a framework for examining the role of values, stories, and ideals in shaping the social world and reflecting change and conflict. In order to understand these concepts and the way they inform myriad social–cultural–political attributes that shape contestations within cities, we need to explore changes in the urban landscape. These changes should be seen as both the medium and the outcome of different identity-shaping sets of values, which different groups bring into being within their cities. It is my overarching argument that religion-based conflicts are increasingly evident in these contested urban spheres. Furthermore, I contend that the urban landscape is increasingly influenced by external forces fomenting these conflicts.

This chapter seeks to further our understanding of the role of religion in conflicted cities and how it informs and shapes these cities. To illustrate my argument, I look into the ways the Haram al-Sharif (meaning "Noble Sanctuary"), the most iconic sacred Islamic site in Jerusalem, is produced, represented, and perceived, not only as an important Islamic religious symbol but also as a renowned site of Palestinian national revival. As we will discuss, urban and ethnonational conflicts are shaped by the sacred as well as other external forces. Given the fact that Jerusalem is often at the heart of national and international stories about how religious processes influence urban development, it may be regarded as an extreme case study; nonetheless, in this chapter I will demonstrate how this site illustrates a much broader phenomenon (AlSayyad and Massoumi 2010; Gómez and Van Herck 2012).

Jerusalem serves here as a prism through which we may see the potential ramifications for the future of urban contestation in conditions of religious resurgence within increasingly globalized urban landscapes. To illustrate these issues, this chapter will firstly examine the ways the sacred site is being produced as the most iconic religious–national landmark and explained against the background of a minority struggle for empowerment through the cityscape. Secondly, it will contextualize the symbolic (and often highly material) struggle over Jerusalem as a space of flow, where the urban is increasingly influenced and influencing different scales and informing a Palestinian national revival mythology. This will mostly entail a discussion of public representations and declarations about the Haram al-Sharif from Israeli-Palestinian public figures. Thirdly, the chapter will discuss the implications of religiously based conflicts within the contested city and explore the political implications of the spatialization of the sacred in a highly conflicted city, mainly through the prism of religious rituals and manifestations. Before embarking on this analysis of the most important Islamic and Jewish sacred site in Jerusalem, however, I would like to place the conflict over Jerusalem's sanctity (as a metaphor for the broader national struggle) within the context of the struggle over sacred sites among Palestinian communities in Israel in recent years.

Minorities, Sacred Sites, and the Judaization of the Israeli Landscape

In order to put the activities related to the Islamic sacred site in Jerusalem in context, it is useful at this stage to address Israel's cultural–political geography. It should be noted from the outset that the following are only rudimentary observations about issues relevant to our discussion of Jerusalem's Islamic shrine (Hilal 2006; Kimmerling 2001; Rouhana 2004; Yiftachel 2006).

The Palestinian (or Israeli, beginning in 1948) landscape experienced dramatic changes and transformations during the nineteenth century, mainly due to the growing interest and activities of European powers and an influx of new ideological groups to the region (Pappe 2004; Wagstaff 1985). One of the most influential and meaningful changes was the growing presence of Jewish settlers and settlements, which later served as the crucial basis for the emergence of the state of Israel. This was a direct outcome of the advance of the Herzlian concept of practical Zionism, i.e., the return of Jewish people to their historical homeland (Vital 1975). The years under the British Mandate (1917–48) were particularly transformative, witnessing a massive influx of Jewish immigrants and refugees. The land was nonetheless far from deserted, and the Arab population living between the Jordan and the Mediterranean Sea did not sit idly by as Zionists put down roots in the area (Pappe 2004). In opposition to the Jewish nationalist project, the local Arab population promoted its own national Palestinian movement (Muslih 1998). Tensions between these two opposing ethnic groups and ideological movements grew following the UN vote for partition of the land, with both sides realizing that a war for Palestine was imminent (Dowty 2005; Laqueur and Rubin 2001). Shortly after the final British withdrawal on May 14, 1948, a full-scale war was launched between the Jews (soon to be the state of Israel) and their Arab neighbors. As a result of the war, Israel was established as a Jewish state and imposed its rule within its sovereign territory, now comprising 78 percent of Israel/Palestine (Yiftachel and Ghanem 2004). The majority of the Arab-Palestinian population fled or was forced out of the new Jewish state, thus transforming the native Arab majority into a dispersed and marginalized minority in its previous homeland (Ghanem 2001; Morris 2001; Pappe 2011).[1] Israeli-Palestinians have become a "trapped minority," meaning that their Arab-Palestinian identity contradicts the hegemonic Jewish character of the state in which they are supposed to be equal citizens with equal rights (Rabinowitz 2001a).

As a sovereign state, Israel launched a policy of "Judaization," building over five hundred new settlements and cities in areas previously inhabited by Palestinians (Benvenisti 2000; Yiftachel 2006). One of the most important results of this project has been the disappearance of non-Jewish cultural artifacts, landmarks, houses, villages, and other cultural or spatial representations of Arab-Palestinian heritage (Falah 1996; Shehadeh 2010). As an outcome of this state-hegemonic project, the Arab minority is by and large deprived of (or lacking access to) a public space with which it can identify outside of Arab settlements. Arguably, the public space—the national cultural landscape—is dominated by Jewish-Zionistic icons and symbols. Israeli historian and public figure Meron Benvenisti, a strong advocate of Israeli-Palestinian reconciliation and mutual recognition of the loss on both sides, summarizes the contemporary Israeli landscape vis-à-vis its Arab-Palestinian origins with the following words: "One need only read Israeli textbooks or see the albums of 'before and after' photos—the land of 1948 and today–to realize how close we are to the point when the vanished Arab landscape will be considered just a piece of Arab propaganda, a fabrication aimed at the destruction of Israel" (Benvenisti 2000, 5). Since the Oslo Accords (1995), the Israeli-Palestinian minority has become increasingly involved in the Israeli public sphere. This has followed the realization that negotiations between Israel and the Palestinian Authority have not contributed to any significant improvement in their civil status or rights, paving the way for activities that "localize the national struggle" (Rekhess 2002). Issues that have haunted Palestinian communities for decades, such as the right of return, accessibility to heritage sites, the "opening of the '48 files,'" refugees, land ownership, and the communities' very definition as a national minority are coming to the surface more and more in public media, the courts, and the Israeli parliament (Rabinowitz 2001b; Reiter and Lehrs 2013).

In recent years, Palestinian citizens and groups in Israel have also become increasingly active in struggles over heritage sites, most of them of a religious nature (Luz 2013; Reiter 2010). Deserted mosques, religious endowments, graveyards, and other cultural landmarks are being contested both publicly and legally. To support these efforts and as part of an emancipatory process, several NGOs have been established. One of the most prominent is the al-Aqsa Association for the Development of Islamic Endowment Property, an offshoot of the Israeli Islamic Movement. According to Sheikh Kamal Rayan, its former director, the organization focuses its activities on "the demand to apply *Waqf* assets to the conservation and development of neglected sites" (cited in Ghanem 2001, 128). Arguably, sacred places are highly effective in the ongoing "cultural war." Due to their religious connotations and social relevance (including a deep sense of place), they are less susceptible to yield to the state's hegemonic machinery and the Judaization-cum-Israelization of the landscape. Places which are framed and perceived as sacred are highly evocative and therefore successful as platforms for bringing together people and groups who, on a day-to-day basis, do not necessarily agree or cooperate. Indeed, this should be understood against the backdrop of the increasing nationalization of the sacred among Palestinian communities (on both sides of the Green Line) which is often part and parcel of the struggle against the Israeli occupation and its current hegemonic position (Bowman 1993; Lybarger 2007).

Following Gramsci, I claim that relations between dominant and subordinate groups are a process in which boundaries and consensual norms are always shifting and being negotiated (1971). Tangled in a web of political and social relations, dominant and subordinate groups are constantly competing and transforming the spaces they are sharing (or competing for) in accordance with their cultural, economic, and political stances. The struggle for a particular place and the changes in the sociospatial boundaries of that place are inexorably linked to politics of identity. The struggle (or resistance) of a subordinate group over a particular place involves, by and large, a spatialization of identity conflicts and, at the same time, identity constructions around a particular object. Thus, in recent years the Palestinian minority in Israel has become more and more involved in various projects of different scales concerning sacred sites. From a political and cultural geographic perspective, it is engaged in a constant struggle—indeed a battle—against the state's ongoing project of Judaization. The struggle over the sacred and especially Muslim sacred sites is highly effective, as it challenges the very core of Israel as a Jewish state. As put succinctly by Nadim Rouhana, a Christian Palestinian who is also an Israeli citizen: "The holy Islamic places are more important to me than the Christian ones … I would pay good money for a mosque to be built atop Mount Carmel because it challenges the political Jewish identity of the State of Israel" (Nadim Rouhana, interview with author, August 2002). It should come as no surprise that the heart of these struggles is in Jerusalem, Israel's capital as well as the location of the most important and iconic sacred site for both parties: the Haram al Sharif, or Temple Mount. This sacred site in Jerusalem serves not only as the most holy site for the Israeli Muslim minority but also as the most conflictual place within this highly divided city.

The Sacred as Spatial Resistance

In a recent op-ed, Ra'id Salah, the leader of the Islamic Movement, made some intriguing statements which linked the Palestinian national struggle with the religious role of Jerusalem in contemporary Islam and Palestinian nationalism. In what follows, I will paraphrase from this essay, written with Salah's usual candor and eloquence:

> It is no secret that the eyes of the Islamic Movement are set towards the issues of Jerusalem and the al-Aqsa Mosque as they are to be found at the height of Islamic, Arabic and Palestinian concerns. It is no secret that the Islamic Movement was highly successful in promoting the problem of Jerusalem and

the al-Aqsa Mosque as surely it is not a secret that the Islamic Movement was able to cultivate great awareness to this issue among Muslims, Arabs and Palestinians. This success notwithstanding, there were those in the Arab public space and Palestinian Public space that tried to transform this achievement of the Islamic Movement into its guilt and a reason to question the Movement. Additionally, we were under duress to give up on our projects of al-Ribat[2] and Masatib al-'Ilm[3] at the al-Aqsa Mosque ... those opposing us have found no better way to support Jerusalem and the al-Aqsa Mosque but by casting doubts on the accomplishments of the Islamic Movement in the Jerusalem and the al-Aqsa Mosque issues. (Salah 2015)

These allegations against some of Salah's political and religious opponents tell a spatial story of how the sacred is influencing the urban, and how forces to be found on different scales (and at times external to the city) are in vogue. Since the 1980s, there has been an abundance of activities among Israeli-Palestinian Muslim citizens in and around Jerusalem. The driving force behind these activities are by and large the Islamic Movement in Israel (Ali 2018; Larkin and Dumper 2012; Luz 2013). This is especially true regarding the section of the movement headed by the author of the above quote, Sheikh Ra'id Salah (Larkin and Dumper 2012). Under his leadership, the movement has radicalized its stance against cooperation with the state authorities, constituting one of the more extreme presentations of political Islam in the region (Mustafa 2013).

The most prominent contribution of the Islamic Movement is to be found at the southern tip of the platform below the al-Aqsa Mosque, commonly known as "Solomon's Stables." In recent years, save for an occasional visit by archaeologists, the place was mostly closed to the non-Muslim public. Known also as *al-Aqsa al-Qadima* (ancient al-Aqsa), it was not part of the pilgrimage routine at the site. Since 1967, the management of the Haram al-Sharif, like other Islamic religious buildings in East Jerusalem, has been in the hands of the Jordanian Ministry of Endowments (Reiter 2008). This arrangement was haphazardly agreed upon, as silently as possible, by the Israeli government shortly after 1967. Thus, the actual daily routine of the Haram was kept by an administration that was paid and followed instructions coming from Amman. The creation of the Palestinian Authority (PA) following the Oslo Accords in 1993 heavily distorted this arrangement, since the Palestinians under Arafat were constantly striving to better their position and to undermine both Israel and Jordan's control of the Haram (Berkovits 2000).

In 1996, the Israeli-Palestinian Islamic Movement sought to prove that it was also a significant player, in addition to the triad of Israel, Jordan, and the PA.

In the summer of that year, the Islamic Endowments Authority (by now a scion of the PA) received approval from the Israeli government to carry out necessary maintenance works in the underground halls. Under the leadership of Ra'id Salah, the Northern faction of the Islamic Movement mobilized thousands of volunteers, along with money and materials that were indispensable for this building project. The movement was responsible for the execution of a large-scale renovation project that ultimately transformed the halls into one of the largest mosques in the Middle East (Abd al-Malik Dahamsha, interview with author, September 2002). This was a live demonstration that the power of this particular place, combined with the movement's organizational skills, could bring about massive public support among Israeli-Palestinian citizens. One of the outcomes of the 1996 al-Aqsa campaign was the establishment of an annual rally called "al-Aqsa is in Danger" (Arabic: *al-Aqsa fi khatar*). The rally was initially organized as a fundraiser for the 1996 renovation campaign; however, it was such an astounding success that it has since become the biggest and most meaningful regular event held by the Northern faction. This attests to the importance assigned to the Haram by Israeli-Palestinians but is also a sign of the movement's role and its significance in contemporary politics.

The Islamic Movement is engaged year-round with various social activities targeted at bringing the Haram al-Sharif closer to its constituency. Throughout the year, pilgrims from around Israel are provided with bus services to facilitate their visit to the Haram. This is not a sporadic or occasional effort but rather a continuous project (Kamal Khatib, interview with author October 2002). Thanks to such efforts, the movement is reaching more and more people, including those without regular access to written or electronic media—particularly women. In Sakhnin, a town of 25,000 people in central Galilee, no fewer than twelve buses (carrying roughly 600 people) depart regularly to Jerusalem on weekends (author's observations). During an April 3, 2011, visit to a mosque in Ibbellin, a village of some 11,000 inhabitants in the Lower Galilee, I saw a handwritten note on the inner door of the mosque inviting the public to participate in prayers in al-Aqsa. This meant that thousands of visitors (possibly pilgrims) were being transported to the Haram al-Sharif from around Israel on a weekly basis, rather than awaiting special occasions. In 2004, the movement was responsible for bussing about 350,000 people to Jerusalem (Larkin and Dumper 2012). This suggests that since the beginning of the movement's activities, over two million people have been provided transport to Jerusalem.

The al-Aqsa Association for the Upkeep of Islamic Endowments and Sacred Places initiates numerous projects to maintain a public connection with al-Aqsa.

Established in 1990, the Association's raison d'être is the preservation and defense of religious endowments (*awqaf*) and Islamic sacred sites throughout Israel (Kamal Rayan, interview with author, October 2002). However, special attention is given to projects that concern the sacred center in Jerusalem. Two such projects directly involve commemorating the Haram and connecting as large an audience as possible with it. The first is called *Shadd al-Rihal* ("fastening the saddles"). The name is derived from a well-known tradition (*hadith*) according to which Muhammad acknowledged that saddles could be fastened to beasts for holy pilgrimage to only three mosques (those of Mecca, Medina, and Jerusalem) (Kister 1969). The importance of this tradition is primarily the fact that it establishes Jerusalem's status as equal to the other two most important sanctuaries in Islamic piety. According to former director Rayan, the project's objective is to establish a direct and unobstructed connection between Israeli-Palestinian Muslims and the al-Aqsa mosque, especially now that "dire days that are upon us" (Kamal Rayan, interview with author, October 2002). A second project involves planting trees around the Haram. These two projects have been developed so as to ensure a connection between the sacred site and Israeli-Palestinian Muslim devotees on a practical and quotidian level, solidifying their commitment. Indeed, in recent years there has been a growing tendency among Israeli-Palestinian Muslims to decorate new houses—mostly above the main entrance—with signs and pictures of the Dome of the Rock. The casual and everyday manner in which this has become a convention clearly indicates that the Islamic Movement is making headway among its constituency with its objectives regarding the Haram and Jerusalem. These spatial activities are part of a wider range of activities which transform the city into a "space of flows," allowing forces of different scales to actively influence the city through its sacred site. In recent years, the al-Aqsa Association has become the key actor in these activities, initiating various projects which aim to enhance the importance assigned to the site by Muslim believers (Larkin and Dumper 2012; Luz 2004).

Scaling the Struggle for the Sacred: Transforming the City into a Space of Flows

The concept of geographical scale has come to the fore in recent debates among political, economic, and urban geographers (Brenner 2001; Jonas 2006; Marston, Jones, and Woodward 2005). In light of the discussion among scholars in the field, I would suggest the following: scale is the spatial configuration where sociopolitical relations are contested (Swyngedouw 1997). Spatial scale must be understood as something that is produced and, as such, is primarily a political and social project. It is a process that involves politics and is therefore constantly contested by opposing forces. Scalar configurations are not predetermined platforms upon which social life simply takes place but are continually remade through sociopolitical struggles. Scale is socially constructed, which implies that in each and every level of analysis—from the personal to the global—our understanding of scale is the outcome of social processes and political struggles (Jonas 2006). The question of scale and the setting of scale is a matter of political struggle involving power relations and shifts in existing power geometries (Smith 1993). Scale demarcates the site of social or political contest, providing a context for each struggle. It is an active progenitor of specific social processes; it sets the boundaries for struggles over identity and spatial control. In the face of a scale imposed by a hegemonic power (such as the state), subaltern groups may opt to thwart this power by actively jumping scales.

To illustrate this argument, let us explore the following remarks from an Arab-Israeli leader, at the time an elected member of the Israeli parliament. On September 28, 2000, MK (and future Israeli prime minister) Ariel Sharon made a highly controversial visit to the Haram al-Sharif. In the days that followed the visit, the Second Intifada was underway and civilian acts of resistance against state authority were spreading among Palestinian communities both within and beyond the Green Line. When interviewed about the riots and reactions among Israeli-Palestinians, Abd al-Malik Dahamshe, then head of the Islamic party in the Israeli parliament, supplied the following rejoinder:

> It is a war that every Muslim should be part of. There is no Green Line when al-Aqsa is concerned and this [the reactions] will continue throughout Israel …
> I cannot see this murderer transgress the most holy place in this land and idly observe from the sideline. Am I not a human being? Am I devoid of emotions, am I not a Muslim? He entered the most holy mosque of the Muslims in order to defile it as a murderer, as a powerful man, a Zionist. Do you honestly believe that we will not face up to it? This act is addressed against our very existence, but we do exist. Our sole culpability is that we are humans and that we have a life and that we have a mosque and a land. (Gal 2000)

Here, Dahamshe uses an intriguing spatial language. He weaves a complex multi-scalar configuration, from the global to the local via the supranational. Against the backdrop of Israeli control over the sacred, he moves between scales to subvert and resist a pregiven geographical production of scale in that specific place. Indeed, jumping scales allows subordinated or controlled parties to dissolve superimposed spatial boundaries. The intense struggles of the Second Intifada further supply us with a number of declarations, deeds, and representations regarding the Haram and the way it is produced and spatialized by Muslim Israeli-Palestinians. In a similar vein, Tawfiq Muhammad 'Ari'ar presents us with an uncompromising view of the Islamic character of the holy precinct in Jerusalem (2002). The conflict over the site is essentially a religious one, 'Ari'ar claims, and since it is one of the three most important Islamic shrines it cannot be negotiated, nor compromised. The author exploits all the standard religious justifications to warn PA officials against concessions when negotiating with Israel over the place. He is particularly averse to the idea that Jews will be allowed to continue to pray at the Western Wall. An even more confrontational and adamant approach is advanced in an article authored by Ra'id Salah. He vows to defend the Haram al-Sharif with his life and warns against even the smallest concession of any of its parts:

> This is the destination of the nocturnal journey of the Prophet (Isra'a) and from here he ascended to heaven (M'iraj). This place witnessed the conquest of Jerusalem by Umar ibn al-Khattb and the liberation of Jerusalem from the hands of the Crusades by Salah al-Din … and because it is so important it is beyond negotiation and no voice will rise higher than the voice of al-Aqsa. And those of feeble character that say that America is stronger than them the blessed al-Aqsa answers and says God is Stronger. And the Western Wall from within and from without is part of al-Aqsa and so are the other buildings and mosques within it, including al-Musalla al-Marwani. This being the true nature of al-Aqsa, we will renew our covenant with God and our covenant with al-Aqsa and we will pin our hopes on our Islamic nation (*Umma*) and our Arab world and our Palestinian people and reiterate: we shall redeem you in spirit and blood. (Salah 2002)

Rhetoric of this nature positions the Israeli-Palestinian Islamic Movement as the most hawkish faction, reluctant to make any concessions with Israel regarding the Haram al-Sharif. Salah's attitude, which at the time was backed by daily tangible actions, not only produces the public image of an al-Aqsa zealot but also reflects badly on anyone willing to consider a less obstinate approach. Salah makes the connection among the local, the regional, and the global as part of his strategy to thwart or resist Israeli control over the place. He thus not only promotes himself as the "true" sheikh of al-Aqsa but also successfully fuses the sacred (religious) with the nation and national goals. The promotion of the sacred site in Jerusalem as a symbolic national site allows for external intrusion and influence on the urban landscape.

The implication of this scalar configuration is the making of the sacred site into an ethnonational (and supranational) Islamic landmark. In doing so, Israeli-Palestinians are first and foremost constructing ways to resist the Israeli state and the Jewish majority's construction of the space, producing instead a different understanding and conduct within the place. This is precisely the transformation of cities that Castells defines as constituting a space of flows as opposed to a space of places (Castells 1996). Using these terms, he addresses changes in contemporary societies which, due to numerous technological innovations, are constructed around flows: flows of capital, flows of images, flows of information, and even flows of religious symbols. The city is thus being produced and constructed at different locations and on different scales. Such technological developments allow for a growing dissociation between the production and performances of everyday life and the locations where these processes are spatially located. In the case of Jerusalem, the way the sacred site is being produced and perceived is mostly organized by players external to the city who inform, influence, and transform the city, even though they are spatially disconnected. Thus, the spatiality of the sacred and the spatial discourses revolving around it are responsible for reinventing traditions that structure a new urban perspective, which in turn informs new modes of actions. The city is subject to claims and counterclaims over symbolic places. Newly attributed allegorical meaning is charging the urban scene with an evolving sense of local identity, which allows for the fusion of a certain history and geography to construct new means of struggle through the sacred for the minority. While it is outside the scope of this chapter to delve into the topic further, this spatial discourse mirrors a project currently conducted by the urban Jewish majority on both the citywide and national scale (Azaryahu and Kellerman 1999).

Conclusion

At the outset of this chapter, I raised a question regarding the intricate connections among religion, materiality, and sacred places in the context of an ethnocratic urban regime. Subsequently, I sought to explore the ways sacred places are being produced and narrated among minorities as spatial means of struggle and empowerment and the ways they are inscribed into the landscape in contested geographies. I focused on the most iconic Islamic site in Jerusalem, al-Haram al-Sharif, and how it is being produced and explained against the background of a minority struggle for empowerment through the cityscape.

I followed the processes through which the site is being narrated and produced in public representations and religious rituals. I demonstrated how within the highly contested urban sphere—as well as the Israeli ethnocratic context—the Palestinian minority is claiming the urban landscape and (more precisely) its most revered sacred site through religious narratives, religious rituals, and by fusing this sacred ground into the process of national revival. This chapter therefore illustrates how religion can provide a useful framework for competing narratives and spatial logic as well as for the construction of new political geographies in the city.

In his seminal work on highly contested cities, Scott Bollen introduces his concept of "polarized cities." He defines them as "sites of enduring and consistent interethnic violence laden with political meaning, capable of destabilizing both city life and larger peace processes" (2000, 10). Jerusalem indeed represents an extreme case study of an urban milieu that is yielding to flows of religious and political radicalization. However, Jerusalem is also part of a broader and growing class of religiously contested cities worldwide. Indeed, religion and faith-based struggles loom large in urban conflicts. Therefore they undoubtedly serve as spatial meanings and metaphors for claiming the city. Urban divisions between communities of faith are readily apparent in cities around the world that have suffered from ideological or ethnic separation, conflicts, and violence (Becci, Burchardt and Casanova 2013). Various distinct groups thus weave new patterns into the urban landscape as ways of claiming the city through religiously based identity politics (Hervieu-Leger 2002; Orsi 1985). As a case in point, Mike Davis has demonstrated how Latino immigrants are reinvigorating religious urban communities in the United States and changing the North American urban landscape on a grand scale. Through his analysis of the Mexican Virgin of Guadalupe parades in Los Angeles, Davis demonstrates the linkages among cities, culture, and religion, and the city can be claimed through religious rituals (2001, 13–4). Returning to the subject of Jerusalem, Friedland and Hecht explore current political contestations in the city while emphasizing its sacred character and the growing influence of religion on how the city is managed (2014). This exploration of what they describe as "Sacred Urbanism" reveals the immense impact of religion and sacrality on the current urban landscape.

Within the body of studies on "religion in the city," I would also point to discussions of the spatial behavior of religious minorities (Dodds 2002; Metcalf 1996, among others). In this chapter, I therefore asserted the idea that the construction of alternate spatial discourses among minority groups not only constitutes a powerful strategy to reinforce identity and power, but also allows for intricate spatial politics that render the urban vulnerable to a plethora of influences within a multi-scalar setting. Through the cracks of increasingly oppressive urban governance, religion is enabling marginalized groups to challenge and infiltrate the social, spatial, and political center. The Islamic sacred site in Jerusalem is being produced as a place that informs and strengthens identity for a minority facing a highly problematic power-geometry within a discriminatory state. It is being used as a location that serves as a symbolic anchor for a dispersed community. The Islamic sacred site in Jerusalem serves in this case as the most iconic and meaningful place for the Palestinian community in Israel. The struggle over this place is part of a cultural and political struggle for autonomy and self-determination. In today's Jerusalem, the Islamic Movement capitalizes on specific religious interpretations and successfully transforms them to create a space of exception. The urban becomes a micro-site of the national struggle and succumbs to more radical and reactionary ideas in order to accommodate needs that traditional religious norms fail to meet. Allegedly, the commodity is sacrality, but the stakes are highly political and the consequences are far-reaching in a range of multi-scalar settings, starting from the personal and reaching the national and global via the urban. The current understanding of the sacred site and the ways it is being produced is congruent with the current trends of polarization, religious radicalization, and the development of a highly fragmented urban landscape in Jerusalem. In many ways, the various—and at times opposing—spatial interpretations of the most sacred site in Jerusalem encapsulate the very essence of contestation and conflicts in this troubled city (Yacobi 2015). Moreover, my exploration of the Haram al-Sharif in Jerusalem follows a growing interest in a new form of religious "urbanity" and the ways in which material religious presences may refashion and alter contemporary cityscapes. Religious place-making—the appropriation and experiencing of space through various religious activities—is clearly a multidimensional and a multi-scalar process. This grounding and "production" of religious space (Knott 2005) through the conception, representation, and lived experience of the sacred by a minority community needs to be seen as a means of empowerment (through an alternative understanding of sanctity as part of countering hegemonic constructions of the urban and its sacred meaning).

I will conclude by suggesting that religion is becoming more and more relevant in the urban landscape. This is spatialized and manifested in religious rituals as well as sociopolitical contestations over sacred sites. It is particularly apparent in regions where disputes over national territory permeate the urban space and inform its power geometries. My analysis also demonstrates how representations, discourses, and tangible manifestations of sacred places within the urban sphere—and the way they inform and sustain group identity and materialize within the sacred landscape—are highly indicative of a plethora of sociospatial processes. Therefore, I argue that these representations and discourses need be looked at as lenses for urban (and national) politics, since they provide a framework for examining the role of values, stories, and ideals in shaping the social world and reflecting change and conflict. In order to understand these concepts and the way they inform myriad social–cultural–political attributes that shape contestations within cities, we need to explore changes in the urban landscape and, more precisely, materialities of sacred places. This is certainly true in cities where such processes render minorities and marginalized groups more susceptible to scrutiny and suspicion as they intensify their contest with hegemonic discourse, constructing visible signs (i.e., religious sites) that rise from religious alterity, different spatial logic, and different understandings of the city. I hope that my analysis fosters new approaches to interpreting these complex processes, with a focus on both long- and short-term developments in contemporary religious manifestations.

Decoding Strategic Secularism in Madrid: Religion as Ambience in Three Scenarios

Mónica Cornejo-Valle
Complutense University of Madrid

On April 15, 2018, I arrived on Serrano Street in Madrid to join marchers for the International Day of the Unborn Child (unofficially established by Pope John Paul II in 1999).[1] Serrano Street is the main high-end shopping area of Madrid, and on that sunny Sunday, many people were walking in the middle of the road, since the traffic had been diverted for the occasion. I arrived by subway and walked through Colon Square toward Prada, the fashion shop, to find the first attendees. Then I walked with them toward Gucci to find the meeting point. For several days before this event, Spain's Catholic media called citizens to march "for life." The scene seemed less explicitly religious than, for example, the huge Holy Week processions just a few weeks earlier. Still, some people carried big national flags with the flaming Sacred Heart of Jesus on them. There was also a two-meter-tall white cross, several priests and nuns here and there, more crosses, and other iconic references such as small posters and banners from Catholic associations and personal Catholic adornments. However, the dominant aesthetic of the scene was the color green, meant to symbolize hope. At the meeting point, in the square of St. Francis Borgia's church, a throng of teenagers were exchanging green balloons for small donations. They also sold caps, necklaces, and T-shirts, but many attendees wore their own green clothes, bought for previous marches or meetings. The clothes displayed the motto "Sí a la vida" (yes to life), but the light green matched that of the official T-shirts worn by participants in a run against cancer that was happening at the same time and place. When we were in the first half of the march, the race against cancer had just finished, and the runners met and crossed the wave of posters of fetuses while they walked back home. For a moment, the march was flooded by the runners (also wearing green T-shirts) and the antiabortion activists seemed to double their numbers. The religious dimension of the event was not easily visible, and the strategy was ostensibly secular (marching through a commercial street instead of praying in a worship place). Nonetheless, this scene was as good an example of the contemporary religious landscapes in Spain as a traditional Catholic procession.

The aim of this chapter is to explore the blurred boundaries between the religious and the secular, focusing on how secular means are employed to implement a confessional agenda. More specifically, in this chapter I explore how different events and practices work together and share strategies and social actors, even when these forces and actors seem to be advancing entirely different agendas when viewed separately. To illustrate, I will consider three cases: the celebration of the International Day of the Unborn Child in 2018, the scandal of the fashionable Wise Men in 2017, and the nativity scene protest around Christmas 2016. In order to explore these cases and their theoretical relevance, I will first discuss some concepts such as strategic secularism, ambient faith, and the semiotics of relevance. Then I will explore how Catholics manage their public expressions, recognition, visibility, and invisibility in a strategic way which deliberately blurs the boundaries of the secularist imaginary of the city in order to address their confessional agenda.

Before going further, I would like to address the ambiguous visibility of Catholicism in Madrid. Catholicism is everywhere in the city: there are Catholic buildings, statues, crosses, images, and processions, as well as the names of saints, bishops, and the Virgin Mary in streets, squares, clinics, schools, companies, and more. Considering only the sites in the municipality, there are 356 parishes and churches in addition to 1,071 Catholic associations, schools, and communities of religious life, sometimes housed in historic buildings that are labeled and protected as cultural heritage.[2] The four contemporary local holidays are Catholic. Eight of the twelve national holidays are Catholic too. It is useful to note here that 58 percent of local inhabitants described themselves as Catholic in 2019,[3] and that the presence of Catholicism in the city is extensive for historical reasons. Thus, it is generally accepted that Catholic names, buildings, processions, and decorations are "traditional," the legacy of a particular history that has a value as cultural heritage, regardless of the confessional dimension. However, despite the material and symbolic presence of Catholic elements, the locals are usually unaware of the extensive presence of confessional tokens in the urban landscape, which makes such tokens somewhat invisible. According to my fieldwork experience, only those who know the religious field of the city very well have it in mind; more often than not, locals only perceive breaches in the symbolic and sensorial *continuum* of Catholicism when other expressions of religiosity (Jehovah's Witnesses offering their Watchtower, Pentecostals preaching, women in hijab) show up. Thus, the material and symbols of visible Catholicism are paradoxically invisible.

This portrait could be the obvious picture of religious hegemony in a city, but the Catholic Church is in fact worried about the loss of their cultural and political hegemony in society, the loss of the spiritual and moral meaning of their symbols and their condition of visibility/invisibility. This is particularly the case in Europe and Latin America, territories that Catholics consider part of their spiritual patrimony (John Paul II 1999, 2003). In the Spanish context, democracy and pluralism have decreased the cultural and political hegemony of the Church in society. Until 1975, National Catholicism was the official ideology of Francisco Franco's dictatorship (1939–75); priests were part of the government, and 99 percent of the population declared itself to be Catholic (CIS 1965). Today, 67.5 percent of Spaniards describe themselves as Catholic (CIS 2019) and 84.1 percent think that religious authorities should not participate in government decisions (CIS 2017). However, some Spanish Catholics are working to reposition the Church and gain public influence and visibility through multiple repertoires of collective action (Cornejo-Valle and Pichardo 2017, 2020). These repertoires are complex and sometimes contradictory, as I will show, but the more complex and flexible they are, the wider the range of social, cultural, and political contexts they reach and affect, extending their influence into different public debates. These repertoires include traditional religious practices in a logic of heritagization that links Catholic identity with nationalism and collective memory. However, they also include new actions along the lines of the "eventization" of the sacred (Knoblauch 2014a; Pfadenhauer 2010), as manifested in antiabortion celebrations, which are also part of a global dynamic of deprivatization (Casanova 1994) and repositioning of Christian actors in the public realm.

Strategic Secularism and Ambient Faith

In his study on religious deprivatization and the role of gender and sexuality in that process, Juan Marco Vaggione introduced the notion of "strategic secularism" in 2005. The concept refers to the deliberate articulation of secular discourses and practices by religious actors in order to defend their doctrinal positions in public affairs. According to Vaggione, there are at least two different dimensions in which strategic secularism is visible: discursive and organizational. On the one hand, the present-day defense of the "natural family" (against a liberal regime of sexual and reproductive rights) is articulated in scientific and legal terms instead of centering the discussion around morality or revelation (Morán Faúndes and Vaggione 2012; Vaggione 2005). On the other hand, religious activism is not only carried out by churches or the clergy in religious settings, but also in courts, parliaments, streets, TV shows, and wherever faith-based organizations participate as legitimate civil society actors, without the need to invoke any sacred authority to speak and act in these arenas. Vaggione (2005) named this the "NGOization of the religious" to draw attention to the secular affiliation of the new religious activism. Similar displacements have shown up in other sites of intersection between sexuality and religion, like the discourses and practices around AIDS, as Marian Burchardt has explored in depth (Burchardt 2015). However—at least in the case of Catholics—strategic secularism seems to go beyond sexuality, and we can find the same tendencies described by Vaggione in other aspects of the Catholic bio-agenda, including euthanasia, abortion, or stem-cell research. The unifying adversary in these forms of Catholic strategic secularism is the so-called culture of death (Bracke and Paternotte 2016; Cornejo and Pichardo 2017; John Paul II 1995; Vaggione 2012). However, although many scholars have argued that the secularization of discourses and the strategies of religious actors are related to the deprivatization of the intimate (Dobbelaere and Pérez-Agote 2015; Vaggione 2017) and the politics of the intimate as the place to reallocate religious moralities in society, I suggest that the notion of strategic secularism opens up additional avenues of inquiry.

Vaggione's early and well-developed conception of strategic secularism has impacted several feminist and gender studies scholars (Bessone 2012; Carbonelli et al. 2011; Miskolci and Campana 2017; Morán Faundes 2012; Morgan 2014; Rodríguez Rondón 2017), while additional authors have used this notion in other fields. In 2009, Matthew Engelke applied this concept in a more general sense as the "use of secular subjects and objects as part of an overarching religious agenda" (Engelke 2009, 52), as practiced by Christian actors to address their perceived social marginality. Other scholars have used strategic secularism to refer to the dynamic of church–state relationships, as well as their evolution and ambiguities (Berg-Sørensen 2013; Rahim 2009). These independent conceptions of the same expression point to the deliberate and ambiguous intersections of the secular and the religious with the public and the private. However, for the purpose of this chapter, I am interested in Engelke's notion of strategic secularism because it leads our attention to the micro-level (improving upon Vaggione's notion in this sense) and allows us to advance further into a semiotic approach.

Matthew Engelke describes how the Bible Society of England and Wales developed a "Campaign to Culture" to visibilize themselves through secular means, presenting Christianity and the Bible as moral common sense and cultural heritage (Engelke 2009, 2011, 2012). One of the most interesting episodes of the campaign was the intervention of the Bible Society's arts officer, who organized a display of kites as angels for the Christmas decoration of a shopping center (Engelke 2012). Through the angels display, professionally designed by a reputable (and non-Christian) company in London, the officer wanted to create an "ambient faith," an aesthetic atmosphere and sensory experience of the spiritual that could bring some reenchantment to the Christmas season. Just as the Bible Society sought to bridge the sacred and the religious, the notion of "ambience" reminds us that the sacred and the religious are not only modern ideological narratives, but aesthetic and sensorial experiences that can coexist in the same environment (a shopping area or a traffic intersection).

Through this approach, we can extend the meaning of strategic secularism to the reinterpretation of traditional symbols and practices (decoration, nativity scenes), especially to observe reinterpretations that religious actors carry out in order to keep the religious meaningful and relevant in secular contexts. In this "semiotics of relevance" (Engelke 2011), traditions are invoked in different ways (values, sensorial experiences, objects) while tradition, symbols, and identities are reinvented and transformed. In this line of reasoning, strategic secularism is also a semiotic game where concrete objects, bodies, and movements in the public space can be read as indexes and markers that create relevance, but also play, or enact, what is believed to be secular and religious, as Susan Gal (2002) suggests in her approach to the public–private dichotomy. Through this extension of strategic secularism toward a semiotic perspective, we gain a theoretical framework to analyze multiple cases which do not present the same strategies and games.

Religion as Ambience: Three Scenarios

Despite the differences among these cases, all of them are connected by the so-called New Evangelization, a project that aims to regain the public relevance of the Catholic agenda. The original idea of the "New Evangelization" comes from a speech by Pope John Paul II delivered in 1979 during his first apostolic trip to Poland, where he preached against secularism and pointed out the need for the Church to convert the unconverted in Europe, the very heart of Christendom.

Several decades later, Pope Benedict XVI developed the idea in his Apostolic Letter *Ubicumque et semper* (Benedict 2010) and focused on the topic for the XIII Ordinary General Assembly of the Synod of the Bishops (Synod of the Bishops 2012a, 2012b). Through several documents and a special commission, Pope Benedict XVI created the doctrinal frame for the new role of Catholics in the world, mainly devoted to individual conversions and institutional support. The Catholic New Evangelization is the pastoral framework for the postsecular era, and urban spaces are a recurrent concern. As established by the XIII Ordinary General Assembly of the Synod of the Bishops in 2012:

> The Church acknowledges that human cities and the culture they express [...] are a privileged place of the New Evangelization. Putting in practice an urban pastoral plan, the Church wants to identify and understand those experiences, languages and styles of life, that are typical of urban societies. She intends to render her liturgical celebrations, her experiences of communitarian life, and her exercise of charity, relevant to the urban context. (Synod of the Bishops 2012c, proposition 25)

Pope Francis repeated the same ideas in *Evangelii Gaudium* (2013), and they have developed into a robust doctrinal and pastoral framework that supports different expressions of religiosity, including all kinds of creative secular strategies to reach urban dwellers in their own language. I will now introduce three case studies in Madrid, different in nature and implications, in order to explore how they work together and how secular means are employed to implement a confessional agenda.

(1) The People's Nativity Scene Protest from December 3, 2016 to January 9, 2017, Puerta de Alcalá

Every year since the nineteenth century, Madrid's city hall has managed Christmas street decorations. In 2015, after twenty-seven years of right-wing politics in the city, a new left-wing government was elected, taking office in 2016. The following Christmas season, the commission governing city events decided to adorn the triumphal arch in the Plaza de la Independencia (a big traffic roundabout generally known as Puerta de Alcalá) with several lights in abstract geometric shapes. Psychiatrist Jose Miguel Gaona, a regular guest on conservative media outlets whose office is in the same square, placed a domestic nativity scene (the "Holy Family" in the Catholic tradition) underneath the triumphal arch. He tweeted a picture of it, texting, "Puerta de Alcala has its nativity scene, finally. Small in size but big in meaning."[4] In the same post, he used the Twitter handle for the Catholic Church's radio station (Cadena COPE). Immediately, his friend and the director for the Catholic radio's weekend show, Cristina Lopez-Schlichtin, spread the message, inviting all listeners to put their own domestic nativity scenes in the same place. The message was relayed by all conservative media outlets within a few days and the square became crowded with small *belenes* (nativity scenes) as well as Spanish flags, children's paintings, Christmas greetings, and messages on paper. The longest note stated:

> Many people in Madrid feel proud of being Catholic, Christian and Spanish [...] and we enjoy Christmas as the coming of Jesus, the center of these celebrations, to which other people are giving another meaning. [...] Mayor Carmena,[5] allow the Christmas celebrations and respect the Spanish tradition and culture by not removing the nativity scenes.[6]

Small slips of paper read "The first refugee" and "Welcome Jesus," in reference to the refugee crisis and the big banner that was hung on the city hall façade with the motto "Refugees Welcome." Another large poster read, "We build the fatherland" (*hacemos patria*). In several interviews published by conservative media, anonymous citizens said that they were surprised and hurt by the absence of the Holy Family under the arch, and some of them thought that "the nativity scene has always been in Puerta de Alcalá, and it has become a symbol of the city."[7] However, this was not really the case; the figures of the Holy Family had never been placed there until 2006, when conservative Mayor Ruiz-Gallardón put several light shapes in the three openings of the arch, including a nativity scene for the first time. Nonetheless, the hashtag *#PontuBelenPuertadeAlcala* (put your nativity scene in Puerta de Alcalá) succeeded, and the call attracted around 500 *belenes* according to the Association of *Belenistas*, which voluntarily removed the little figures in January 2017.[8] Ultimately, the figurines became a protest against the secular style (i.e., abstract shapes instead of biblical scenes) of the city government[9] and an exhibition of citizens' faith in response.[10] A representative of the municipality stated that the government appreciated the people's participation in the streets with their small decorations, and Mayor Carmena noted that they "want[ed] to celebrate a Christmas for everybody, and everybody's vision of Christmas is welcome."[11]

This vignette is very much like Engelke's example of ambient faith, involving the same decoration themes and the notion of creating a familiar atmosphere to feel the presence of the Christian legacy in contemporary scenarios. While the chosen location for the angel kites was a shopping center, in our case study it was just a roundabout, which is a typical urban nonplace in the tradition of Marc Auge (1998)—a space where drivers and pedestrians pass by. In this case, both the place and the psychiatrist who claimed the religiosity of tradition can be interpreted as secular means for delivering a confessional agenda, in line with strategic secularism. As in Engelke's example, there was a shared feeling among Madrid's Catholic activists of not being sufficiently visible or recognized. In fact, as suggested by the reactions (particularly the invented memory of the roundabout as historically linked to the nativity scene), it seems there was a feeling that Catholic identity was vanishing from Christmas, and that this was a disrespectful political calculation on the part of leftist officials in the local government. When we consider the explicit political dimension, more secular means appear to address the religious agenda; national symbols and references to refugees, the mayor, and the fatherland are used to merge Catholic identity and concerns with other general affairs.

(2) The Three Wise Men Parade, January 5, 2016, Castellana and Recoletos
      Avenues

The Three Wise Men Parade (*Cabalgata de los Reyes Magos*) is one of the most popular Catholic traditions in Spain. Every year on January 6, thousands of families attend the parade in downtown Madrid (as in every Spanish city), but several neighborhoods in Madrid also have their own small parades in the days preceding the main one in the city center. The event usually consists of several flatbed trailers carrying the Wise Men and their courts (in the Catholic tradition, they are kings and come with many pages to assist them in delivering presents and candy to children). As companions of the court, other fantasy and historical characters also take part in the big celebration, including fairies, famous scientists, artists, characters from Disney and Star Wars worlds, and other personalities from TV shows and popular culture. They march together, waving to the families, until they arrive at a huge final stage where the mayor receives them. Then the Wise Men say some kind words to the families and ask the children if they behaved during the year. The main parade is organized by the municipality without the participation of the Catholic Church, and it is widely accepted as a secular urban tradition, as expressed by the presence of Mickey Mouse and Darth Vader. The different styles, aesthetics, persons in the parade, and other details of the organization are usually a matter of public commentary and, from time to time, the Church or Catholic media and activists have criticized it, concerned by what they consider a secularization of the event and the corruption of its "true" (religious) nature.

One relevant conflict occurred in 2016, becoming the first clash of the progressive Mayor Carmena's mandate.[12] That year, the Wise Men exhibited very colorful robes designed by the fashion celebrity Agatha Ruiz de la Prada, who changed the traditional costumes (an orientalist fantasy) of the parade. Instead of reserving the seats of the front row for VIPs and celebrities, as usual, Mayor Carmena invited kids and families with disabilities to occupy them for the first time. That same year, the municipal government fostered gender equality in two of the neighborhood parades by allowing the participation of women as Wise Women, replacing the male characters. There were neither camels nor a star, which are iconic elements of the Wise Men's representation (in parades but also in nativity scenes, Christmas postcards, and other decorations) in the Catholic tradition.

The Catholic media, religious activists, and the right-wing People's Party (in the opposition role at that time) interpreted the changes as a secularist campaign to dechristianize the tradition.[13] The dresses of the Wise Men were compared to bathroom curtains,[14] the Wise Women were accused of being a feminist attack, and the style of the parades was considered an ostentatious artifice that disappointed children and offended Catholics.[15] The councilors of the People's Party denounced the "leftist phobia of Christianity" and "lack of common sense," challenging the local government with Islamophobic statements such as "They wouldn't dare to organize a secular Ramadan."[16] The most widespread statement was a tweet posted by a People's Party's deputy in the national parliament, Marquess Cayetana Álvarez de Toledo, who tweeted: "My 6-year-old daughter: 'Mom, the clothes of the Wise Men are not the true ones.' I will never forgive you, Manuela Carmena. Never." The declaration was contested by numerous jokes and memes questioning what the "truth" of the clothes was and other elements of a tradition that pretends to recreate biblical events, even though the Bible says nothing about kings, courts, the number of the men, or how they looked.[17] In the following years, the style of the parade returned to the patriarchal orientalist fantasy that many residents remembered from their childhoods, with no more protests.

Of course, the way in which a fantasy is recreated year after year is always changing, and a superficial search for old pictures of the Wise Men in Madrid will immediately show how untraditional the tradition is, and how different the aesthetic experience has been before. In this sense, the feeling of continuity in tradition is not really supported by a literal conservation of customary dresses, gender roles, VIP seats, and other innovations that the conservatives and the Church stressed in 2016. Perhaps the feeling of continuity relies on something as volatile as the ambient faith, which includes at least two dimensions here: (1) the atmosphere of the experience, in the sense of aesthetics and meanings of the symbols, as well as the legitimacy of the participants (can Star Wars characters serve as members of the Wise Men's court if women cannot play the part of the Wise Men?); and (2) the fact that it is not only a matter of how the ambient faith is recreated, but also who (or what) delivers the faith experience. Following this logic, when an ostensibly Catholic event is recreated as ambience, religious activists question whether an agnostic mayor leading a left-wing government is the proper manager for a performance of biblical narration. According to these Catholics' criticisms, the legitimate keeper and interpreter of the "true," "credible" nature of the experience was the tradition itself, in an abstract sense (it was not clear in their discourses), instead of those they described as a secularist force organizing a fake parade. While the municipal organizers were framed as secular actors who might use secular administrative means to recreate a biblical story, it is interesting that Catholic critics did not claim that the municipal government ought to turn the organization of the event over to the Church to restore its spiritual meaning. Indeed, what was explicitly claimed was that the municipal government (admittedly a secular actor) ought to uphold the allegedly confessional character of the event. As the Wise Men parade is widely accepted as cultural legacy in Spain, tradition was invoked here to support Catholic hegemony by secular means, in the logic of strategic secularism.

(3) March for the International Day of the Unborn Child, April 18, 2018, in
     Calle Serrano (toward Puerta de Alcalá)

As described at the beginning of this chapter, Spanish antiabortion protesters have met around March 25 in several cities for many years now, assembled by the platform "Yes to life" (*Sí a la Vida*, a group of faith-based NGOs and associations). Their numbers are not large (500–2,000 people in Madrid, according to our fieldwork), but Catholic and conservative media coverage generally shows such demonstrations in their best light, as if they were always crowded. During the marches, people usually carry banners and posters— some bearing fetal ultrasound images—as well as Spanish national flags and other symbols (such as elements from specific pro-life associations or Catholic schools). In 2018, demonstrators displayed a variety of slogans: "Woman, you are not alone, you can count on me," "Yes to families with a purpose," "Each life matters," "Right to life," "Thanks to life," "Do not kill the body with abortion. Do not kill the soul with sin," "Mother, let me live! It is God's will," "Feminism kills," and "I was an embryo, and you?" among others. Demonstrators also sang and shouted their slogans: "Spain united will never be defeated," "Life is wonderful," and "No to abortion, yes to life." The marchers, organizers, and celebrities within the antiabortion movement (including some members of the conservative People's Party and the far-right party Vox) walked behind a banner displaying the motto of the march: "Yes to life." Several meters ahead, a woman in a pickup truck shouting mottos through a loudspeaker cheered on the demonstration. Teenagers dancing in the truck and on the ground surrounded her. A big part of the staff in charge of the occupation of the street were teenagers, and it was common for the leaders to repeat through their loudspeakers how young the demonstrators were, and how hopeful this was for the future of the antiabortion movement.

The first part of the event was the march and the second was a show. The march led us to a large (10-meter) stage with a powerful sound system, a giant (3 × 2-meter) screen, a green and white hot air balloon, and a big "Yes to Life" sign that could be seen from far away. As we arrived at the stage, we could hear the music thundering and the voices of two masters of ceremony cheering through their microphones and shouting over the loud music. Then the show started, with a complex combination of antiabortion testimonies, slogans, live music, reminders of how to donate, manifestos, a doctor's speech, a minute of silence, and the release of green balloons that flooded the sky and were meant to represent the ascension of unborn souls to heaven. This kind of event is not "traditional," and its religious dimension is invisibilized as an explicit strategy to reach out to audiences beyond Christian believers. This is done by presenting antiabortion issues as a secular concern about human life, based on scientific premises about the origin and purpose of that human life. The connection between this case and Vaggione's notion of strategic secularism is obvious since the antiabortion movement is one of the processes that Vaggione analyzed. In short, strategic secularism consists here of translating doctrinal content (the *Evangelium Vitae* Encyclical) into a scientific rhetoric (with an emphasis on the notion of "life," the introduction of doctors as witnesses, fetal ultrasound images) and legal demands delivered by NGOs and associations (such as antiabortion organizers).

The three cases outlined above depict contradictory political scenarios where the religious and the secular—as well as the public and the private—are related ambiguously, but social actors deliberately work to create particular ambiences and experiences (sometimes through criticism), developing different intersections between a confessional agenda and secular means. The first case can be read as a demand and effort to reunite the sacred (the Holy Family) and the secular (the traffic intersection, national flags) in the same ambient experience;

the second case displays the demand of the Catholic point of view (presented as "tradition") for the secularized version of a biblical narration; and the third case represents efforts to secularize what is believed to be sacred (fetuses according to Catholic convictions, and pro-life rhetoric in general) to expand the public influence of a confessional agenda.

The secular-religious dichotomy is, as it were, performed or articulated not only in discursive and political terms but, interestingly, through particular urban atmospheres and interactions with the public space as ambiences of faith. In the nativity scene protests, small objects, flags, and messages interacted with the everyday traffic jam in the roundabout, marking the space by claiming their own fake tradition. Perhaps the Wise Men parade is a more obvious case of re-enchantment of the city, even if this is only because the event is designed to stimulate children's imaginations and because the tradition itself is about illusion and magic (the Wise Men were magicians, after all). Despite the obvious ideological dimension of the Day of the Unborn Child, it is also designed to create emotional moments through typical emotional triggers like slogans, touching testimonies, loud, thundering sounds, catchy music with lyrics about life, survival, and hope, minutes of silence, the release of balloons and, at the end, a moving political manifesto which gives the whole experience not only an ideological framework but also a crucial sense of mission.

Toward a Semiotics of Relevance

Finally, the ambiguous combination of ambient faith and strategic secularism that we see in these three cases can be understood as a "semiotics of relevance." Engelke (2011) introduced this expression to refer to the secular strategies (symbols, actions) that religious actors use to imprint places with religious visibility, but I think relevance is a better word than visibility. As discussed in the introduction to this chapter, Madrid is a city in which the traces of Catholic hegemony are so familiar that they seem invisible and have no cognitive salience for locals. This is just a characteristic of the scene, something to work with. Sometimes that invisibility feels uncomfortable, but other times invisibility is the key to achieving relevance and reaching particular doctrinal goals. In fact, the three cases analyzed here reveal how different Catholic events deal with religious relevance and what kind of relevance they demand: the nativity scene protests demanded the visibility of Christianity in the Christmas season, a critique of the more secular decorations preferred by the city officials; the Wise Men parade demanded conformity to the Catholic version of the tradition; and the Unborn Day demanded public acceptance of the confessional bio-agenda. In different disguises, these scenarios all imply a plea for relevance (as different than visibility) that is aligned with the aims of the New Evangelization, and make sense as expressions of the deprivatization process.

Certainly, the fight for relevance is about making the religious meaningful. The notion of semiotics is related to signs as vehicles for meaning, but it also reveals that meanings are conventional and made of collective agreements, especially when we are dealing with processes of negotiation like political contestation, which is pertinent in each of our three cases. Hence, I suggest a semiotics of relevance whose focus is not on meanings (like Engelke's) but on signals. Such an approach suggests paying attention to the display of particular tokens and the strategic presence of symbols in the city, as well as the use of bodies (clothes, adornments, traffic) as symbols to create relevance and to fight for such meanings (i.e., fight for the religious or secular relevance of one image, one object). Therefore, the nativity scenes, the clothes of the Wise Men, their companions, their sex-gender assimilation, the fetuses on posters, the anti-abortion testimonies, the manifestos, and the silences performed as indexes, markers to establish emotional reactions to particular tokens, concrete material objects that had been confessionally defined as religiously relevant. The meaning of what is religious (or secular, or traditional, or public) is not always clearly defined, but these signs came to mark the streets with what is believed to be sacred for Catholic activists (fetuses, the Holy Family, biblical scenes) and, when the signs were not perceived as sacred enough, criticism arose (as occurred in the Wise Men episode).

This semiotic also reveals the use of public spaces in the fight for relevance. The three episodes considered in this chapter took place in important central locations of the city: the high-end Calle Serrano, the business and historic avenues of Castellana and Recoletos, and the monumental roundabout of Puerta de Alcalá. As indexes, these locations mark the Catholic hegemony and stand for history, scale, and distinction. The first two elements communicate aspects that are important in Spanish Catholicism's demand for relevance: historical roots and the size of the Catholic population. The third, distinction—considered in a Bordieuan sense (Bourdieu 1984)—is an expression of the sociocultural background of those behind conservative Catholic activism in contemporary Spain. These activists express themselves by occupying exclusive and wealthy areas of the city that are also economically and culturally relevant: these richer neighborhoods are also more elegant. Hence, the older, bigger, and more elegant public spaces are, the more they create and communicate relevance. The hegemony of the Catholic community in the city is thus not only created by the use of space; certain locations are used to demand relevance in a particular way, by bringing history, wealth, and size together. At the same time, they are not particularly religious or Catholic places, or no more so than the rest of the city. They are oriented to activities as secular as business, luxury shopping, traffic, and tourism, making them perfect backdrops for a semiotics of relevance, understood as strategic secularism. If strategic secularism is about the use of secular tools for religious agendas, certain public urban places (just like the rest of the signs displayed in the streets) should be considered part of the symbolic repertoire available to religious actors.

Part Three

Public Religious Events, Urban Transcendence, and Embodied Spirituality

Urbi et Orbi: Pope Benedict's Visit to Berlin and the Emplacement of Communicative Events

Hubert Knoblauch
Technical University of Berlin

In this chapter, I want to focus on the visit of Pope Benedict XVI to Berlin in 2011. This marked the first visit of a German pope to the (new) capital of Germany, and in this sense it was a unique event. As opposed to John Paul II's visits in the 1990s, this was a German pope visiting the German capital—an event which had not happened for centuries (if ever). While in the 1990s, the majority of John Paul II's audience came from Poland, Benedict's 2011 appearance mainly drew congregants from Germany, with the whole journey framed as the pope's visit to Germany. In addition to Berlin, Pope Benedict traveled to a Catholic area in former East Germany and to the city of Freiburg in southwestern Germany, one of the core regions of Catholicism. Over the course of the day, he visited a Holocaust memorial, met with representatives of the Jewish community, gave a speech in the German parliament, and celebrated a Mass at the Berlin Olympic Stadium.

The presence of the German pope in the German capital may be of interest regarding the relationship between nation (politics) and religion (Catholicism)—a relationship which the local tabloid, *Bild*, made very public in the skyline of Berlin, as Figure 10.1 shows.

Although we have addressed the national dimension—the pope's speech in the parliament—there is another issue which is more interesting for the study of urban religiosity, and it is that issue which will be examined here. Berlin is probably one of the clearest examples in the world of a "secular city." Even though a large number of West Germans (who are more religious in terms of church membership) were integrated into Berlin before the fall of the Wall in the 1990s, and despite a recomposition of the city's population (currently 3.7 million) since

Figure 10.1 "We are the pope."

then, the vast majority of Berliners are nonreligious. Therefore, we will focus on the public presence of religion in a highly secular urban setting.

The Catholic pope's public presence was not continual, but rather expressed in a series of localized communicative events in various places throughout Berlin. Of these events, the papal Mass at the Olympic Stadium was the most notable, exhibiting the standard features of what I call *communicative events*. In our common understanding, social events may be seen as a temporally bounded gathering of people who are usually oriented as an audience toward a performance of actors or an artifact. As opposed to mere "social occasions" (Goffman 1963a), events are characterized by an (active) audience, typically creating a spatial focus. This spatial focus may imply a performance, but it can also be an artifact, such as a painting, or some other objectivation, such as a film (Kolesch and Knoblauch 2019). Over the last decades, events have become subject to organized and strategic planning, or event management. In an event, audiences are witnessing a performance, artifact, or object in a way which allows them to have an (exceptional, unique, or "authentic") "experience" (Pfadenhauer 2010); the same applies for urban events (Betz, Hitzler, and Pfadenhauer 2011). In addition to their temporally bounded form and ritual performance, I would emphasize that events involve physically delimited public spaces where performers, objects, and audiences gather and interact. (The peculiarity and relevance of these public spaces has become particularly salient during the novel coronavirus pandemic—at which time this text was corrected—considering that, while the public sphere still exists, public events have been prohibited in almost all countries.)

Because events are strongly bounded and localized, they acquire an additional element which is constitutive of what I would call "communicative" events. Communicative events are characterized by being mediatized to secondary audiences and other co-participants who are not locally co-present.[1] While this may hold true for all events, the specific new aspect of communicative events is the simultaneity of locally co-present and mediated secondary audiences: secondary audiences relate to the same performance, and co-present audiences are observed by secondary audiences—be it collectively via mass media or individually via interactive media. Communicative events therefore exhibit a double orientation, both to the present audience and to media audiences, in a way which affects the very performance and associated actions. This "liveness" of events (Auslander 1999) produces an added value, making it clearly relevant to various kinds of economic commodification (in what is called "cultural capitalism") as well as to marketing. It is also relevant to branding in various cultural spheres, such as religion (Stolz 2010). Due to the impact of mediatization on event performance, even well-established religious rituals and ceremonies are transformed. The dissemination of digital media among an increasing number of audience members allows these orientations to multiply independently of mass media, which are subject to governance by organizing institutions.

Mediatization accounts for the translocality of events in ways which are no longer shaped by mass media, but rather co-produced by participants using new media and distributed within their networks. With the increasing role of mass and digital media, local events are allowed to transcend scales of participation in a live "event." In fact, the current form of eventization seems to consist of a network of organizations, communication technologies, and material infrastructures emplacing events rather than local happenings represented through media.

Mediatization therefore allows for the simultaneous encroachment of symbolic communication at various scales: gestures, audience settings, buildings, cities, countries, and perhaps even continents can be objectified and disseminated not only via mass media (facilitating simultaneous participation among people not present at the event) but also by audience members themselves (via mobile phone and internet). Media communication technologies are also part of an assemblage, including organizations (such as the Catholic Church) and sociotechnical infrastructures (such as transportation systems), through which the communicative event becomes emplaced.

The evolution of mediatization means that media such as video monitors in stadiums or on the street (for "public viewing") have become essential features in large-scale events. Mediatization has a particular spatial dimension in that it relates communicative actions, actors, and their objectivations or significations to other things.[2] While events have been studied in the social sciences mostly with respect to their temporality, the stress on mediatization allows for a focus on the spatial features of the communicative event. Following Löw (2016), one can assume that any social phenomenon always takes on a spatial form; therefore, a study of contemporary popular religion can be addressed by looking at its spaces, i.e., the spatiality of its communicative forms of action.

In this chapter, I will focus on the spatial aspects of communicative events and, more specifically, on their emplacement (Valentine et al. 2010) and its mediatization. Emplacement here refers to (a) the local setting, and (b) the strategies of stakeholders for staging the focus with respect to various media. Emplacement also includes (c) the material "location" of an event (e.g., a building), how it is embedded in a larger context on a different scale, such as a neighborhood, city, region, or country, and (d) the spatial arrangements of bodies and things within the (temporal) course of events—in this case, the stadium as the material setting for crowds—and whatever is happening onstage. By examining place-seeking strategies (Becci, Burchardt, and Giorda 2016), this chapter will address the governance and management of religious events (Getz 2007). This includes not only the discourses surrounding a particular event, but also the setting within a constructed urban geography, the building and, finally, the performative aspects of the (mass-mediated) communicative actions which characterize the event. By analytically distinguishing various spatial scales, I want to ask how urban space figures in the event, how the event is emplaced in the context of Berlin, and how it is staged locally in a chosen location.

Empirically, this analysis is based on intensive field research on Pope Benedict XVI's visit to Germany, including participant observation in the organizational committee as well as videography of the event. In addition, it involves discourse data about the event from German newspapers.[3] Incidentally, this study draws on comparable events that have been studied videographically, such as the visit of Pope John Paul II to Vienna, the Reformation anniversary events of 2017, and the 2017 World Youth Day in Krakow. I participated as an observer in these events, recording videos and making analyses which can inform an understanding of the Berlin case.

In a great deal of contemporary research, the relationship between religion and space is framed by the binary scheme of substantialist religious theories. The eventization of religion not only underlines how religious space is constructed in communicative actions, but also exemplifies what I would call a "popular" religion. As opposed to folk religion, popular religion accounts for the increased relevance of the market and politics to religion. Moreover, it is characterized by the interactive mediatization of religious communication, the adaptation of pop-cultural elements by religious organizations, the empowerment of subjects (including a tendency toward spirituality) and, as a reaction, the re-marking of sacrality or distinction from secularity, as Wohlrab-Sahr and Burchardt (2012) argue. The rise of communicative events and their dissemination constitute one of the most striking features of this popular religion, found not only in small religious movements (Favre 2014) but also, as we witness here, in mainstream churches.

The structure of this chapter follows a pattern of spatial scales. After sketching out the ways in which the pope's visit was emplaced in the urban space of Berlin, I will focus on the Olympic Stadium as the built setting for the event. The next scale of observation will draw on video recordings of the event within the stadium, including a view of collective actions by large audiences as well as selected glimpses of the participants (even simple gestures). As we shall see, it is on this level that the event is distinctly marked as religious and, even more specifically, as a Catholic event. As "micro" as these observations may be, they constitute the focus of the mediatization of the event. Mediatization does not only imply media; it is also a major strategy for linking spaces, transcending scale, and turning the Mass into a global Catholic event, as I will argue in the conclusion.

Decentering, Insulation, and Isolation: The Pope in the City

As per Simmel's analysis, Berlin has become one of the "paradigmatic sites of modernity" (Berking, Steets and Schwenk, 2018). In terms of sociological indicators for religion, Berlin can be said to fit this analysis if we consider modernity to be linked with low participation and membership in religious organizations. In 2016, 16.1 percent of the city's inhabitants were Protestant, 7.5 percent were Muslim, 2.7 were from other Christian denominations, and over 60 percent did not take part in formal religious organizations. Even though Berlin hosts an archdiocese, Catholics only make up 8.9 percent of the local population and are sometimes said to be part of a "diaspora."

While the city accommodates regular religious events, religious activities are rarely visible in public. As in other European cities, however, religious

architecture features prominently in Berlin.[4] The Catholic and Protestant
Churches have historically tried to be present in all of the city's quarters, which
were built during Berlin's rapid nineteenth- and twentieth-century extension,
and religious architecture is also prominent in the historic center of the city.
Following the unification of East and West Berlin, the historic center became
the focal point of a unified Berlin in 1990. Religious activities have since
increased, such as the reconstruction of the central synagogue, the expansion
of the Catholic archdiocese, and the rise of the Protestant cathedral as one of
the locations for symbolic state ceremonies. If one focuses on Catholicism, the
spatial arrangement of architectural symbols is quite telling. While the Protestant
Berlin Cathedral is located alongside Berlin's most prestigious avenue (Unter
den Linden), seated next to the State Opera, Humboldt University, and the
German Historic Museum and facing Museum Island and the Prussian castle,
the Catholic St. Hedwig's Cathedral, built after the occupation of Catholic Silesia
by the Prussians, is practically hidden in a minor street off the major avenue.

This situation provides the context for the considerations that went into
choosing locations for Pope Benedict's visit—indeed, the spatial strategies
which produced ephemeral spaces (Becci, Burchardt and Giorda 2016). These
deliberations met with a great deal of public interest when it came to finding a
location for the Mass. Despite the Catholic cathedral's centrality, its proximity
to Benedict's accommodation and the parliament where Benedict was to give
a speech, and the fact that a large square in front of the cathedral was available
for public use (and was the site of regular open air orchestral concerts), the
organizers never considered this church nor the square surrounding it (as one
would consider St. Peter's Square in Rome). Rather, public debates as well as the
planning committee initially focused on the square in front of Charlottenburg
Palace to the far west of the city (several miles away from the Center West
neighborhood, the most Catholic part of Berlin). The reason for this may have
been that the western part of the city still harbors much more of the Catholic
population than the center or east (which were formerly under socialist control).
Many months into the planning of the event, it became clear that the number
of interested participants could exceed 10,000 or even 20,000. At that point, the
event organizers (which consisted of a collaboration between the Vatican, the
German Bishops' Conference, and the local archdiocese) accepted the suggestion
to use the Olympic Stadium. Even though it had recently been refurbished
into a modern sports stadium, the location was quite controversial due to its
fascist origins. The Olympic Stadium is located even more to the west than
Charlottenburg Palace and has remained almost completely undamaged since

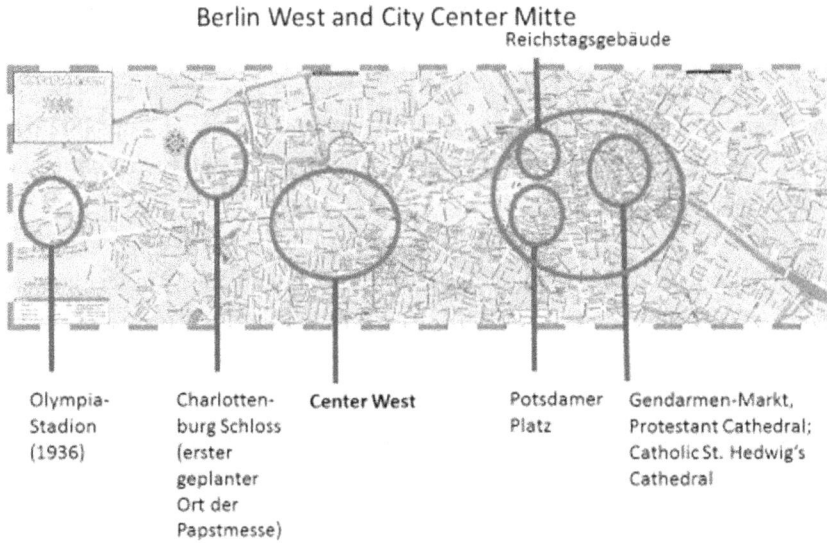

Figure 10.2 Locations (both considered and utilized) for the public events in Berlin. Reproduced with permission of Hubert Knoblauch.

its construction in the 1930s by the Nazi regime. The surrounding Olympic Park sits along the western fringe of Berlin's City West, the formerly nonsocialist and bourgeois part of Berlin. The *decentrality* of this location is made clearly visible on a map as shown in Figure 10.2.

There were, in fact, several good reasons for choosing this location, such as ease of access via public transport or car and proximity to the airport. This may have been a factor in the enormous turnout of Catholics from outside of Berlin, with faithful arriving from Bavaria and Poland (the border of which is only 80 kilometers away).

If one looks not only at the topography of locations but also at the movements between locations, a comparison between Pope Benedict's visit to Berlin and (to choose an example) the visit of John Paul II to Vienna in 1998 is quite telling. As opposed to Vienna, where the pope cruised past crowds in the streets with his "popemobile," in Berlin there were no crowds on the street waving to the pope at all. Indeed, Pope Benedict made no appearances in open public places. He appeared only at *insulated* locations: at the airport where he was received as the head of the Vatican state, at the parliament where he gave a speech, at the Olympic Stadium where he presided over a Mass, and at the residence of the Nuntius where he stayed overnight. In addition to insulation, we could even speak of *isolation*; when the pope traversed the city from the center (Reichstag) to the west (the Olympic Stadium), the streets were evacuated and protected by high-security personnel, including snipers on the roofs along the main roads of his route. The locations where he appeared were gated and heavily secured, such as the parliament and the Olympic Stadium (which is, like any modern stadium, a strictly separated and highly controlled public space).

If we look at the spatial order in the urban geography related to the papal visit, it is important to mention one final location, which was in fact an open public space. During the first day of Benedict's visit, a large crowd gathered in the city center to protest against the pope, Catholicism, and religion in general. It is quite symbolic that this crowd gathered at the newly rebuilt Potsdamer Platz, a square which had formerly been bisected by the Wall and, since reunification, had come to represent a united Berlin (see Figure 10.3). The group included not only critics of Catholicism and atheists but also gay and lesbian groups, and was accompanied by techno music and a carnivalesque atmosphere (ironically reminiscent of carnival processions in Catholic countries). In this way, the protests constituted an anti-event. It is highly significant for the role of religion in public space that this anti-event was held openly in postwar Berlin's most paradigmatic central neighborhood, while the pope's appearances in central Berlin only occurred in isolated locations cut off from the city (but transmitted to media everywhere).

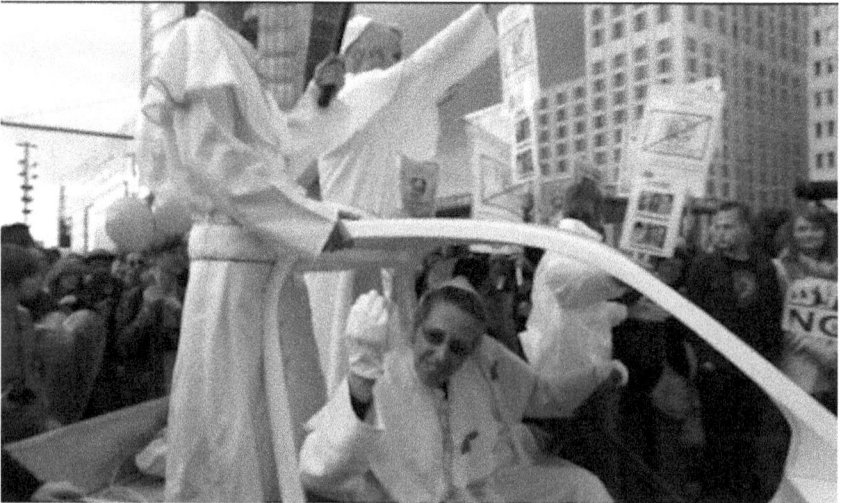

Figure 10.3 Carnivalesque parade of "popes" at Potsdamer Platz (Photo Hubert Knoblauch).

The Stadium and the "Mass Ornament"

One might conclude that the selection of the stadium was a rational decision in order to house the 60,000 to 70,000 people expected to attend (after initially registering). Then again, there are many other locations in the city which could have accommodated such a crowd. To give an example, Protestant Church Day, which took place in Berlin a few years later, involved the gathering of a large public crowd in the very center of the city at the Gendarmenmarkt, a square which is sometimes used for political rallies. This square may have been considered as too strongly marked by Protestantism, as it is bordered by two architecturally prominent Protestant churches; on the other hand, the 2016 Catholic Church Day celebration in Leipzig (a city with far fewer Catholics and a larger Protestant presence) was set in the inner city.

The selection of the location was linked to strategic reflections about the number of people who would join the Mass and whether or not they would "fill" the space. Despite the presence of some 400,000 Catholics in the Archdiocese of Berlin and the fact that many visitors from elsewhere (such as Bavaria and Poland) were expected to come see the pope, it was quite clear that the mass of people would not amount to the number necessary to "fill" the most prominent symbolic place in Berlin, the Brandenburg Gate.

Since the fall of the Wall in the 1990s, the Brandenburg Gate has become one of the most prominent international "landmark buildings" (Jones 2006). It is one of the global symbols of Berlin which, cut off from international tourism until 1989, has since become the third most popular city for tourism in Europe. It is also the site of highly symbolic national and global events, such as the globally renowned New Year's celebrations as well as festivities surrounding the Football World Championships and National Championships. Furthermore, it was chosen as the location for Berlin's largest event during the 2017 Reformation Anniversary. Nevertheless, the location was hardly discussed for Pope Benedict's visit because no one believed that the square in front of the Gate would be filled. The importance of this mass effect becomes obvious in cases where it fails; one recent example is the debate over the size of the crowd in front of the White House at Donald Trump's presidential inauguration where, despite Trump's claims, photos clearly proved that the crowd was much smaller than it had been at Barack Obama's inauguration. A similar problem of "filling the space" occurred at the 500th Anniversary of the Reformation, for which the German Protestant Church had planned a "central" celebration on a field close to Wittenberg. They expected (and arranged for) some 250,000 people, but only 120,000 turned up—leading to a dispersed crowd rather than a dense mass of people facing the impressive constructions, choir, and television cameras (Haken 2019).

As opposed to the Brandenburg Gate, the Olympic Stadium is symbolically a much more ambiguous building. It hosted the Olympic Games in 1936 and figured prominently in Nazi propaganda on a global scale. Its "fascist" architecture is expressed in its grandeur and the use of classical symbols. The "Marathon Gate" inside the stadium is particularly striking, having contributed to turning the stadium into an international landmark building. Any "fascist" associations with the building were somewhat loosened after the war, and the stadium was even harnessed for religious uses; indeed, the first postwar national congregation of the Evangelical Church in Germany was set in the Olympic Stadium. More surprising still, in 1954, the evangelical pastor Billy Graham (who may be considered one of the inventors of what we call the communicative event) came to Berlin to receive some 100,000 people in the Olympic Stadium, converting more than 20,000 (Balbier 2010).

In 1996, Pope John Paul II held a Mass in the Olympic Stadium. While he could be distanced from the association with German fascism due to the fact that most of the Mass participants came from Poland, there was some debate about the German Pope Benedict holding a Mass in this building, as Joseph Ratzinger (Pope Benedict's civilian name) had been a member of the Hitler Youth. Even though the stadium had been modernized in the early 2000s, the scenography of Benedict's Mass emphasized the prewar symbolism of the stadium rather than downplaying it; exclusively for the Mass, a huge sanctuary was constructed and placed directly in front of the Marathon Gate, bringing it to the center of the audience's (as well as the camera's) focus. The altar was positioned so high that the Marathon Gate became a frame for it (and an elevator had to be built so that the pope could enter the sanctuary).

Frank and Steets (2010) show how the stadium can serve as a particular material form of communication. As it is a materially closed circuit, it separates the inside from the outside while also uniting the crowd at one location. In this sense, the stadium exhibits what has been called isolation and insulation, gathering and condensing the diasporic Catholic community locally. It is also a gated setting which is highly controlled by the organizers. Moreover, as it arranges audiences in a circle, it materially creates a spatial focus along with a kind of spatial reflexivity. Attendees are able to witness what is happening on both the ground and the stage, and, because of the stadium's circularity, they can monitor others in the audience. This monitoring also engenders crowd psychology; masses of people can act together and simultaneously ensure that they are indeed acting together by keeping an eye on others—a reflexivity which may be represented by media and extended by mediatization (e.g., to public viewing audiences of religious events).

Although stadiums, like any other spatial setting, can be manipulated to a certain degree (for instance, by covering the upper rows of seats), the optics of the crowd depend, of course, on the number of people and the density of the gathering. Density is especially important if we move down the scale, from the building to the embodied actions in the stadium. It becomes most visible in the staging of the event within the stadium during the pope's visit. Although Benedict quite clearly (and very much in accordance with his ritualistic theology) announced that he would emphasize the spirituality of his Catholic Mass (entitling the event "Mysterium fidei"), he allowed for the event to include several crowd-pleasing features before and after the Mass. Most impressive was his triumphant entrance into the stadium.

He slowly rode around the blue tartan track of the stadium in his popemobile, eliciting loud cheering and standing ovations from the audience as he passed by. I would remind the reader that the pope did not ride publicly through the streets of Berlin in his vehicle, as John Paul had done in Vienna, passing thousands of people on his way to the Mass. Instead, the popemobile only entered the stadium, substituting the tartan track for the public street and the stadium audience for the broader public. In this sense the audience was an "ornament" to the media representing it as the public, as Kracauer ([1927] 1995) argues with respect to political mass events. Instead of presenting the pope passing empty roads, the media presented the pope amid cheering crowds of people. Before we go on to analyze the specific mediatization of the audience, the Mass, and the event, I first want to look at how religion figured into the event.

Framing (Catholic) Religiosity

Even though the pope's "triumphant" entry in his popemobile presented him as a (very famous) celebrity, the Mass at the core of the event was framed in a way which emphasized its general religious and "high church" character as a Catholic gathering in the midst of this sports stadium. During the early stages of the event organization, the pope himself had made it very clear that he wanted to avoid any kind of popular religiosity.[5] The religious framing was defined early in the Mass when, after the pope had entered the altar and sat down on the *sedilium*—the priest's chair—a speaker approached the microphone on stage and asked the audience not to clap, cheer, or shout during the Mass; the last choruses of "Benedetto!" abated, and clapping only set in again when the pope left the stage at the end of the Mass. The abovementioned sanctuary clearly marked the religious features of the event spatially. Although its general construction did not differ significantly from the artificial stages built for pop concerts or comedy shows in the stadium, its distinctive symbols were the altar, the *presbyterium*, and the large cross.

While the appeal to avoid forms of popular audience expression concerned the stadium's acoustics, the link between religion and space was also made clear in that several rows on the left side of the stage were occupied by bishops, whereas the right side accommodated high-ranking German political figures (such as Chancellor Angela Merkel, several state ministers, and the president of Germany). In addition, the attendees with stadium floor seating had been selected by the organizers and mainly included religious personnel and members of religious organizations. The religious framing was also marked by the fact that, unlike during events like the World Youth Day, the seating order in the stadium followed the general pattern of St. Peter's Square (see Figure 10.4).

Figure 10.4 St. Peter's Square spatial arrangement (Photo Hubert Knoblauch).

As the images suggest, the Mass was very formal. Before it began, a highly ceremonial performance was staged: 2,000 acolytes entered the stadium, walked down between the rows, and lined the tartan track during the ceremony. In addition, there was a second entry of 100 clergy members in liturgical dress from the base of the sanctuary. In order to "fill" the stadium acoustically, some 2,000 singers from church choirs covered the stadium's northern galleries. Even though the choir was complemented by a jazz-pop singer and ensemble who filled the service's pauses, the Mass exhibited many elements of pre-Vatican II rituals, such as Latin prayers and songs (supported by the choir and a missal book made available to the audience). The contrast to John Paul's public appearances was no accident. Pope Benedict was and remains a vigorous supporter of liturgical reform—or rather, restoration. He not only supports pre-Vatican II rituals, but also stresses a kind of ritualistic fundamentalism, with the theological relevance of these rituals as one of the core elements of Catholicism. To him, it is the tacit meaning of the common ritual which exalts Catholic music—and consequently the Mass's motto, "Mysterium fidei"—as enacted in the liturgy.

Mediatization

It would be misleading to suggest that these rituals were restricted to the stadium. On the contrary, the Mass was televised by the Berlin branch of German state television. As with sporting events, state television had a monopoly on transmission from the stadium, and their central leadership decided which images would go on air. It is significant that what was aired was called the "global picture" (Weltbild)—that is, the image that was sent out to other stations reporting on the event.

It should be noted that such events are anything but minor stories for radio and television stations. When the pope visited Vienna in 1998, the Austrian national broadcaster (ORF) reported with the largest number of cameras they had ever allocated to one location at one moment in time. Thirteen years later in Berlin, the television broadcaster still laid an exclusive claim to the stadium broadcast. Their exclusivity, however, was somewhat diminished by the fact that most audience members could make use of their mobile phones, and indeed began using them extensively upon the pope's entrance. A sense of the pope's celebrity was co-produced by the audience who, instead of showing reverence in the traditional way as the pope passed (by making a sign of the cross), raised their mobile phones to take photos and videos of him in his vehicle. Because ritual actions in Catholicism are not accessories but rather essential performances of belief (an idea very much espoused by the theology of Benedict himself), the audience's substitution of recording photos and films for the making of the sign of the cross is highly significant (Knoblauch 2014a).

We should also keep in mind that the audience members were not only involved in the stadium's activities. During the event, they were connected to people outside the stadium through various networks and platforms such as "WhatsApp." Two photos we had accessed may give an indication as to the visual representation produced by participants. It seems that to more conventional Catholics, the majestic image of the pope on the huge screen during the Mass was more important, while more liberal Catholics found the representation of devoutly praying persons more relevant to the religious character of the event.

The fact that audience members themselves have become more represented in media is an important development. When television and mass media dominated media coverage, as was the case when Austrian television covered the 1998 papal Mass in Vienna, filming focused mainly on what was happening on stage and hardly ever faced the audience; fourteen years later (and following the rise of digital media), German television regularly focused on the participants at Benedict's Mass. In the media coverage of the Vienna Mass, the broadcast only showed audience members for sixteen minutes per hour covered, while in Berlin it was forty-eight minutes per hour, with close-up shots increasing from seventeen per hour to seventy-nine per hour. While the official broadcast from Vienna included only one audience reaction, in Berlin there were twenty-nine— that is, seventeen per hour.

The reason that the audience was so prominently featured at the Berlin papal Mass may have been related to a deviant case of audience coverage. During the Mass, the pope requested two minutes of silence. The German television commentary emphasized that having two minutes of silence was quite an exceptional phenomenon for television, while the camera (and the production) clearly tried to find images representing the silence in the stadium, with a camera flying over the heads of the audience members. The camera, however, clearly solicited waving hands, smiling, and cheering from the audience, gestures which obviously contradicted the requested "solemn silence." Production quickly changed cameras twice and finally focused on a priest sitting next to the altar— who himself quite noticeably started to smile when he realized that the camera was focused on him.

Conclusion

The smiling gesture of the priest, which almost ironically broke with the expectation of solemnity announced by the television commentator, might be on the "nanoscale" of sociological analysis, yet it exemplifies how spatial scales are transcended by mediatization: through the television camera, his smile was immediately projected onto the giant screen in the stadium and, as a "global image," was simultaneously transmitted around the world. As part of the event, mediatization extended the focus of the proceedings from micro-sociological details all the way up to the global audience. Interactive digital mediatization by the audience simultaneously contributed to rescaling the event in unprecedented ways. Rescaling in this context suggests that the relationships between spatial scales, from local to global, were changing in a manner which was strategically intended by the Catholic Church as a "politics of scale." Through mediated communication, the event was allowed to surpass the various spatial scales with its recipient design of the Catholic oriented toward a global audience and, consequently, the "orbis," or whole world.[6]

   When talking about the global, we should distinguish this "global event" from a "global mega-event." While a global mega-event (such as the Olympic Games) demands large interventions in urban space (Gaffney, Wolfe and Müller 2018), a papal Mass is set in an existing sociospatial frame. It is interesting to see that its specific emplacement in an urban space (east, west, etc.) does not figure prominently in media representation of the event. There is no doubt that the mere existence and use of a stadium requires some urban context (a large number of people and infrastructures). The event, however, is emplaced in such a way as to use a landmark building to underline the "singularity of the event" (Reckwitz 2020). It is a "singular" event—and at the same time it is one in a series of events (papal Masses) which are organized all around the world. By reason of this seriality, the event turns into a "field configuring event" (Lange, Power and Suwala 2014). This transformation does not take place in the religious field, of course, but rather in the field of the Catholic Church as a global actor. Through the performance of a series of spatially singular communicative events, the Catholic Church demonstrates both its presence and its relevance in different places, contexts, and regions in the world—and thus its globality. It is by way of the media's globalized dissemination of the spatially dispersed and globally emplaced papal Mass that Catholicism demonstrates its "presence" in the world.

But what does this mean for the relationship between space and religion below the global scale? As we have mentioned, the Berlin Mass did not address the city itself, but rather used the stadium in a general symbolic context, framed by signs of Catholic religiosity. Through its decentralization, the emplacement of the event demonstrated the irrelevance of the specificity of Berlin. Neither east nor west nor center nor periphery played a role; rather, a select handful of event "islands" represented the singularity of the city. The events were therefore characterized by a massive insulation within the space of the city and isolation from the urban population. Indeed, while the center was symbolically taken over by opponents of Catholicism or religion in general, the pope appeared only at certain locations. Despite the fact that the German pope was visiting Germany and Berlin, his Mass was neither an urban nor a national event, but rather (successfully staged as) a religious and clearly marked Catholic event. In this sense, it was not truly a form of urban religiosity, i.e., "distinctly and specifically urban forms of religious practices, experience and understanding" (Orsi 1999, 388). Because the papal visit in general and the Mass in particular were staged as events, they were instead a matter of (the emplacement of) religion within an urban setting, helping to relate the singularity of location to the seriality of the event.

For the sociology of religion, the very nature of such a global event series may appear as a reaffirmation of religion. In fact, the "mass ornament" in each event serves as a Catholic collectivity communicating to the global Catholic *communitas*. However, eventization itself is by no means specific to the Catholic Church. As with any event, it competes locally as well as in media with other events (and even with other domains, not just religion) (Stolz 2010); it is therefore no surprise that it may have popular consequences beyond the religious sphere, such as in politics (as John Paul II demonstrated in Poland). The event studied in this chapter, however, followed almost the opposite path. It ignored the national as well as urban contexts and marked the papal Mass as a local and—at the same time—*trans*local communicative event, in the kind of specifically religious ways that Haken (2019) calls "religious celebration." Religious celebration, therefore, seems to be one of the newer and increasingly relevant forms of communication with which contemporary religiosity constructs its (temporary) presence in (temporary) spaces across a variety of societies and cultures.

Turning Spirituality into a Public Event: The Popularization of Collective Meditations in the Urban Space

Mar Griera
Universitat Autònoma de Barcelona

Anna Clot-Garrell
Universitat de Barcelona

It is September 21, and the Barceloneta—the beachside neighborhood of Barcelona—is busy and full of people.[1] There are gatherings on the beach accompanied by loud music, sights and smells from lively tapas bars, and groups of bikers, runners, and young people walking around. At 7:30 p.m., a group of about seventy people of different ages and profiles meets in a neighborhood square. They sit cross-legged, close their eyes, and start to meditate. A flash mob meditation for Global Peace Day has been announced on Facebook, WhatsApp groups, and other social media. Many meditators have responded to the call in Barcelona, but also in London, Buenos Aires, New York, and Singapore. Most of the participants do not know one another. In Barcelona, they meditate in a circle for approximately thirty minutes. A strange quietness surrounds the event. Some passers-by observe the meditation and take pictures; others spontaneously join the meditation. A small group of tourists whisper while two local police officers watch the scene at a distance in a respectful manner. The sound of a Tibetan bowl being struck marks the end of the meditation. Gradually people stand up and smile at one another; some engage in conversation. Minutes later, they are all gone, as if the meditation had never happened. The square is again full of noise and crowds. This public meditation, which we attended in September 2015, is one example of the manifold spiritual flash mobs and encounters that have been spreading in Barcelona since 2011, following a global trend.

This chapter is borne out of our interest in exploring the emergence of these "urban spiritual events" in contemporary Western cities. Drawing on the case study of Barcelona, we aim to address the singularity of these events and unravel their sociological significance for broader understandings of contemporary forms of urban religion. Our argument moves along three different lines. First, we demonstrate that the *public* and *collective* character of these events stands in contradiction with the classical portraits of holistic spirituality which have tended to emphasize its private nature (Luckmann 1967, 1990). We argue that this suggests the emergence of *new forms of sociability*, which are being created out of global and virtual networks, along with ephemeral forms of face-to-face interaction (Molnár 2014). Second, we highlight the importance of the *spatial* and *embodied* dimensions (Fuller and Löw 2017; Löw 2016) through which the urban character of these events is shaped and displayed. Third, we observe both the interrelatedness between spiritual and activist discourses and the affinities of these urban spiritual events with new social movements aimed to *decelerate* society (Rosa 2013). The main argument is that these spiritual events creatively combine repertoires from different religious and urban cultures, generating new spatial practices.

This chapter is anchored in a four-year research project aimed to map and analyze public religious events in the cities of Madrid and Barcelona. The main data source for this chapter has been participant observations and ethnographic interviews in spiritual public events in Barcelona. A total of ten participant observations were conducted between 2015 and 2018. These observations have been complemented by six in-depth interviews with the promoters of these events.[2] In addition to participant observations and interviews, we have traced and collected documents and information about these events on social media. We have applied tools from "grounded theory" (Corbin and Strauss 1990) to analyze the data collected. To respect the confidentiality of the people interviewed, all names are anonymized.

The chapter is structured in four sections. First, we conceptually address *urban spiritual events* in order to understand the novelty, meaning, and relevance of this phenomenon. In the next section, we contextualize and describe the evolution of urban spiritual events in the context of Barcelona. We then move to the analysis of the three interrelated dimensions that bind these events (public/collective, spatial/embodied, and political/spiritual). We conclude by discussing their hybrid nature and main characteristics.

Conceptualizing "Urban Spiritual Events"

In recent years, there has been a growing academic engagement with the notion of events and the idea of the "eventization of society." In his book *Event: A Philosophical Journey through a Concept*, Slavoj Žižek defines an event as "something shocking, out of joint that appears to happen all of a sudden and interrupts the usual flow of things; something that emerges seemingly out of nowhere, without discernible causes, an appearance without solid being as its foundation" (2014, 1). This conception of events as *interruptions* relates to Erving Goffman's concept of "infractions" (1971), which refer to those kinds of actions that break with the taken-for-granted rules of interaction in a specific setting. Similarly, Harold Garfinkel's ethnomethodological concept of "breaching experiments" (1967) alludes to those actions that disrupt, interrupt, or transgress the "normal flow" of a certain social reality. From this point of view, events are temporal interruptions that contravene everyday courses of action and ordinary assumptions, while revealing implicit social norms.

However, not all infractions or breaching experiments are events, nor are all events impromptu. Events are generally planned in advance and are usually carefully organized by a specific group of people. The preparation of an event comes together with certain expectations and involves an organizational effort despite its apparent disruptive and spontaneous character. The idea of the event as a fortuitous happening is, as Monika Salzbrunn puts forward, powered by the media that "constructs the event as an unexpected phenomenon, random, unpredictable. There is a trend to isolate the event and deal with it in its immediate context" [Authors' translation from French] (2017, 2). However, an analysis of contemporary events shows that the idea of the event as a fortuitous and effortless happening is far from true. Organization is crucial for the success of a public event (Molnár 2014).

Events generally take place in cities, and their manifold configurations are intimately related to urban culture. In contemporary cities, there are multiple types of events with notable differences in scope, objectives, and context (Smith 2015). Urban studies scholars have noted the growing importance of events (Spracklen and Lamond 2016), which are manifested in the following trends: (a) the eventization of leisure, sports, or music (Spracklen et al. 2013); (b) the celebration of mega-events (e.g., the Olympic Games) which provoke a rapid urbanization and transformation of urban centers; (c) the commercial practices of organizing events to promote certain products; (d) the eventization of political protests (Rojo 2014); and (e) the emergence of ephemeral, playful, and sometimes subversive events such as flash mobs, which are "public gatherings of complete strangers, organized via the Internet or mobile phone, who perform a pointless act and then disperse again" (Molnár 2014, 44).

The literature on events, however, does not refer specifically to religious phenomena, although there is a growing interest from the sociology of religion in exploring the growth of religious events in relation to faith traditions and spirituality. Michaela Pfadenhauer (2010), for instance, has considered the celebration of Catholic World Youth Day as a marketized event that emerges as an innovative response to secularization and pluralization.[3] Evangelical events are also gaining worldwide popularity; some of them have become mega-events that gather thousands of people in the same setting, such as the concerts of evangelical pop singers or the massive prayer meetings of acclaimed and charismatic pastors. The eventization of faith runs parallel to what Hubert Knoblauch has identified as the "popularization of religion," which "underline[s] the fact that the boundaries of marked religiosity claimed by the great institutions are being dissolved in two ways: the lay are actively creating religious communication and the communication of religious organizations is going beyond culturally marked religiosity" (2008, 148).

Holistic spiritual events are also a growing phenomenon. In the countercultural Glastonbury Festival (Bowman 2009) or the international Burning Man festival (Gauthier 2013), to name just two examples of wildly popular events that have been gaining ground around the world, we see very clearly the eventization of spirituality.[4] However, we argue that beyond these massive spiritual events that usually take place in natural, remote, or rural environments, holistic spirituality events, such as the meditation flash mobs described above, also take place in cities.

The Emergence of Urban Spiritual Events in Barcelona

The emergence of meditative flash mobs in Barcelona relates to a global trend. Fleeting and playful[5] urban events have proliferated globally. As illustrated by Virág Molnár's research (2014), flash mobs have spread worldwide since their emergence in 2003. This is observable in the diffusion of flash mobs in social media, like amateur videos and photos on YouTube and Facebook, but is also reflected in the word's inclusion in the 2004 *Oxford English Dictionary*. Along with their temporality, the spatiality of these ephemeral events is also important. Flash mobs usually take place in public spaces, such as city squares, parks, or train stations, but they are also organized in semi-public settings such as stores, shopping malls, subways, or university campuses (Molnár 2014, 49).

The Advent of Ephemeral Urban Spiritual Events (2011–14)

The appearance of urban spiritual events in Barcelona follows this worldwide urban trend, but these events are articulated in ways that reflect the local sociopolitical context. Meditation flash mobs in Barcelona emerged in 2011 as part of the May 15 *Indignados*[6] movement that occupied the main city square, Plaça Catalunya. Amidst political and social debates, workshops, talks, and discussions, a group of people in the *Indignados* assembly formalized their involvement in the protest under the name *Harmonia* (harmony) and *Revolució Interior* (inner revolution). These groups organized meditations and harmonization exercises such as yoga or *Jin Shin Jyutsu* for the people involved in the everyday organization of the movement, framing the activities in terms of spirituality and health. Meditation flash mobs started when the square's occupants were cleared in June 2011. As our interviewees observed, these meditation encounters were initially organized by young people who were personally involved in the 15-M protests and promoted these flash mobs under the umbrella of two global organizations based in Barcelona: *WakeUp* and *Medmob*. A few months after the beginnings of 15-M, the first meditation flash mob took place on September 6, 2011, in Plaça del Rei, one of the main squares in Barcelona's city center.

From 2011 to 2014, we observed the organization of these flash mobs with some regularity and following similar patterns: a well-known city square would be selected as the site of an ephemeral occupation through silent meditation, which in turn would be disseminated through social media (mainly Facebook). We counted seven meditation flash mobs between 2011 and 2013, with four events happening in 2012 alone. Since most of the flash meditations took place in the year following 15-M, the emergence of these encounters seems related to the popular power of the *Indignados* assembly. The flash mobs were announced on social media, accompanied by captions such as "Awakening the Peace Here and Now," "Global Peace Day," "the Re-evolution," or "Mother Earth." These first spiritual events were mainly attended by people involved in the 15-M movement, but also by members of Thich Nhat Hanh's *sanghas* and Buddhist groups as well as people linked to Barcelona's diffused holistic–spiritual–therapeutic milieu.

The Rise of Massive Urban Spiritual Events (2014–17)

While the first urban spiritual events followed the model of the worldwide flash mobs, they changed shape slightly in the following years. From 2014 onward, the participation of *Medmob* formally ceased in the announcements, but the meditation gatherings continued under the auspices of Barcelona's chapter of *WakeUp*, the young global Buddhist organization related to Mindfulness and the teachings of Zen Master Thich Nhat Hanh. While the small and almost spontaneous meditation actions in city squares were maintained for certain significant dates, such as the International Days of Happiness and Peace, *WakeUp* also began organizing a new and massive form of the event. A member of this group started to promote large meditation events, which required bureaucratic procedures and public permits. The first public spiritual event was planned when Zen Master Thich Nhat Hanh visited Barcelona in May 2014 and *WakeUp* organized a meditation flash mob in the city's monumental Arc de Triomf (Triumphal Arch). The event was entitled "Sit in Peace" and, according to its organizer, attracted about 600 people. Buddhist communities already had previous experience organizing large events, especially related to the visit of spiritual leaders (e.g., the Dalai Lama). However, the novelty was that this time, the event was planned in an open-air urban space and the emphasis was on the act of meditating in public.

This meditation was followed by three other massive dynamic meditations between 2016 and 2017 that took the form of silent mindfulness marches for peace across the main streets of Barcelona—usually starting at Parc de la Ciutadella and finishing in Plaça Catalunya. Two of these large dynamic meditation flash mobs were organized to mark the visit of Plum Village monks to Barcelona (2016 and 2017). Likewise, in September 2017, along with Buddhist communities and a Christian meditation group, a silent march for peace and nonviolence was organized in response to the terrorist attacks that took place in Barcelona in August 2017. From May 2014 to September 2017, we counted seven spiritual events, four large meditations with the popularization of these silent mindfulness marches, and three small meditation flash mobs in city squares. These spiritual events followed the pattern of earlier meditation encounters: they were announced through social media and had the support of several Buddhists groups, some Christian meditation groups, and other holistic spiritual groups and individuals.

New Political Frames of Urban Spiritual Events (2017–19)

From October 2017 to June 2019, spiritual events continued to take place. However, during this period, the organization of these collective public meditations was deeply connected with the political situation in Catalonia. This was illustrated by the new public meditations that started in October 2017, when the Catalonia self-determination referendum was organized by the Catalan government with the support of several civic entities. The Spanish government forbade the referendum and Spanish police forces intervened violently in many electoral centers. The weeks after the referendum, the political climate in Catalonia was tense and uncertain. As a response to this situation, a group of people, coming from different spiritual milieus, promoted the organization of what was called a *Marathon of Silence*. The *Marathon* consisted of public meditations and the creation of a webpage as well as a channel within the Telegram messaging app to coordinate parallel meditations from home. For the first days, the meditations were held in front of the Catalan Parliament and were explicitly framed as actions aimed to mitigate political tensions and to promote public serenity. Afterward, the group also organized meditations in other significant and "politically charged" spaces, such as Plaça Universitat or the Estació de França (one of Barcelona's historical train stations) near the Catalan Parliament.

These spiritual events were in continuity with previous flash mobs but also had some distinctive features. On the one hand, *WakeUp* was not the main organizer. This time, the initiative came from a group of individuals involved in the civic platform *País Conscient* (Conscious Country), which aims to transform values and promote socially responsible policies in Catalonia, with the support of other entities such as Brahma Kumaris, Buddhists, and the World Community for Christian Meditation, among others. This was a diverse group of people in terms of age, gender, and religious affiliation, who nevertheless shared a role as meditators engaged in social and spiritual movements. On the other hand, while previous flash mobs had a very abstract and general purpose, these meditations had a rather concrete and local goal: confronting the tension in what was perceived as an important social and political crisis through meditation.

These static meditations finished when the Catalan crisis lost momentum.[7] As a result of the new political situation marked by the imprisonment of Catalan politicians and activists, a new spiritual event gained strength. In June 2018 and 2019, a Catalan civic entity organized large silent marches in response to the repressive response of the Spanish government to Catalan pro-independence activists. The aim was to make Catalan society's commitment to peace visible through a silent march, with demonstrators dressed in white clothes. The marches were attended by about 300 people and had the support of several civic and pacifist organizations as well as different religious communities, including local Buddhist, Muslim, Sikh, Catholic, Jewish, Protestant, and atheist organizations.[8] While in previous events, most participants did not clearly mark their religious affiliation—only Plum Village Buddhist monks did—in this case the multireligious character of the marches was emphasized. Meditation, or the conscious practice of silence, was used as a common language to show peace (and commitment to peace) across religions. As Eugeni Garcia Rierola (2017) shows, the practice of silence is extremely useful as a means of ritualizing togetherness in a multireligious context.

Urban Events and Spiritual Choreographies

We distinguish three overlapping features that characterize these urban spiritual events: first, their *public* and *collective* character, which problematizes traditional understandings of holistic spirituality and public space; second, their *spatial* and *embodied* expression, which shapes their urban character; and, finally, their *political dimension*, which emerges from the articulation of a spiritual response to the challenges intrinsic to neoliberal societies.

Public and Collective Disruptions

Sociological literature has mostly portrayed holistic spirituality as belonging to the intimacy of studios and homes (Luckmann 1967, 1990). However, our empirical evidence questions the emphasis on both the private and the individualistic expressions of these events, and demonstrates a much more complex and heterogeneous picture in line with recent research in this field (Aupers and Houtman 2006; Clot-Garrell and Griera 2019; Fedele and Knibbe 2020). The public and collective character of urban spiritual events brings new questions to the fore: What is the intention behind the organization of these events? How are they constituted? What are the implications of these public collective displays?

The first observation we make is that the public appearance of people standing in a silent meditative pose in the middle of a noisy city creates a *disruption* (Goffman 1971). The disruptive power of public meditations comes from the fact that public space is not considered to be a "normal" nor "common" place to meditate. The sight of a group of people meditating in a spiritual center or temple would not generate surprise, nor would it be perceived as an infraction of the rules of conduct (Dixon et al. 2006). Following Goffman, "A rule of conduct may be defined as a guide for action, recommended not because it is pleasant, cheap, or effective, but because it is suitable or just. Attachment to rules leads to a constancy and patterning of behaviour; while this is not the only source of regularity in human affairs it is certainly an important one" (1956, 473). The celebration of a collective meditation in an urban public space breaks the expected pattern of behavior for this setting and becomes an "infraction" in Goffman's terms.

Rules of conduct might affect the individual in direct and indirect ways. On the one hand, rules affect the individual directly "as *obligations*, establishing how he is morally constrained to conduct himself" (Goffman 1956, 473). That is to say, the individual regulates her own behavior to adapt to certain rules of conduct. Therefore, participation in a public meditation represents a conscious act of confronting one's self and one's conceptions of correct behavior in certain urban contexts. This might "lead to feelings of uneasiness" and discomfort (Goffman 1956, 473). As we experienced in our participant observations, it is not easy to stand still, meditating, in the middle of a crowded public space. At the beginning, it is deeply uncomfortable, a feeling which is widely shared among participants. However, the collective dimension of the event is crucial to its public character and can help to mitigate participants' feelings of discomfort while generating a sense of companionship. We observed a camaraderie which develops from the initial stages, when there is a tactful watching aimed at guessing who the rest of the participants are amidst the people near the meditation's meeting point. Likewise, during the silent marches there are also smiling gazes and some gestures of solidarity from observers (who are careful not to disturb walkers physically or by talking too loudly while they pass). Finally, a more visible expression of affect unfolds at the end of the event, when many participants hug each other warmly. Through small gestures and facial expressions, an ephemeral intersubjective community of experience is built.

On the other hand, rules also affect the individual indirectly, "as *expectations*, establishing how others are morally bound to act in regard to him" (Goffmann 1956, 474). Pedestrians, drivers, cyclists, and other users of the public space do not expect to find a group of people meditating in the middle of a square or hundreds of people walking in silence and blocking traffic in the center of Barcelona. As an "out-of-place" event, collective meditation is perceived as "situationally inappropriate" (Goffman 1963a) and might generate surprise, curiosity, and amusement, but also animosity or antipathy in observers. As Monika Salzburnn and Raphaela Von Weichs put forward, "It is important to note that different people interpret and appropriate the same event in different ways" (2013, 1). The perception of the event is highly dependent on observers' experience, knowledge of the spiritual practices they are witnessing, moral arguments about acceptable uses of the public space, and feelings of safety (or danger).

However, in general terms, it is important to state that our fieldwork revealed that these kinds of spiritual events do not generate strong forms of animosity, at least at first sight; indeed, the opposite is true. The perception of these spiritual events as harmless helps to understand why the organizers have not had to face strong bureaucratic obstacles—as some other religious groups, like Muslims, have (Griera and Burchardt 2020)—when organizing these open-air events. In most circumstances, city officials do not even require the organizers to apply for a permit; rather, they watch without asking. It is quite revealing that one of the first promoters of these meditation flash mobs did not even know that it was necessary to request a special permit for organizing such an activity. Public expressions of holistic spirituality are usually perceived with sympathy and considered inoffensive,[9] perhaps because they are not often considered as pertaining to the "religious domain" and are therefore not subjected to regulations on religious affairs (Griera and Clot-Garrell 2015a; Martínez-Ariño and Griera 2020).

Embodied Scenarios

We have suggested that public meditations and mindfulness marches are not—or are not only—spontaneous public disruptions, but planned and contextualized events with what theater scholars would consider to be a consciously chosen scenography and choreography. Not every part of the city could serve that particular purpose. Public spaces are not neutral, but mediated by urban memories, uses, architectural elements, iconic components, sensorial atmospheres, rules, and regulations. As Cresswell notes, "the place of an act determines (as much as it is determined by) the reactions to the act and the meanings accorded to it" (1996, 6). In our fieldwork, we have observed that not only spaces are carefully selected, but also that the selection criteria of these chosen spaces change according to both the sociopolitical context and the intrinsic evolution of these events.

The first meditation flash mobs, which emerged in 2011 as a result of the 15-M movement's experiences, chose city squares as their main backdrop. Inspired by the *Indignados* movement, meditation encounters started to take place in other public sites, a choice that revived and, in a way, embodied the political gesture of the 15-M actions. Two criteria governed the selection of the city squares in which meditation flash mobs took place between 2011 and 2017: their urban centrality and their natural beauty. We have thus distinguished two kinds of flash mobs: first, those performed in city squares of particular political and touristic significance, such as Plaça del Rei, Plaça Sant Jaume, or Plaça dels Àngels, that make meditation not only visible but also disruptive, as discussed above; and second, events staged close to appealing natural environments, such as the Mediterranean beach (e.g., Plaça del Mar) or Barcelona's urban parks (e.g., Ciutadella), which can draw large groups interested in visually attractive locations.

The large flash mob meditations that began in 2014 abandoned this idea of "occupation" due to the high number of participants expected and the need to request a special permit. Meditation encounters thereafter began to take place in more monumental places, such as the Arc de Triomf, yet still followed a similar pattern of attentive and meaningful deliberation regarding the existing meaning of the space and the objectives of the event. The promoter of these events, who explained the choice of the Arc de Triomf for the massive meditation flash mobs with the Zen Master in 2014, illustrated this as follows:

> They [the City Council] offered us several places, that is, in front of the Old Port, they offered us Montjuic, the area of Plaça Espanya or the Arc de Triomf, and then we thought that the best was the Arc de Triomf, and then they were studying the issue and they said "well," because the Arc de Triomf is not a war arch, it is a welcome arch for all people, it was the gateway to the Universal Exposition at the beginning of the century, and then we were investigating and I said, of course, this is an open door, it is a welcoming door. [Authors' translation from Catalan]

However, we observed that the "natural element" of the city—that is, the effort to seek out nature in the urban context—was also included in the dynamics of these massive meditations. For example, the silent mindfulness marches started in Parc de la Ciutadella, a beautiful green space in the middle of Barcelona, before moving to dense city locations such as the streets of Ronda Sant Pere or the well-known boulevard Les Rambles. This route was followed by the silent marches for peace that occurred between 2018 and 2019, which conversely began near the iconic Arc de Triomf and ended in Parc de la Ciutadella. These urban spiritual events, therefore, either begin or end in quiet and beautiful park-like sites, despite moving through loud urban thoroughfares and major urban squares.

The meditation encounters that started in October 2017 with *The Marathon of Silence* rearticulated the political dynamics of the first flash mobs, but in different locations marked by the political climate of the Catalan self-determination referendum rather than the 15-M protests. These included the garden in front of the Catalan Parliament or university campus locations in which political demonstrations were also taking place.

Despite differently evolving forms and spatial criteria, the common and central element in all these urban spiritual events is the body. The body becomes the actor in these ephemeral encounters and the boundary that distinguishes participants from nonparticipants. This boundary, while porous and enabling people to freely join the meditation, also has social markers. In this regard, most participants fit the profile of holistic spirituality outlined by researchers

(Heelas et al. 2005; Sointu and Woodhead 2008)—that is, mostly urban white middle class, with a higher proportion of women. However, while this pattern was evident in the first spiritual events, it was less pronounced in the last ones— especially those explicitly including members of different religions. Nonetheless, it is worth noting that beyond the materiality of bodies in terms of body postures and social class, there is also a related and important sensory dimension (Degen 2008). This sensorial aspect of a group of people was illustrated by one of the organizers:

> There is a collective energy between people who participate, and people watch us. For instance, in the case of Plaça Sant Jaume, I arrived, and I could not see anyone, so I decided to sit [in meditation position] alone so that they could identify me. It was such a strong feeling, even a social claim, of being able to sit there in the middle. (Authors' translation from Catalan)

While the silent bodily disposition either in collective meditations or mindfulness marches can be disrupting, it is also a way of subverting regular uses of public places and bestowing new meanings upon certain places, particularly those which are dense with commercial and touristic activity, as exemplified in the previous quotation. The particular bodily posture of meditation, coupled with silence in these public spaces, creates a sacred atmosphere through which the space is not only lived but also appropriated. What makes these spiritual events distinct, therefore, is not only the choice of a location that could confer, in different ways, public visibility to meditation, but the ways in which the site is reimagined by the presence of meditating bodies.

The Religious, the Spiritual, and the Political

Holistic spirituality has emerged as a category that describes the increasing presence of people who do not define themselves as religious or nonreligious but rather as spiritual, as well as to make sense of the increase in groups and individuals promoting body–mind–spirit practices inspired by Eastern traditions and ancient Western religions and philosophies (Sointu and Woodhead 2008). The category encompasses a wide variety of groups, beliefs, and practices that have an "air of resemblance" (Wittgenstein 1921) and are related to what Charles Taylor (2007) calls "the massive subjective turn of modern culture." However, as outlined above, the boundaries between holistic and Western Buddhist groups are difficult to establish. Moreover, the analysis of the silent mindfulness marches in Catalonia that have included members of different religions (Jewish,

Sikhs, Muslims, Christians, and Buddhists) has shown both that members of other religious groups feel comfortable using what we frame as a "holistic spirituality repertoire" (Clot-Garrell and Griera 2019; Griera 2017) and that, at least in the performative moment, boundaries between other religions might become diluted.

In addition, in our interviews it became clear that meditation flash mobs and mindfulness marches were not only framed and justified through the language of spirituality. These events were also interpreted as being part of a political genealogy of protest related to nonviolent action repertoires and pacifist movements. References to Gandhi often appeared in the interviews, and local leaders who fought against the Franco dictatorship in Spain[10] (especially Lluís Maria Xirinachs)[11] were also widely considered as role models. Linking these events with these political genealogies opens the range of potential participants and fosters an idea of spirituality suitable to everyone sharing similar political commitments. In addition, despite the fact that each event is framed as oriented toward a specific and distinct goal (peace, happiness, ecology, or calming down the Catalan political climate) there is a certain common thread that binds these events together.

Through our fieldwork, we have identified a shared narrative vis-à-vis the contemporary world and its main problems. In general terms, the narrative follows a basic diagnosis: the impacts of modernity and capitalism, and subsequent processes such as urbanization, mass production/consumption, and the speculative economy have generated a global ecological and humanitarian crisis—a crisis that is accentuated by what Hartmut Rosa (2013) terms the *acceleration of society*. This acceleration has both an external dimension (in the constriction of both time and space in contemporary societies) and an internal one (in the internalization of time pressure, especially within the middle class). Mindfulness marches and collective meditations are devices aimed at counteracting both dynamics: internal acceleration is challenged by slowing oneself down and external acceleration is challenged by symbolically disrupting the accelerated flow of the city.

Departing from this narrative, the performance of meditations in the public space is perceived as serving a twofold aim. The first is to cultivate and foster the experience of meditating in a public space as a form of "connecting with the collective energy of the surroundings" and with like-minded participants. This generates a sociability that forms spontaneous communities. These communities get empowered by breaking rules of public space together and showing that "there is another way of walking, a conscious way of walking, a peaceful way of doing everything," as one of our interviewees put it. The events are ephemeral, but the idea of being a big group of people doing something *disruptive* together—even more so when these events are held simultaneously in different cities and are portrayed in social media afterward—contributes to sustaining a mindful and spiritually conscious worldwide community; an imagined community united by the spiritual and political commitments of its members. In her research on global yoga events, Anna Koch has shown that "the multiple event spaces bind together on a particular day, and the global imagination of a chain of people standing together can offer an 'invigorating social space' providing empowerment" (2015, 554). This empowerment holds a political dimension, as it emerges as a form of critique and resistance but also as a moral critique of an unjust system. As Koukal explains it, "of all of the various forms of political dissent, the most dramatic as a form of expression is that which places lived bodies in tension with the prevailing social order (…) They are a collective will concretized, an intersubjective mass animated by a common purpose that fills a public space and obstinately makes their shared demand" (2010, 109). However, as Paul Bramadat illustrates in another chapter of this book, public spiritual events do not always take the form of political dissent. As his examination of the bridge controversy related to the International Day of Yoga events in Vancouver reveals, the political configurations of the context in which these events take place is also important in shaping the form that they take and how they are perceived by public audiences. In the case of Vancouver, yoga was publicly pictured as "a risible elitist activity" disengaged from its spiritual character.

The second purpose of the meditations in public space is more spiritual in tone but also has a political dimension. There was a shared belief among the interviewees that collective meditations have a thaumaturgical character, since the act of a group of people meditating and devoting their "spiritual energy" to some particular cause might "unlock healing energies" and foster an "energy of peace." Therefore, the act of meditating in public is perceived by many of them as thaumaturgical in the sense of being able to produce consequences that go beyond ordinary reality. We also observed a widespread conviction among the participants that the act of meditating in public space has an "irradiating" effect, since the "good" and "powerful" emotions that might be generated in a collective meditation have the capacity to affect the people in the surroundings and positively light up the atmosphere of a place.

Hartmut Rosa's considerations on "resonance" (2013) help to illuminate how political, spiritual, and personal aspirations get entangled in the organization of a collective spiritual event. Rosa refers to "resonance" as the opposite of alienation and notes that "tied to this encounter in which I experience a transformation of myself, I experience this other, which transforms me" (Lisjter, Celikates and Rosa 2019, 73). This is similar to what Charles Taylor (2007) identifies as an aspiration, or experience, of fullness in the secular age, an emotional and lasting connection with oneself and with others. The "irradiation" that participants search for in these collective public meditations should be understood in terms of an individual involvement with social purposes. There is an aspiration to deeply connect with oneself while, simultaneously, connecting with others. Turning inward is not perceived as a form of isolation, but the opposite. Participants consider that in order to make "authentic connections with others" and be able to create "powerful alternative communities," individuals need to cultivate their inner self through meditation. This relates to Rosa's emphasis on the collective and social dimension of resonance, since he underlines that rituals, such as the public meditations examined here, "actually play a strong role in creating conditions for resonance" because they generate the necessary disposition toward "being open to hearing the call, being affected, and [having] the expectation that you can reach" (Lisjter, Celikates and Rosa 2019, 74). Indeed, our research shows that the social aim of "affecting society" beyond those involved in the meditation is precisely reached through the aforementioned public character of these spiritual events.

Conclusion

As Fedele and Knibbe suggest, "In many countries 'spirituality' has emerged as a category that is relatively 'silent,' at least in the public domain" (2020, 3). Most research frames holistic spirituality as belonging to the private sphere. Luckmann's (1967) view of the privatization of religion was very influential and prevalent among sociologists for many decades. This privatization thesis was questioned, especially by José Casanova in his work on *Public Religions in the Modern World* (1994), but his objections seem only to apply to world religions and the ways they might enter and redefine the public and political spheres. Holistic spirituality was considered to be the privatized form of religion par excellence, representing the most individualized approach to transcendence and often caricatured as narcissistic and self-referential (Carrette and King 2004; Liptoviesky 1983).

The urban spiritual events examined in this chapter defy this classical portrait, since they have a clear aspiration of being public and being in public.

This public character is at the very heart of their existence: they do not exist beyond the public space and, more specifically, beyond the urban public context. They are phenomena embedded in particular cities, and yet in many ways they resemble events that have spread worldwide. Furthermore, the spiritual events described here not only take place in public spaces, but also aim to act and intervene within them, provoking social but also thaumaturgical effects. The holistic spirituality repertoire has melted into the script of contemporary urban culture's choreographies and shows discursive, practical, and sensorial forms of appropriation, even disruption, of public spaces. As Virag Molnár underlines:

> Flash mobs also highlight a variant of the spatial tactics that de Certeau (1984) argued were so essential for the sociocultural production of urban life. Whereas de Certeau exposed the everyday creativity concealed in routine practices (such as walking), flash mobs illuminate how everyday technological tools can be used ingeniously to create urban interventions, to break the routine of the everyday, by reframing public space around unexpected outbursts of sociability. (2014, 55)

Most of these urban spiritual events, like most flash mobs, gather a group of individuals with no previous community links but who share certain spiritual and moral views. Collective public meditations are ephemeral experiences that unite people for a specific purpose but do not respond to classical forms of community. The ambition of these events, however, is not only playful and communitarian but also political and even subversive, since they aim to contribute to a "better world." In holistic spirituality groups, there is a prevalent conception that personal transformation is the first step for social transformation, and that meditation might thus serve to activate social change by changing oneself (Clot-Garrell and Griera 2019). Public collective meditations aspire to enact both individual and collective change. Their framing is very similar to that of social movements, and they might be read as a social movement themselves, as they have been developed in terms of "deceleration" movements following Rosa (2013).

Our research, therefore, has revealed these new urban spiritual events as creative assemblages that blend together languages and practices from different milieus, such as urban culture, holistic spirituality, popular religion, and social movements, which in turn generate new public interventions and spatial practices. Likewise, we have demonstrated the sociological relevance of these events in informing broader understandings of contemporary forms of urban religion. Further research is required to expand the discussion on the evolution and transformation of the category of spirituality in the public domain, and on the interdependence between popular, religious, and protest languages in contemporary urban rituals. Furthermore, it would be especially interesting to interpret this phenomenon from a global comparative perspective to grasp the interplay between global and local dynamics and the role of social media in diffusing and propagating this type of event.

God's Warriors: Embodying Evangelical Brazilian Jiu-Jitsu in Rio de Janeiro

Raphael Schapira

Graduate Institute of International and Development Studies

At the end of a Brazilian jiu-jitsu seminar on a street in João's Hill,[1] a community[2] located in Rio de Janeiro's northern outskirts, a local female pastor takes off her flip-flops and steps onto the mats. She raises her arms and begins preaching, facing the students who are sitting on the ground. The four coaches standing beside her close their eyes and assume a praying posture, either crossing their arms in front of the chest, putting their right hand on their heart, or raising their hands—although lower than the pastor's—as if to respect the momentary primacy of religion over sports. Most students follow the coaches' example, closing their eyes and bowing their heads as they listen to the sermon. Parents, siblings, and residents who have been watching the training session sit outside the nearby grocery store, bearing witness to the transformation of the small street into a space of evangelical Brazilian jiu-jitsu.

I remember the excitement I felt while observing how some thirty children and teenagers remained silent while the voice of the pastor filled the air. During that moment, I perceived an otherworldly layer of significance added to the usual meaning given to Brazilian jiu-jitsu, which my interlocutors see as a life-transforming activity that leads to a righteous life. The young athletes have been told that they are God's warriors in deciding not to fall for the evil forces of drug-related criminality, in particular the temptation to become child soldiers in the trade. What to my eyes began as an only socially motivated Brazilian jiu-jitsu seminar had turned into an evangelical intervention in the public space, showing the whole community the devotion of the young athletes.

Brazilian jiu-jitsu is a martial art that focuses on grappling without the use of striking with arms or legs. It developed in Brazil during the twentieth century out of the intersection of several martial arts, principally judo, with influences from other sports such as different wrestling styles and capoeira (Silva and Corrêa 2020).[3] Brazilian jiu-jitsu became internationally known in the early 1990s due to the Ultimate Fighting Championship (UFC), a televised show in the United States that pitted fighters representing different martial art styles against each other. Winning the first edition of this new form of championship, the Brazilian jiu-jitsu representative proved the effectiveness of this fighting style, transforming overnight a little-known martial art into a mass media phenomenon that continues to influence the way practitioners and fans move all over the world (Downey 2006). Since then, Brazilian jiu-jitsu has been growing steadily around the world as a sport in its own right and as part of a new martial art called mixed martial arts (Alonso and Nagao 2014). Due to its great versatility, Brazilian jiu-jitsu is practiced for recreational, fitness, and self-defense purposes, and many practitioners also compete in tournaments in their respective category divided by age, gender, weight, and experience.

The great success of Brazilian jiu-jitsu and mixed martial arts has led evangelical churches to embrace these sports in the United States (Schneiderman 2010) and Brazil (Barrionuevo 2009). For example, the Bola de Neve church,[4] which has chapters all over Brazil, actively promotes Brazilian jiu-jitsu and fighting matches (Rivers 2011). Although there exist no exact numbers for Brazil, given the popularity of Brazilian jiu-jitsu and evangelical churches, it is reasonable to believe that evangelical Brazilian jiu-jitsu is a widespread phenomenon. In 2013, Brazilian jiu-jitsu was Brazil's most popular martial art, with approximately 1,907,724 practitioners (Ministério do Esporte 2015).[5] Given that in the 2010 census, 22 percent of Brazil's population self-declared evangelical (Instituto Brasileiro de Geografia e Estatística 2010), it is reasonable to estimate the number of evangelical jiu-jitsu practitioners to be around half a million.

At the beginning of my fieldwork in Rio de Janeiro, which lasted from September 2017 until July 2018,[6] I was told, "in Rio, you can find a church and a Brazilian jiu-jitsu club at every corner." Following this line of thought, the main interest of this chapter is the impact on public urban space resulting from the encounter between the two. I ask how evangelical Brazilian jiu-jitsu coaches and practitioners transform public space through the practice of their sport, seeking an answer by analyzing the entanglement of the urban, religion, and sports. I discuss how the location of Brazilian jiu-jitsu projects in communities greatly affects their characteristics. The Brazilian jiu-jitsu coaches of these projects consider their students' social backgrounds, adapting their religious and spiritual guidance accordingly. The peculiar interpretation of Brazilian jiu-jitsu by evangelical coaches and pastors imbues the practice of Brazilian jiu-jitsu with religious meaning. I argue that the moving body becomes a medium for expressing and producing religious identity, by which evangelical Brazilian jiu-jitsu practitioners transform the public space of sports halls and communities.

Urban Violence, Empowerment, and Evangelical Brazilian Jiu-Jitsu

"Collecting Souls—Uniting the Flock in Brazilian Jiu-Jitsu" is simultaneously a sports, religious, and social project. Gabriel Machado founded this youth project in his church in the neighborhood of Pombal, in the North Zone of Rio de Janeiro, at the beginning of 2017 after having been invited to do so by the president of his church. However, just when he was about to start giving classes, the church hired a new pastor who stopped the project. The new pastor positioned himself against teaching Brazilian jiu-jitsu in the church, arguing that the space of the church should only be used to do God's work and that martial arts were inappropriate to spread the gospel. He feared that the practice of a martial art like Brazilian jiu-jitsu would stimulate violent behavior in the participants.[7] However, after many discussions, Gabriel and the church's president were able to convince the new pastor that Brazilian jiu-jitsu is an effective outreach tool that does transmit values in line with the church's teachings, and the inauguration class was held in April 2018.

A typical class at Gabriel's dojo[8] consists of about ten students aged between six and fifteen, with slightly more male than female athletes, who live in the surrounding neighborhoods. It starts and ends with the jiu-jitsu greeting ceremony, for which the students line up in order of belt rank[9] with the coach facing them, followed by a short prayer. Before the class starts, the students put on their training uniforms and tie their belts accordingly. They are supposed to leave their flip-flops lined up at one corner of the mat and to bow when stepping onto the mat, signaling their recognition of the dojo rules. After the greeting and the warm-up exercises, students practice specific techniques shown by the coach. This is followed by several one-on-one rounds of sparring lasting between two and six minutes (depending on the athletes' age), in which two practitioners wrestle each other for training purposes with the intent to apply techniques to control their partner, eventually forcing him or her to give up. This wrestling requires a technical understanding of the body and its limitations, physical fitness, willpower, patience, and humility to ensure that no one gets hurt. Participants must take care of themselves and others, always negotiating the appropriate amount of force with the danger of hurting someone else or oneself.

Much like similar evangelical Brazilian jiu-jitsu projects, Gabriel's project is located at the margins of the state (Das and Poole 2004), where the notion of "public space" is a complicated one. If we understand public space as freely accessible to anyone, created and protected by the state's "monopoly on the legitimated use of physical force" (Weber 2015, 136), then the de facto parallel spaces of marginalized communities under the control of drug cartels are not public spaces. In public discourse, Rio de Janeiro's communities are described as war zones with equally dangerous inhabitants who must be contained within, even though they de facto form an essential part of Rio de Janeiro's social fabric (see Perlman 1979). Nevertheless, the streets and little squares of communities often have "the quality of public space in which daily interactions, economic exchanges, and informal conversations occur, creating a socially meaningful place" (Low 2000, 33) in the sense of Lefebvre's lived space (1991, 362).

Evangelical Brazilian jiu-jitsu projects intervene meaningfully and directly in marginalized public spaces, not only through public training sessions but also by having students pass through these spaces dressed in their white training uniforms and displaying the projects' patches. Given the location of Gabriel's project, the students' walk to and from the gym in their training uniforms is a way for them to show others, especially the police, that they do not form part of the local drug cartel. This is important since the church is in the neighborhood of Pombal, which forms part of a complex of communities to which Irisópolis and Tocaia Grande belong. Although the residential buildings of Pombal were initially projected for members of the military and despite the neighborhood's neutrality, barriers erected to hinder the military police from entering are visible, indicating that Pombal forms part of the neighboring community complexes controlled by drug cartels. Nevertheless, Pombal is considered neutral territory, not belonging to any drug faction dominating the neighboring communities. Therefore, Brazilian jiu-jitsu students from neighborhoods controlled by different drug factions can attend training there.

However, it is often too dangerous for children and teenagers to come to class. The police might be conducting operations inside the communities, or rival drug factions might be fighting each other for control over the territory. For this reason, simply coming to training already shows the students' dedication, as a situation which appears to be peaceful might change at any moment. A police helicopter can suddenly appear, forcing inhabitants to run for cover. When Wilson Witzel took office as Rio de Janeiro's governor in 2018, he authorized the police to use draconian measures against the drug cartels, leading to the highest number of people killed by the police in two decades, among them many innocent civilians (Santoro 2019). Apart from Witzel's dubious success in combating crime, the measures have resulted in an even higher level of militarization and incarceration of community inhabitants (Machado da Silva 2008).

Gabriel Machado was already fascinated by martial arts as a child when the Brazilian *vale tudo* and mixed martial arts heroes became famous through the UFC hype at the beginning of the 1990s. However, growing up in the slum-community Tocaia, his family was too poor to be able to pay for martial arts classes. Although his family's situation got better after moving to Tocaia Grande, a neighborhood built as part of a governmental urbanization program, it was not until Gabriel already had a family of his own and a stable job that he began practicing Brazilian jiu-jitsu. At that time, martial arts professor Carlinhos Silva was giving classes in a community center nearby, and Gabriel took the chance to realize his childhood dream and started learning judo and Brazilian jiu-jitsu with him. Due to his dedication, he became Coach Silva's assistant and was eventually authorized by him to lead his own project. When the opportunity arose to offer classes in his church, Gabriel decided that it was time to give back: "You know, I am a very spiritual person. I think God gave me the opportunity to learn jiu-jitsu and judo. So, if he gave me the opportunity, I have an obligation to give others the opportunity, too, and serve as an example." Gabriel's main reason for dedicating himself to his project is that he wants to allow children and teenagers to get to know something other than drugs and violence. He says that in the surrounding communities, people are either consuming drugs or working for the drug business. Giving them the opportunity to get to know something different means to break the "chain of evil" through the "current of good" and to achieve this, he says, all you need is "strength and will." Couched in evangelical metaphors, Gabriel points to the strong social component of his project aimed at changing social reality.

This makes Gabriel's sports project an example of how evangelicalism in Rio de Janeiro's communities can act as a means for extremely marginalized people to generate resources through informal means (Lanz 2016). Brazilian jiu-jitsu is increasingly viewed as a form of physical capital (Bourdieu 1978) even beyond jobs that require knowledge of martial arts, e.g., the security business or the police. The Secretary of Sports in São Paulo and at the Secretary of Education in Rio de Janeiro are working on programs aiming to institutionalize Brazilian jiu-jitsu in schools (Machado 2018, 2019). Politicians and aficionados envision Brazilian jiu-jitsu as having the power to instill in students values such as discipline, hierarchy, and perseverance, which will make them "champions, not only on the mats but also champions in life" (Rogério Minotauro, as cited by Machado 2019).

However, despite the wish to change social reality, for Gabriel and other evangelical jiu-jitsu practitioners, positive social change is primarily achieved through personal change. Their social work aims at the individual and his or her capacity to change him or herself, not society. Gabriel wants his children and teenagers to not feel limited by the fact that they live in a poor community and to have trust that their lives will be better than those of their parents, something he would have wished for himself:

> I never had anyone telling me that something big was waiting for me in the future but that achieving it depended only on me. I needed this person, and this is what I am trying to pass on to my students: the future does not need to be that which you see around you, the future can be what you want it to be. Sometimes they do not have the hope to project something big. But this is what I want to show them: think big and your future will be bright.

According to Gabriel, Brazilian jiu-jitsu training is supposed to empower its participants by teaching them self-control, discipline, focus, self-confidence, and trust in God's strength, which will pull them out of their idleness. Given the context of urban violence and poverty as described above, I find it striking that for Gabriel, the primary object of change is not social injustice but the individual. Instead of aiming at changing a discriminatory system that continuously reproduces the "sub-citizenship" of the poor (Souza 2018), he believes that it is the individual who has to change to escape poverty, and that one way to do so is to learn Brazilian jiu-jitsu.

Brazilian Jiu-Jitsu as Embodied Religious Activity

Evangelical Brazilian jiu-jitsu enthusiasts transcend the difference between sport and religion. At the level of speech, this can be observed in the way metaphors related to fighting are used. For example, practitioners sometimes refer to "the everyday battle," stating that "God teaches us how to fight" or that "Jesus was the champion of champions." Pastor Boaventura da Costa, who I met in a gym in Rio de Janeiro's East Zone, used to train in Brazilian jiu-jitsu. He compares the fighting inside the dojo to a theater of operations in which training for the everyday battle of survival in the favela as well as for the everyday spiritual fight takes place. Referring to the biblical passage 1 Samuel 17 (David and Goliath), pastor da Costa narrates that David was trained in combat by fighting with the lion and the bear. Interpreting this passage from the Bible literally, da Costa concludes that life must be understood from the actual practice of fighting—in this case, training in Brazilian jiu-jitsu: "God is teaching us that the preparation for the daily battle, for studying, for conquering a professional position, for being better people with ethics and attitude—this comes from fighting."

However, in da Costa's view, training in Brazilian jiu-jitsu does not only prepare for everyday life in the favela, but it also prepares for what he sees as a spiritual fight against an unseen enemy, which he characterizes as "wicked" and "many times negated." To fight against this enemy, he says, one needs discipline, focus, determination, and faith, and the way to learn this is through hard jiu-jitsu training. "If I want to fight a spiritual army, I need to be well trained," da Costa states and concludes, "hard training, easy combat." The theological orientation da Costa expresses through his martial rhetoric is known as "spiritual warfare," a term used "to denote both the war between angels and demons for influence over humans and the human contribution to this ongoing battle" (Bramadat 2000, 170, n3). It is important to note that pastor da Costa argues that the connection of spiritual warfare and Brazilian jiu-jitsu necessarily involves training the body, too, as this makes it different from other forms of spiritual warfare. Even where it has connected with militarism, the focus has been mainly on a militarized discourse for doing "spiritual battle" (McAlister 2016).

The importance of training the body is also emphasized by Gabriel, who sees Brazilian jiu-jitsu equally as an important, even religious activity. Taking the biblical passage on the body as the vessel for the Holy Spirit, he says that training your body, taking care of it, and knowing yourself as a physical person signifies that "you're doing what the Bible tells you to do." For Gabriel, the teachings of the church and the teachings of martial arts complement each other:

> You have to be aware of your attitude at every moment. Because if not, you end up having your enemy, your ego, passing your guard and defeating you. And then you're totally disconnected from the church, disconnected from God. Jiu-jitsu is the same thing. If you don't take care of the hand gripping you, you can be sure that the grip will become a choke. This is what I connect: the church and the teachings of martial arts and fighting.

In his perspective, Brazilian jiu-jitsu becomes another way to teach God's word. When asked whether the fighting aspect of Brazilian jiu-jitsu stands in contradiction with Christian values in terms of stimulating violence, Gabriel responds that there is a big difference between aggressiveness, which forms part of jiu-jitsu, and violence, which people mistakenly associate with jiu-jitsu.

> People think that because jiu-jitsu is a contact martial art, it generates violence. But when you get into the atmosphere of jiu-jitsu, you don't see or perceive violence. What you perceive is aggressiveness which is biblical. [When] you read the Bible, you will find that there have always been fights and battles. But the problem is not the battle; the problem is whether the heart of a person carries rage. When you fight [jiu-jitsu], you don't use your rage. You use your intelligence, your wisdom, and your knowledge. Jiu-jitsu teaches you to respect the limitations of your neighbor ... [and] the church teaches you to love your neighbor. So, when you respect the limitations of your neighbor, you love your neighbor.

The question of whether it is possible to show "one's love of one's neighbor through hurting one's neighbor—even in a non-rage-filled way" (Paul Bramadat, personal communication) remains disputed among Christian practitioners, fans, and researchers of Brazilian jiu-jitsu and mixed martial arts. From an academic viewpoint, in their endeavor to make "a Christian case" against mixed martial arts, Nick Watson and Brian Brock consider the sport "immoral" due to the violence involved (2018). Christian fans are more ambiguous, expressing "internal moral tensions" between their love of watching mixed martial arts fights and their love for Christianity (Borer and Schafer 2011, 181), while many Christian professional and amateur practitioners of combat sports fuse fighting and religious practice (Rivers 2016).[10]

A close analysis of evangelical combat sports reveals that for evangelical Christians endorsing combat sports, the moving body in training and fighting is imbued with religious meaning, allowing practitioners and spectators to embody the beliefs, ethos, practices, and culture of Christianity. Fit bodies that can fight do not only represent discipline, self-control, and sacrifice; indeed, the "fighting body and its practices *are* the theology" (Greve 2014, 168; italics in original). Justin Greve calls the connection between the Christian mind and body a "theology of the body" in which body, mind, and spirit are inextricably linked (Greve 2014, 143). In practice, this means that religious belief is expressed through fighting and that fighting can lead to believing.

Analyzed from the perspective of embodiment, the practice of Brazilian jiu-jitsu in an evangelical setting not only expresses and transmits beliefs, ethos, and practices of Christianity, but is generative of it. New religious movements such as evangelical churches emphasize experience-oriented forms of transcendence for which sensual-bodily dimensions are paramount (Gugutzer and Böttcher 2012, 11). Here, the body is not just a useless vessel for a disembodied spirit; it is an important medium that permits the experience of spirituality and produces one's identity through the exercise of specific movements. Building on the conception of the body "as the existential ground of culture" (Csordas 1990, 5), Ingold and Vergunst (2008, 2) point to the importance of understanding the body as grounded in movement. It is not just the body as the bearer of signs (Hietzge 2002, 33), but, as Brenda Farnell emphasizes, human movement as a medium other than speech that transmits knowledge and is metaphorical in itself (2012). Movements can be, therefore, "signifying movements" (Farnell 2012, 86) that are not just expressing preexisting knowledge but are generative of knowledge and meaning.

Competing for Jesus in Public Space

Evangelical Brazilian jiu-jitsu practitioners most notably transform two types of public space: sports halls and the public space surrounding their home gyms. It is common for Brazilian jiu-jitsu athletes to participate in public competitions. These competitions, organized by Brazilian jiu-jitsu federations, take place regularly in different sports halls around Rio de Janeiro. They give evangelical athletes a stage on which to demonstrate their devotion to Jesus in a nonverbal way through tattoos, patches on Brazilian jiu-jitsu uniforms, gestures, and the moving body itself. Since "evangelical Christians are keen on making themselves and their religious experience visible (and audible) to others" (Spyer 2017, 8), they widely use online postings of pictures in social networks.

At Brazilian jiu-jitsu competitions, it is normal to see male athletes showing off their trained and tattooed upper bodies during breaks between fights. Crosses or depictions of Jesus figure prominently on the muscular backs of athletes, often together with tattoos referring to Brazilian jiu-jitsu. Jesus might be depicted as a fighter, with a muscular chest and an abdomen displaying the six-pack of someone heavily trained, differing from his bearer only by his long hair and the crown of thorns on his head. One athlete had a huge, crack-filled cross tattooed on his back with "King of Kings" written in English above it, while three Japanese characters were visible on his left tricep.[11] These tattoos are examples of how Brazilian jiu-jitsu athletes are embodying and engraving into their skin the notion of evangelical morality, not only as "the exteriorization of the interior which is simultaneously the interiorization of the exterior" (Gell, 1993, as cited in Schildkrout 2004, 321) but also as a domain of intersubjectivity and agency (Jackson 1996, 33).

A similar process occurs with patches with messages written on them, used by evangelical practitioners on their Brazilian jiu-jitsu uniforms. Retailers sell these patches during competitions together with uniforms and other martial art items. Very prominent is a patch saying, "Athletes of Christ. Believe in the Lord Jesus, and you and your dojo will be saved." Others state, "God in heaven. Jiu-jitsu on the ground" or "Bola de Neve Church—Fight Ministry," expressing the athlete's membership in one of Brazil's most prominent evangelical churches. These patches are worn together with patches indicating the athlete's team and club.

Finally, evangelical Brazilian jiu-jitsu athletes often perform gestures such as making the sign of the cross and silent prayers at competitions before stepping onto the mats. They also point their index finger toward the sky, especially after winning a fight. In Brazilian jiu-jitsu, as in other combat sports such as boxing, the winner of a fight is indicated by the referee by raising his or her arm. This moment is often used by evangelical athletes to point their index finger toward the sky and look up, with their head back and their lips moving silently in a thanksgiving message, giving this moment religious significance by implying that the victory is a victory for God.

Brazilian jiu-jitsu competitions are an opportunity for evangelical Brazilian jiu-jitsu athletes to shape public spaces. Although small, explicitly evangelical competitions that change the secular character of state-owned sports halls through temporal appropriation exist, larger Brazilian jiu-jitsu competitions do not make any reference to religion. This is where evangelical athletes make use of the described practices to shape the public space of sports halls through their actions by producing experiences of "collective effervescence" with religious meaning. At the moment the athlete's victory is pronounced and their index finger points to the sky while the athlete's supporters cheer, the index finger becomes an "appresentation," in Husserl's sense, referring to something else as present (Knoblauch 2012, 37). This brings concrete religious meaning back to Durkheim's concept of collective effervescence as used in studies of sport, which has been transferred to describe "the emotion and excitement generated at a modern sports event" (Dunning 1986, 3).

One of the coaches of João's Hill, described in the introductory vignette, told me with pride the story of how he and his athletes had arrived home after winning a trophy for best team at a competition for social projects. Holding the huge cup they had just won out of the car window, they drove up the hill of their community, announcing their victory to everybody. I understood the deeper meaning of this story only when the coach explained to me that usually, it is drug dealers who drive up the hill. Displaying their assault rifles through the open window, they announce who is in charge. By replacing the assault rifle with the sports trophy, Pablo continued, the kids and teens experienced that it was possible to be respected and admired without belonging to the drug cartel. In this story, young Brazilian jiu-jitsu athletes undermine the common symbolic economy of the community's public space, and this, my interlocutor assured me, was his greatest victory.

Evangelical Brazilian jiu-jitsu also has a concrete impact on the public space of the communities where it is practiced. Since drug dealers and residents share the same public space, drug dealers can easily recruit children and teenagers by giving them simple tasks at first that might subsequently become more important (Dowdney 2003, 123). By allowing children and teenagers to develop an alternative sense of self, this becomes a much harder thing to do. Their involvement in evangelical Brazilian jiu-jitsu results in new forms of appropriating public space, for example, via public training sessions or by walking on the streets in their Brazilian jiu-jitsu uniforms. The success of evangelical Brazilian jiu-jitsu in Rio de Janeiro's communities supports the hypothesis that "religious innovations are concentrated in contexts of material deprivation. Here, religion is used to negotiate hardships and ... [t]he readiness of religious groups to address poverty has shaped their attractiveness" (Becci and Burchardt 2013, 19).

Conclusion

The public expressions of evangelical Brazilian jiu-jitsu in Rio de Janeiro are examples of the capacity of sport and religion in tandem to transform public space. Besides intervening in peripheric urban spaces directed at the inhabitants of disadvantaged communities, the presence of evangelical Brazilian jiu-jitsu practitioners is strongly felt during professionally organized competitions directed at a broader audience. Evangelical athletes and coaches use both as a stage for the production and performance of the evangelical sporting self, expressing and constituting itself through movements, gestures, tattoos, and patches on the training uniform. These give religious meaning to the realms of sports and the urban—both of which are commonly framed as increasingly and often inherently secular—transforming sports halls and streets at the margins of the state into sites for the expression and production of new religious forms.

Feeling Sufis: An Essay on Intimate Religion in Berlin

Omar Kasmani

Affective Societies—Institute of Social and Cultural Anthropology,
Freie Universität Berlin

In a powerful deliberation on religious affects, Donovan Schaefer offers the crucial insight that religion "feels before it thinks, believes, or speaks" (2015, 8). This chapter takes up the matter of in/visible religion by privileging its intimate and felt presence in the city—or, *how religion feels*. It focuses on the Sufi ritual of *zikr* in Berlin and locates traces of saintly traffic in ritual time and through the bodily affective experiences of its participants. I pursue an intimate reading of an Islamic ritual as a way to illustrate how religion, in particular its imaginal–spectral iteration, bears the potential to trouble secular urban logics and brush against temporal ideations of the city.[1] Affective accounts of what Sufis see with eyes closed enriches our understanding of Berlin's hidden religious topographies (Burchardt and Becci 2013) and points to critical coagulations of material and immaterial presence of Islam in Berlin (Burchardt and Westendorp 2018). It is also to say that ostensibly private feelings of love, loss, and longing in ritual atmospheres, even at their fleeting best, cite shared desires and anxieties of its participants within a hetero-affective abundance of intimate relations in the city (Kasmani 2019).

The Sufi circle that I refer to in this text meets on a weekly basis in Berlin-Neukölln.[2] This postmigrant community is at once locally embedded and transnationally configured.[3] Its followers are children of Turkish *Gastarbeiters* whose history in the city goes back to the early 1960s.[4] The grand sheikh, however, is based in Istanbul, as is the group's organizational headquarters. Although women are active contributors in the community's affairs, the ritual setting I was able to access is a men's-only prayer gathering, which takes place on a weekly basis at a neighborhood mosque.[5] The material is drawn from fifteen months of observations and in *zikr*.

In terms of format and structure, this chapter is a diptych. The first section is a composition of fragments. *Feeling in Circles* features long, direct excerpts from interviews with Sufi followers. These have been selected on the basis of two interrelated themes that evolved during fieldwork: feelings of love and affection, and believers' apprehension of the unseen or the saintly during the ritual.[6] However, what my Sufi interlocutors describe in terms of their experiences is neither entirely immediate to the moment of our interactions nor gleaned from a single performance; rather, their views on the affective qualities of the ritual reflect a gathered consciousness that individuals accrue over a period of time. This aligns with my view that affect is not simply a question of what one feels but also serves as its indistinct yet critical elaboration, a gradual form of *knowing by way of feeling* (Kasmani, 2019, 35). The other important point to take into consideration is that *zikr* is performed with eyes closed, shaping how followers learn to see during the ritual and limiting what is ordinarily observable to the researcher in the field (Mattes et al. 2019). This ties with Ann Armbrecht's assertion that the invisible does not always signal, less so, equal an absence, but rather, "invisibility was simply the presence of things that were not readily visible to our eyes, not because they were not present, but because they were no longer valued by the world in which we lived" (2009, 215).

Intimate Religion, the subsequent piece in the two-section chapter, turns to researcher's voice with a mix of ethnographic observations and philosophical deliberations on migrant religion in the urban. I propose critical intimacies of *zikr*, whether spatial or temporal, as a way to approach men's access to the godly in the city. Whereas interview excerpts have been cut and tailored for this section, I have resisted the anthropological urge to embed them in a single ethnographic narrative. I am aware that setting these excerpts apart does not make them *raw* data from the field—that is not my intention. I have employed them alongside my reflective essay as corresponding views on the question of intimacy, which I offer as a structuring principle of religious experience. Here, separating voices for the benefit of the reader—though hardly absolute and possibly artificial—is one way to distinguish and record political divergences in intimate experiences and motivations, both of the researcher and the researched. These constitute and record critical affective gaps which are not easily sutured even through a principle of feeling.

Feeling in Circles

I have never in my life … felt such love. Really, so spiritually. Never have I felt such—and … that's actually really beautiful, because you get intoxicated, get into a frenzy of love, where you … where one … compared to drugs or alcohol, it is completely different, you are still yourself, you have control. But it's really like a frenzy of love, which you experience nowhere else, not for other people, not for the woman you love. It's really completely different, and I find it fascinating. Because it … leads to joy, I feel (Ibi 2017).

****

It's about loving God. You have certain feelings … just put them inside God so to speak … I love God because God loves me. This is a real love relationship. And you simply have to love, for He has made it so apparent; that it can actually be a romantic love relationship with God. I won't say that out loud to our group because then there will be some people who could misunderstand that and understand it as heresy. They say, ah, you have a romantic relationship with God, what does that mean? They can interpret that sexually, or however they want. But in this moment, I see it as love for God. And I think it's good that way.

When I was in love with a woman, I no longer saw the woman but what lay behind her. And I see that … hmm, God has used this person so that I could participate in love. Then, you can experience love. And this love comes from God and not from this woman. And that is essential.

There are those romantic ones [who say]: *what haven't we done for a woman to get her affection?* And how should that be so different from the ones who are dear to God? (Onur 2017)

****

The heart finds peace with *zikr*. And *zikr* is … I can't tell, you know, what meaning it has, in my opinion, but what sort of effects it has, of which I am a witness, let's say. It's really, hmm … it's really a key to another world. It's like a key, so that you can go into a room and no matter what problems you have, you can throw them out. And you're better every time. It's really important. I can't imagine a life without *zikr*. It's one of the most important things in my life.

When one is married and one says the name of the wife often, then she will be glad, the wife is glad. You are glad. There is peace, it's beautiful. That's a woman, and now if you think about it, there's Allah, the creator … when you say His name often it's the most beautiful thing. Because … you love Allah the most. More than any human. And the one you love the most you will mention the most. And because of that … yes, because it's something very mysterious, it's hard to explain certain things—it's really a key to Allah. It opens the doors for everything that you want in life. It's really like that. Well, that's how I see it (Imren 2017).

****

First and foremost is the connection to God. So, one constantly thinks of God. And by constantly thinking of God, it is like being with God all the time ... so, that is the theory behind it. And I just see that as an actual expansion of consciousness for me. In the beginning it was very difficult for me, I have to say, especially the collective meeting on Saturday. I am a very introverted person. I'm not one to yell "Allah" on the outside like that. Or I don't get along when others do that. That's very unpleasant for me, but I've come to terms with it. And I've come to see beyond it, yes, they do that because they get into ecstasy, and that's good for them. And I have learned over time to enjoy *zikr* too.

We have spoken before of the love metaphor. Every person loves differently. For example, I am not a person who, when thinking of his wife or his beloved, pines like *ahhh* or whose love is written all over. I am an introverted person, so, if I love someone, I love them quietly. And that's why I'm quiet and shy. And I'm not screaming. But there are people, who ... when they see their lovers, they scream so much, and suddenly their pulse rises and so on. I become more and more calm and relaxed while others just become more active and dance with joy. I am not a man who would dance with joy. But I know many people who would dance with joy. I interpret that in this way. The other way around, the people who cry ... you have to imagine them longing, like someone you try to get close to but can't make it. And this sadness ... then touches them, such that they start to cry. There, I can also understand, if one says it is an unrequited love. That is a question of mentality, I think. Or a matter of the mind. If someone is more extroverted, then you scream. If you are rather sensitive, then you stay calm or get goose bumps. Or a bit teary-eyed. But I can't grasp it. There might even be people who fall asleep in this moment of ecstasy. Such people must also exist. Everything is in order. So, they have a feeling of closeness and some turn ecstatic.

Our sheikh says that it is a situation where you experience just a bit, a breath of this godly love, so to speak, just a breath of it—this energy comes toward you. And this is so strong, this energy, that it just ... must be let out again. [...] He always tells a story. I don't know if it is true. I can't confirm it. But he says there are people who have had a heart attack from it. Because this energy is so strong and the bodily capacity is not at all able to feel this godly love or this power in its entirety. And that's why they let it out by screaming. There is also this theory. So, in this moment when you experience it, it is really distinct. But how does it go out then? I'm someone who can do tai chi and qi gong and stuff like that and I know, I feel that when the energy comes, I am able to channel it. Or I just let it out differently. And others might be mentally over-stretched by it and they just let it out. It is ... how to say, expected? It is a concealed world. We don't know exactly how it works in theory. We just know, we can judge only on the basis of its external appearances (Onur 2017).

****

You call it *jezbe*. Jezbe—I have no idea how I could translate that into German. Or if anyone has translated it into German at all, I don't know. But j*ezbe* … there are different types of *jezbe*. I will explain first what kinds there are and what they are. For sure there are kinds where people scream. There are kinds where people cry. There are kinds where people laugh. There are even ones where people grow tired. That kind of *jezbe* exists. Different kinds. Of course, I'm not an expert … it is something uncontrollable. He … how shall I say … during *zikr*, the person is … I don't want to say in a trance, because it's not supposed to sound as though we smoke something here and ooh — are gone! Rather, this person is so much within a [condition of] love that it may happen that he cannot control it. So, you could tell that person, don't do that, he would do it anyway. The heart is so filled with love in that moment, it doesn't fit anymore. It explodes. And for one person it's just that he screams … you hear different things with us. One person screams, the other laughs really loudly. And the other cries (Imren 2017).

****

For me, it is about being close to God and feeling this feeling of security. […] And that shouldn't just be on the days when I do this ritual; the goal is always to have it all the time. Because if you have it all the time and are always aware of God, then you just do … then you are more virtuous.

You can also see it in a way that you always have someone, like a patron saint who accompanies you and doesn't leave your side. And I prefer to see it that way. I see it as someone who is always with me, who protects me, who helps me.

Sometimes it happens that you think of God. Or you think of certain things, which actually make your eyes tear up because you are touched by certain things. Normally you don't think so intensively about God. In these moments, it is like that, you think about it and yes, it gets better and better with the development you go through as a spiritual human being. So, it also becomes essential, you need it sometime. You miss that when you don't meet on Saturdays (Onur 2017).

****

There are people who, if they perform *zikr* a little too long—this—they drown in this sea, you understand? And … in this time, they don't know what they are doing, they are not masters of themselves. […] It's like watching a film, you sometimes like to watch … [imitates sport commentator] The final: Germany versus Brazil! Ronaldo, he runs, runs, runs, he's already in the penalty box! You're already starting to shake, hey? You're grasping your table and squeezing. He's tricking the goalie, you're already getting up! But why are you getting up, you understand? This feeling, you're immersed, you love what he's doing. He lands a goal, you're in an artificial ecstasy. You leap. You cry! Ah! You're in a situation that you're not normally in. Because you feel love toward it. And to those people nobody says, what are you doing? No one! But when you do the same thing during *zikr*, your eyes are closed, you know, Allah sees you right now. And there are some—many people out there, who do so many bad things, but you have done this struggle and you have gone from—from home to here, through so many bad things. You have closed your eyes and come here to do *zikr*, do you understand? And he sees you, you don't see him, we're all together, it's love. And at some point … at some point you lose it, you begin to scream, you can't control yourself!

When *zikr* has begun to take its course, and this feeling is so strong, it's possible that one—that a few—see things which one normally doesn't see. Things that, for example, a saint normally sees. He sees angels! He sees people who lived 500 years ago! Saints, they are there and they do *zikr* with us. And when you have your eyes closed, you feel that, but you don't see them. But when all of a sudden you see other figures, you'll get the shock of a lifetime. You can fall over. You know what I mean? There have been many cases like this. Everyone was doing *zikr*, and there was a 9-year-old who also did *zikr*, and his eyes were totally open the whole time. After the *zikr* he asked us, "Where are all the other people, who were just as many as us, who all had green hats and white beards? Where did they go?" We said, "But there was no one here." He really saw people who had died back then, who had always done *zikr*. Allah sends them back to earth, their blessing, because they took the love toward *zikr* so seriously that they are still allowed to taste this love, you understand? And the boy saw all of that. There are so many things. You don't sleep, you see things that normally can't be seen. Because … Allah has placed a veil over our eyes. If you lifted that veil, we would see Satan, the angels. We would see the situation of the dead. We would see other things. […] And it's possible that this veil is briefly lifted in *zikr* (Hasan 2016).

****

[The first reason is that] when you close your eyes, the inner show is more effective. You're not distracted by outside stimuli. That also works when we say we think of death. Then we actually imagine that we die. That's hard when you have your eyes open and are distracted by stimuli all the time. The second reason is that you can't concentrate when the others are all swaying. Some even make strange faces, that's distracting. That's just difficult, it distracts from the meditation. The third is interesting. That's again a bit metaphysical. It is about the fact that it's possible that some people's spiritual channels, so to speak, are possibly broadened or just function more sensitively. And it's possible that a Holy One actually stands before you, since you are calling upon him. It could be that you see one of the saints standing before you, and that you get too big of a fright from that, and have a shock (the Sheikh[7] 2017).

****

I think it's just easier to project images in front of your inner eye. Also, in meditation we close our eyes. With any activity that is about looking inside, the eyes are closed. That way, one is not distracted by external stimuli. I think that is the essential point. The second positive reason is simple. Let's imagine we see all these ecstatic people swept up in this ecstasy. And whenever we think of them, we look at the strange contortions they make. We would probably think badly of them. My first time, I opened my eyes … so, about 7 years ago, the very first time. And then I had a bad dream, really. With all these men and so on, it was a bit creepy—when you see what they look like and so on. I once read a nice article in *Men's Health*. And it was written there … men should not see their own face when they come to orgasm because one's face could never be so ugly otherwise. And I think you have to imagine this in a similar way (Onur 2017).

Intimate Religion

In this half of the chapter, based on my impressions of *zikr*, my conversations with Sufi followers, and my limited participation in the ritual itself, I present intimacy as a way to read religious worlding.[8] By intimacy, I mean the critical structure of feeling that inheres in forms of coming close or drawing near, whether it manifests itself during ritual atmospheres, takes hold through its routine performance or perseveres as an afterlife and in excess to the ritual. On the criticality of intimacy, Lauren Berlant has noted that "the inwardness of the intimate is met by a corresponding publicness" (1998, 281). Taking cue, I am interested in how the *felt* and the *intimate* of a doubly interiorized performance like *zikr*—which takes place in mosque interiors and targets mystical interiorities—permeates the urban. Or, how for that matter, its obfuscating presence gestures at the ways in which migrant/ minority religion might test or even bend normative orders of the city.[9] This follows my earlier assertion that religious affect can accrue—if only to a limited degree—a queer political resonance within a particular field of power relations (Kasmani 2017b).[10] Regardless of any queer currency and irrespective of particular outcomes, worlding, as I evoke it, captures how a world coheres through affective threads of (religious) feeling, suturing the inward and outward, hidden and manifested, material and immaterial, and spatial and temporal dimensions of life.

When it comes to intimate religion, Sufis are perfect interlocutors, and *zikr* is a good place to start. As a way to illustrate this, let me turn to my observations of the ritual and its sequential unfolding. *Zikr* is coupled with *sohbet*, the didactical talk that precedes it. Men gather and listen in these circles. Followers pick the etiquette of the ritual as well as its moral underpinnings, learning Sufi terms and aesthetic concepts important for conducting a virtuous life. This is why the group requires the company of a sheikh, who steers the mood during ritual but also helps create meaning beyond and alongside it. Even though men chant in *zikr*, they must begin by reflecting: with heads lowered, eyes closed and in complete silence, the followers imagine the scene of their death—their bodies being washed and lowered into the grave. The exercise serves as a regular reminder that life is fragile and that the present, though important, is not enough. Then, quietly and with an inward orientation, they recite chains of transmission, sequentially naming a whole line of saints through whom their access to the Prophet Muhammad (and by extension to the holy) is rendered uninterrupted and intact. With such affective groundwork, it is no surprise that the main body of *zikr* tends to be thick in its atmospheric make-up.

Week after week, as men in the *zikr* circle would begin to move and recite names of Allah, the earlier quiet was left behind and a heavy body of rhythm took over the room. The sheikh added layers of song, one melody after the other, lyrically bridging a shrine in Baghdad, the streets of Medina, and the mosque in Berlin. Men cried. Sounds of breathing would become louder with time, exhaustion and excitement overlapped in messy ways. Wading through such a sonic mise-en-scène of affect (Kasmani 2017b), men would come to an opening—find a clearing, as it were—where ghostly and saintly figures bearing other temporal rhythms were rendered coeval, contemporaneous. Sounds also offered sensory traces for how feelings unfolded in the room. Emotions ran high, as did the incremental mood of the gathering, and in these abundant and rising atmospheres—as the followers themselves describe—they would be led to screaming, crying, laughing; some would simply fall over.

Being involved in the ritual as a researcher meant confronting the obvious question: How does one observe with eyes closed?[11] More challenging still was to discern the effecting presences that were folded into affective sequences of *zikr*, but were not ordinarily perceptible more so for the researcher, that is to say ritual dimensions that were differently intelligible or required insider knowledge. In Sufis' experiences of the ritual, intimate feelings of godly love stand out, as do their charged encounters with saints, angels, djinns, and spirits. Equally significant is the emotional–moral import of their perceptions of the in/visible on routines and rhythms of daily life. For instance, when in August 2016, the Sufi circle lost its mosque of eighteen years, *zikr* continued without interruption (and incredibly so). For over half a year, the group met regularly in private homes and shared spaces until a more long-term solution was found. During this period, conversations with followers revolved around the role of *zikr*, its cleansing powers, and its ability to protect them from the contaminating affects and effects of the urban (Dilger et al. 2018; Selim 2015).

With or without the mosque, it became clear that the ritual offered occasions for communing and a sense of continuity in the context of migration. At the same time, the deep sense of loss that the followers felt for a mosque that no longer existed provided a sense of how the spectral dimension of the urban, or its ghostly traffics, were not entirely independent of the material settings they required to haunt the city. Not only were non-corporeal presences or saintly figures critical extensions to tangible realities of the urban, but the two also relied on each other. Continuity meant that the Sufis did not view themselves as acting alone in the contemporary, but rather as acting within a chain of saintly masters. Similarly, communing was not simply the act of mortal men coming together to perform a ritual. To commune was to ally with human and more-than-human figures, to feel at one with wider affective companies, to communicate via sensations of touch and contact, to revive by way of immersion, exhaustion, and release, and to come close to a deeper sense of time and place. The point I am laboring is this: amid a displaced and disaffected geo-chronology of migration, the spectral traffic of historical and more-than-human figures in and through collective acts of remembrance installs an enchanted and thus familiar geography while enabling believers' critical intimacy with specific pasts otherwise foreign to their places of migration (Gordon 2008; Rohy 2006). This is to say that in their efforts to navigate conditions of the present, believers engage as much realms *Elsewhere,* to borrow from Mittermaier (2011), as they draw nearer to "times other than the contemporary moment," which Taneja has named the *elsewhen* (2018, 60). Nonetheless, one might still ask: To what end?

Zikr is commonly described as a mindful remembrance of Allah.[12] However, both through my observations of the ritual and based on what followers have described, I take the position that *zikr* is more about communing by way of feeling in affective companies than it is a sensational format reserved for religious mediation (Meyer 2013, 2012)—that the intimate shapes and inter-corporeal forms it takes bear implications which exceed the divine scope of the performance. This is to say that what men feel during ritual time cannot be contained by the ritual itself, just as much to bring to mind that what lies beyond is to recollect, re-gather by way of affect, that which has been or is at risk of being lost to the world. *Zikr* is a touching reminder that to belong is "a matter of how one feels or one might fail to feel" (Ahmed 1999, 341), even more so in the context of migration. Remembering, it follows, is a collective act through which a *feeling* of "we" is formed "in the absence of a shared knowledge or a familiar terrain" (Ahmed 1999, 331). Less transcendence, if you will, and more worlding. While the two notions don't necessarily work against each other, the distinction I draw here is to push for religious experience as that which is not in service of transcending material realities or forsaking mundane realms in favor of the divine, but rather a condition of being embroiled, staying entangled *in* the world, and becoming worldly as a result of that experience.

For Sufis, worlding is informed by the notion that the outwardly manifested world, or *zahir*, is removed only insofar as a veil separates it from *batin*, its true and hidden dimension (Kasmani 2017a). Intimacy thus points to believers' desires to draw near to the affective knowledge and apprehension of that which lies removed, veiled. Insofar as affect is not merely a synonym for feeling but a form of consciousness, it is also a route to becoming worldly and wise through affective relations, an otherwise way of knowing. Saints are perfect guides for such intimate quests. So long as intimacy concerns the affective relation that thrives in the critical distance between close but distinct objects, saintly companies in the ritual help believers suture the outward world with its inward dimension without necessarily transcending it.[13] Thus, despite its ostensibly religious bearings, affective labors involved in *zikr* draw in diverse life experiences, cite manifold motivations, and impact how one feels in the world. Similarly, evoking sacred histories and geographies, especially in the context of migration, is necessarily imbued with the complex politics of longing and belonging, homing and the loss of homes, and thus best not reduced to concerns of a pious life (cf., Lenhard and Samanani 2019). To the extent that urban aspirations cross-shape with religious aspirations (Burchardt and Westendorp 2018), Sufi conceptualizations of *zikr* impinge on everyday routines and inform individuals' moral and desired ways of being in the city. This is to say that when inward feelings and dispositions break out in public forms and genres, religion is no longer set apart, pressing from the outside onto the city, but rather interwoven into its breathing geographies. Furthermore, saintly intimacies point to allied and critical forms of resistance which believers acting in tandem with historical figures bring to aspects of the present, and these outlast both the duration and the setting of the ritual. In this sense, a ritual such as *zikr* offers its participants routine occasions to dip into heterotemporal worlds, if only in passing, refracting in a sense the secular logics of progressive, linear, or godless time in the postmigrant city. It follows that Sufi performances of inward godly remembrance, especially its collective iterations, make present subliminal figures and migrant inheritances that otherwise remain undervalued and thus not ordinarily visible. The spectral is also imbued with the aspirational, especially in a place like Berlin, where migrant forms of religion cannot carry forth long-standing material histories in the conventional sense of historical or material presence.[14]

This chapter has mainly focused on a single ritual in a highly particular Sufi setting within a postmigrant community. However, I remain interested in advancing, in broader terms, intimacy as a structural principle of religious worlding. Such emphasis on the intimate and the felt complements, but also refracts, the material bent in the study of urban religion: bodies, objects, relics, rituals, processions, and architecture are all evidentiary units in a perception of religion which rests, at times disproportionately so, on the logic of visibility (see Garbin 2013). This also applies to the affectivity aroused by religious symbols and dress in the public sphere, the pop-up politics of religious events and prayer activities in the streets, and the spatial politics and anxiety around religious architecture and the repurposing of buildings within urban environments (Beekers and Tamimi Arab 2016). Visually determined, material–spatial readings of urban religion carry the risk of overlooking "religious expressions that are spatially unstable, unfixed, evanescent or ephemeral" (Burchardt and Westendorp 2018, 165). Spectrality as I evoke it is less an argument for the invisible or the immaterial and more a case for how affect sharpens our understanding of material lifeworlds. Focusing on the intimate, the felt, and the ghostly helps capture what evades the eye when it comes to diverse presences in the city, religious or not, but—more critically to this discussion—it also tempers the terms under which religion may come under the purview of the state (Kasmani 2017b). I would therefore suggest that ghostly affective encounters with saints and spirits offer more than the immaterial. As oblique modes of presence, they bear the potential to queer norms of religion's visibility in urban space and thus also elude its surveillance and governance. This is critical if we consider how becoming present is increasingly demanded of migrant religion—particularly in the case of Islam—or how its veiled, closeted, or differently visible forms arouse suspicion and public anxiety. Thus, when we assign political salience to the intimate or trace its oblique affects in the urban, we also temper the assumption that visible expression is somehow more political than its other variants or counterparts.

This intimate reading of an Islamic ritual has in large part relied on feeling textures that interlocutors have chosen to share with me. Believers' experiencing of love or expedient relations of coming close does not mean, however, that such intimacy is always marked by affirmative feelings or feeling welcome. Neither do conditions of closeness yield comfort without fail, nor does intimacy always result in desired or desirable outcomes. Even in their implicit divergence, love (in believers' terms) and intimacy (the notion I employ) are both relations haunted by failure, contoured by feelings of loss, doubt, hurt, fear, and so on; participants in *zikr* were, after all, also caught screaming and shouting. Often in awe of what they might experience during or beyond ritual time, they could feel envious or in doubt vis-à-vis what others saw or felt. Intimacy, it follows, can also endure as violence, a condition of indeterminacy or *cruel optimism*, or it can keep persons and/or communities tied to troubled objects, traumatic pasts, or embroiled in difficult relations with the present—all equally significant affects that remain underexplored given the scope of the material and the purview of this text. To proceed, intimate religion is therefore the name I give to an affect-driven and feeling-centered idea of worlding, whereby believers move and are moved in space and time as they long for, draw near to, or come into contact with religious objects, figures, and places. Insofar as coming close to an object involves moving away from another, intimacy, however personal or interiorized, is always political. Learning from the *Public Feelings Project*, intimate religion embraces the idea that inward feeling and interiorized affect bear outward political resonance, just as the political affects and shapes how and what we might feel on the inside. To render intimacy as the structuring principle of religious worlding is to capture how believers' relating to notions of the divine threads im/material, in/visible, political, moral, and affective dimensions of the world, while folding up (a) the variously tactile, fleshly, inter-corporeal, sensorial, and sensational forms it takes; (b) the aesthetic routines and emotional repertoires it authors; (c) the structures of intimate communing and coming together it supports; (d) the temporal distances it mitigates with sacred histories and imagined futures; (e) the more-than-here geographies it brings forth in the present; and (f) the moral–political distancing that conditions of religious intimacy might demand or uphold. To be religious as such is not simply a matter of piety or of transcending the earthly, but a desirous condition of communing with and extending into the world with feeling and affect. It involves longing in and of the world, which in Freeman's (2007) terms is a growing bigger in spatial and temporal ways, here made possible by virtue of one's affective ties to an object of religious, sacred, or spiritual value. Intimate religion is not religion as matter but a matter of worlding, religiously sutured.

Postscript

Was will Niyazi in der Naunynstraße (1973) is a book-length poem by Aras Ören composed around a single street in Berlin-Kreuzberg. Its opening images are stark, imbued with competing temporalities of *Gastarbeiter* life: an empty, linear, and measured time produced by capitalism, and that which lies underneath it—hidden or perhaps filled, experienced, immediate time. When the poem's protagonist Niyazi leaves for his night shift, his German neighbors are already asleep, his migrant labor invisible to many. In my cross-musings on religion and migration, I am led to wonder if in a place like Berlin, as insufficiently sacralized as it is, Muslim saints can be thought of as migrants of some manner. Present for some, invisible to many. They do not roam around freely, nor are their figures anchored in the city's tomb-shrines—at least not yet. Akin to night shift workers, the saintly figures I speak of in the context of *zikr* slither sheepishly in the urban, likewise suspended between folds of empty and filled time. They are made present only through effortful performances of remembrance—not durable outside them, and barely intelligible in the city save to those who let themselves be affected by way of feeling.

Epilogue

Sophie Watson
Open University

As the editors explain in their introduction to the book, the concept of "urban religious events" is at the center of their argument. These events are defined as public expressions of religiosity that take place in urban public spaces which transform a religious ritual or practice into a cultural experience, which aim at heightening the emotional and aesthetic dimension of the ritual and offer a sensory experience to participants and audiences, and which are new forms of re-enchantment which foster the creation of a sense of unity. These are important dimensions of the chapters here. So too is Bramadat's suggestion in his chapter that "religious and spiritual claims are not *sui generis* but always part of larger social discourses that reveal a great deal about quite this-worldly concerns, interests, and values." In this short epilogue, rather than focus on these specifically, I consider several themes—by no means an exhaustive list—that seem to emerge across and within the chapters (only some of which I refer to directly here): visibility and the interconnections with public–private and politics, affect, and the secular/religious dichotomy.

Visibility, Private–Public, and Politics

At first sight, to use a rather apt metaphor—the notion of visibility is relatively clear—it is to be seen. But interrogating visibility further, questions arise: to be seen by whom?; with what effects?; and when does it matter or become a cause for concern? Many of the chapters of this book implicitly or explicitly shed light on these questions. Connected to visibility is another trope—that of the public–private, in that much of what passes as visible, or which moves from invisibility to visibility, shifts from private to public space, notwithstanding the porous nature of these boundaries. And in so doing, the public in some sense is reconfigured as private, or is enacted as private in that religious actions that are normally out of sight in private spaces constitute public spaces as private at least for the people involved in some of the spiritual and religious activities. So visible–public and invisible–private overlap and shift in complicated ways in the performance of religious acts and practices in urban spaces. Once actions that are private enter urban public spaces, they are open to scrutiny, regulation, misunderstanding, and contestation. On the other hand, their visibility enables greater understanding, acceptance, and even appreciation. Indeed, both of these forces may be present at the same time.

These dynamics are strongly at play where religious events are concerned. Different elements were revealed in the discussions here. These questions of visibility are also a matter of politics. Who has the right to be in public space, and who has the right to be seen, let alone speak, are political matters. Hannah Arendt is a key thinker here; for her the polis constitutes a "space of appearance," in which being-in-public, or "publicity," is effectively synonymous with politics. In Arendt's thinking the space of appearance goes beyond the public square or forum. It is potentially ever present: "appearance—something that is being seen and heard by others as well as by ourselves—constitutes reality" (Arendt 1958, 77). What is crucial here is that publics are only formed in the presence of others, where everyone is equal and where everyone has a right to speak even if they hold different views and perspectives. In this sense, claiming the right to hold urban religious events, and have them accepted by others who do not share your views, is a deeply political act. Where a religious group is more accepted in a society the more central and visible its site of worship is likely to be and the less politics of resistance are involved in the religious practices. In this book, Giorgi and Giorda point out less accepted religious groups can either locate their places of worship in the peripheries (or outskirts) of the city, or they can downplay their visibility. They do not, in other words, enter the public sphere as equal citizens (on this dynamic, see Luz's and Suárez's chapters).

One element of politics is thus the extent to which these religious events are allowed. As Becci and Okoekpen suggest, urban ecological festivals in urban parks are subject to social control. For them, gaining full visibility and space are only achieved through performing certain ideas and discourses on ecological activism and spirituality, where visitors are much more inclined to appreciate spiritual aspects of the movement and to participate in spiritual activities, when these are seen as "subtle," smooth, and non-invasive.

Making Jewish celebrations public and visible in two public squares of Barcelona, blurring the boundaries between religious and secular—a binary which is also mapable onto private–public—has a very particular force and meaning. Here the invisibility of Jewish practices since the time of the Inquisition and the expulsion of Jews from Spain, renders their visibility not simply a poignant event but also a political one, I suggest. Martínez-Ariño attributes the possibility of these events, in particular, as enabled by the legal framework which protects the right to religious freedom and its collective expressions in public and by the change of the political majority in the municipal government which is aiming to promote a message of diversity. Moreover, she argues that the appealing discourse of the "return to normality," which overcomes the abnormal situation produced by the Inquisition and the expulsion of Jews from Spain, is used to frame these religious celebrations.

Visibility, though contesting dominant representations and dominant practices in the city, also creates the possibility of ossifying the otherness or difference that it is seeking to expose and celebrate, or generating contested responses in its turn. That is, as the different and unusual practices are made public, such as meditating in public space (Griera and Clot-Garell), or practicing yoga on the bridge in Vancouver (Bramadat), the more likely it is that onlookers, or those that object to the events in the first place, see these diverse practices as exotic or threatening, strange, or outside of everyday life, rather than seeing them as practices in process and likely to change.

Affect

Each of these urban religious events mobilizes significant affective responses, either on the part of the actors or others in the city. In his chapter on the Sufi ritual of Zikr, Kasmani discusses how religion feels and foregrounds the notion of intimacy as the structuring principle of religious experience and presence in the urban. This also is a question of politics since it draws attention to migrant inheritances that are normally undervalued, at the same time as the political affects and shapes participants' interior feelings. Politics then is also deeply connected to this thread of concern through many of the chapters. Drawing on Foucault's thinking, he suggests that affective relations and capacities become object targets for discipline and forms of biopower, thus constituting a space of politics where opposition emerges through processes of normalization or outright hostility. For example, we see how the spiritual practice of postural yoga on a bridge in Vancouver led to fierce local hostility and opposition even though it was framed by organizers as a way to find "inner peace and harmony, a sense of oneness, a unity of mind and body." Critiques of the event included its presumed elitism, its cost implications for the public purse, inconvenience, its coincidence with the timing of Canada's National Indigenous Peoples Day, as well as a number of other factors. It is almost as if affect itself, the affective and spiritual life, is too "other" to contemplate or accept for many urban residents who encounter these events (see Bramadat's chapter).

The Secular and the Religious

The urban religious events discussed here disrupt conventional binary notions of the secular and the religious. At the same time these events challenge the notion of the modernist secular city, a view that has been subject to critiques at least since José Casanova's (1994) argument that religion is in no way losing its importance in modern society. More often though, the challenge to this previously dominant representation of the city has come from more established religions such as Islam and Evangelical Christianity.

One element of the disruptions discussed in this book is their often temporary character, where the events render spaces religious or spiritual that are normally everyday spaces of commerce, leisure and residence, which return to their former secular nature with no trace of the events that have occurred. There is almost a ghostliness in the silence left behind, reflecting their liminality and marginality to everyday life in the modern city. Other interventions, as we have seen, have a more lasting presence.

For example, in Barcelona the practices of lighting the *hanukkiah* (the nine-branched candelabrum) and constructing the *sukkah* (or hut) in two public squares of Barcelona have a twofold effect. They temporarily mark a part of the urban territory as Jewish, and at the same time blur the boundaries between secular and religious spaces (see Martínez-Ariño's chapter; cf. Luz's chapter). As we see in Becci and Okoekpen's chapter, urban parks represent more fluid and contested spaces of everyday life, used for different purposes at different times, but often conceived of as an imaginary space of nature for city residents, despite the fact that they are manufactured and designed.

Martínez-Ariño makes the point that the expression of religion in urban public spaces is "intertwined with the dynamics of 'eventization,' branding, and 'heritagization' of the sacred." This notion of eventization suggests a focus on the spatial dimensions of events, but also on the temporality and embeddedness of actors, their networks and processes in particular configurations, where specific activities and processes are framed as a cultural experience, a performance, and a spectacle, which often involve a heightening of the senses and emotions. Eventization also bears some relation to the notion of place making through the temporary appropriation of parts of the city which seeks to turn places into something special, or reimagine them from the everyday ordinary places that they might otherwise be considered.

As with all interventions into urban public spaces, the question arises around the different meanings of such events, to both the actors involved and the onlookers. For whom is the place made and with what effects? Who is included and excluded when places are made? The selection of forms of religiosity that are put on display contributes to their acceptability, or not, in the public sphere, as well as promoting exotic versions of religion (see Cornejo-Valle's and Giorgi and Giorda's chapters). This concurs with many aspects of multicultural settlement, where diverse cultures and practices that can be represented as exotic to the dominant groups in society, are more often permitted—restaurants featuring cuisine from different parts of the world being the most obvious illustration.

The chapters in the book illuminate such questions. In their exploration of collective meditations in the urban spaces of Barcelona, Griera and Clot-Garrell propose three different lines of thought: the public and collective character of these events, the importance of their spatial and embodied dimensions, and the affinities of these urban spiritual events with new social movements aimed to slow down society. They argue that what defines these events are the complex ways in which they draw together different subcultures in the city, not just popular versions of religion and spirituality, but also social movements and urban cultures in creative new assemblages that have the potential to transform cities.

This attention to embodiment also finds its place in all of the chapters, since at its simplest level the production of urban religious events necessarily implies bodies in public space—that is, however contemplative or spiritual the practice may be, these are embodied processes. As such, what we might call eventized bodies occupy spaces (Philippopoulos-Mihalopoulos 2019) that are typically empty or used for other things; as such, they are "bodies out of place." Nowhere is the embodiment of religious practices more explicit than Schapira's discussion of Jiu-Jitsu in the favelas of Rio de Janeiro. In these often poor and violent parts of the city, dominated by drug cartels, the evangelical coaches seek to teach their students Jiu-Jitsu as a way to come to terms with their violent surroundings by "understanding the earthly and the spiritual world as a world of fighting." They achieve this, he suggests, by making the body in motion a medium for expressing and producing religious identity.

In the cases that are so beautifully illustrated in this book, we see clearly the complexities of urban religious events. There are tensions of the enactment and exposure of any minority practices, and beliefs, in public. Here we see parallels with social movements around LGBTQ struggles. In the early stages of gay liberation, "coming out of the closet" in a public manner was seen as an important strategy. But at the same time, once gay people became more visible, they exposed themselves to potential hostility, or worse, violence, from the wider community, who either objected to, or felt threatened by, the visibility of a divergence from normative or dominant sexual expressions.

It is interesting that in the discussions here, no cases of actual violence were reported to have occurred, though in the post Soviet re-casting of the secularscape discussed by Rychkova it is not hard to imagine how forceful the removal of religious practices would have been in an earlier era. Going further afield, however, urban religious events do indeed cause a violent response. In China for example, the practice of Falun Gong which combines meditation and qigong exercises with a Taoist influenced philosophy emphasizing morality and the cultivation of virtue has been subject to violent crackdowns by the Chinese state. Arguably then, this collection reveals a greater tolerance to new and different religious practices, often brought by migrants into settler countries such as Canada, Spain, Germany, Switzerland, Italy, Brazil, and Russia. This has to be a good thing.

Notes

Chapter 1

1   The forthcoming "Rite and Stone: Religious Belonging and Urban Space in Global Perspective," a special issue of the journal *Space and Culture* includes several cases on African and Asian cities, which show how the eventization of the sacred and heritizagion of religion interact with local and contextual forces.

Chapter 2

1   This document was produced thanks to a fellowship granted by the Programa de Apoyos para la Superación del Personal Académico (PASPA) of the Dirección General de Asuntos del Personal Académico de la UNAM. The reflections contained within stem from three sources by Suárez (2015, 2017a, and 2017b). Translation: Joshua Lund, University of Notre Dame.

2   For the most precise data on these questions, see Chapters 4 "El campo religioso en la colonia Ajusco" and 5 "La encuesta sobre la experiencia religiosa" of *Creyentes urbanos* (Suárez 2015).

3   See http://hugojosesuarez.com/creyentesurbanos/site/index.html.

4   See http://hugojosesuarez.com/creyentesurbanos/site/centros.html.

5   See http://hugojosesuarez.com/creyentesurbanos/site/altares.html.

6   See http://hugojosesuarez.com/creyentesurbanos/site/procesiones.html.

7   See http://hugojosesuarez.com/creyentesurbanos/site/evolucion.html.

Chapter 3

1   The authors recognize the valuable help received from colleagues who commented on previous versions of this text. Special thanks to Christophe Monnot, Jens Koehrsen, Fabian Huber, Julia Blanc, Alexandre Grandjean, and David Garbin.

2   This survey allowed us to observe that the participants display a similar profile to that of members of European urban holistic milieus (see Becci, Monnot, and Wernli 2021).

3   The data presented here is part of a larger ongoing research project supported by the Swiss National Science Foundation (SNSF), entitled "Towards a spiritualization of religion?" and headed by Irene Becci.

4   Initially, eco-festivals took place outside of urban contexts, such as the highly successful and popular "Grün 80" exhibition in Münchenstein (next to Basel). *Grün 80* was a Swiss Landscape and Garden national exhibition that lasted six months (April 12 to October 12, 1980). A 46-hectare park with 13,000 newly planted trees and shrubs was created for the occasion. This park is now twenty minutes away from Basel city center by tram. https://www.migros-culture-percentage.ch/history/1980-100-years-of-gruen-80 (accessed July 18, 2019).

5   More precisely, the first editions of *Alternatiba* lasted several days and were attended by about 30,000 visitors, while the *Festival de la Terre* hosts between 30,000 and 50,000 visitors. The two festivals are also composed of over 100 stands, with dozens of organizations represented.

6   Nonetheless, they are very different in terms of the discursive, bodily, and spatial strategies used to connect ecology and spirituality.

7   Original text in German, our translation. "Location" is in English in the text.

8   See Koehrsen, Huber, Becci, and Blanc (2019).

9   Our translation from German.

10   The questionnaire was made up of twenty-three closed questions, three of which were similar to the Swiss Household Panel (SHP) questions, allowing a comparison with the Swiss population (regarding religious/spiritual orientation and political position). See www.swisspanel.ch. We handed out sixty-five questionnaires at the *Festival de la Terre* on June 8 and 9, 2018, and fifty-two at *Alternatiba* on September 22, 2018. See Becci, Monnot, and Wernli (2021).

11   For this and the following quotes, see their website and program: http://www.festivaldelaterre.ch/ (accessed July 18, 2019).

12   For this and the following quotes, see their website and program: https://www.Alternatibaleman.org/editions-precedentes/ (accessed February 18, 2020).

13   For a more detailed description of our participation, see Becci, Grandjean, Serlavos, Swaton (2018).

14   When we informed the participants and festival organizers about our research, the latter even encouraged us to take pictures that we could share with them to post on social media.

15   In its first two years, *Alternatiba Léman* took place in a very central square of Geneva, the plain of Plainpalais, and in a couple of smaller juxtaposing parks, then moved to Cropettes Park (a smaller timbered lawn close to the main railway station) in 2017. Since 2018, it has been taking place in Bastions Park, the green area around the historic university buildings. In this article, we will focus on Bastions Park, as it is the most recent location and the one that the organizers hoped to use from the beginning.

16 *Wilhelm Tell* (in German) or *Guillaume Tell* (in French) is the main Swiss folk hero upon whose legend the founding myth of the Helvetic Confederation (Switzerland) was built.

17 "L'atome ou la vie, à vous de choisir" [our translation in the text].

18 The program mainly proposes non-Western music from around the world—often called *ethnic*—which is described in an essentializing and exoticizing way as: "De la musique qui vous fera voyager très loin mais aussi très à l'intérieur … "

19 The Sea Shepherd Conservation Society (SSCS) is an international nonprofit marine wildlife conservation organization, while Fairphone is a company based in the Netherlands that produces modular smartphones following strict sustainability guidelines.

20 Inner transition is the individual counterpart of the (collective) transition movement. It is described as follows by the Transition Lab of the organization Bread for All, which is very active in French-speaking Switzerland on these issues: "On a spiritual level, it promotes the quest for meaning and sacredness, and values such as altruism, diversity and sobriety. It offers sources of inspiration and tools to move from discouragement to hope and from apathy to a new form of commitment: the meditation activist who combines contemplation and action in the creation of local alternatives and resilient territories" [our translation]. See https://painpourleprochain.ch/transition-interieure/#1486376095663-76f89d71-2e52 (accessed February 18, 2020).

21 These included Bread for All, an important Protestant NGO and pioneer in fair trade, a Caritas sale stand, and an urban gardening action promoted by a Protestant woman pastor in charge of a nearby parish.

22 Interview held in Geneva on March 7, 2016.

23 Nice Future, the organization responsible for the first edition of the *Festival de la Terre* in Lausanne, was present in the "responsible consumption" area, and Zoein, a Lausanne-based foundation promoting ecological and solidarity-oriented transition and resilience, was present in the "social solidarity economy, shared economy and ethical finance" space.

Chapter 4

1 See also the introduction to the 2014 special issue of the journal *Social & Cultural Geography*, in which Martijn Oosterbaan writes about a similar understanding of the postsecular perspective (Oosterbaan 2014).

2 For instance, architects published a book about the architecture of Pushkinskaya Square, which described among other things the history and architectural characteristics of the Strastnoy Monastery (Melihova and Tsekhanskii 2013).

3   See https://www.kommersant.ru/doc/4243596.

4   This public organization was established in the Russian Soviet Federal Socialist
     Republic in 1965 and continues to function in modern Russia. The main goals of
     its activities are the protection, revival, and popularization of the cultural heritage
     (historical and cultural monuments) of the Russian people.

5   The first leader of the community was a participant in the All-Russian Society for
     the Protection of Monuments of History and Culture, who recalled having thoughts
     of reviving Strastnoy Monastery in 1970—thoughts he and his colleagues vocalized
     in the 1980s. They planned to restore not only the Strastnoy Monastery but also
     the Church of Christ the Savior, a Russian Orthodox cathedral in Moscow (http://
     www.borodino2012-2045.com/tag/страстной-монастырь) which was eventually
     restored in the 1990s thanks to the efforts of the Orthodox community.

6   The name of the Strastnaya icon literally means "Our Lady of Passions [of Christ]."
     It is a Russian version of the "Passion" type of Theotokos icons, known in the
     Catholic Church as "Our Lady of Perpetual Succor" or "Our Lady of Perpetual
     Help." See https://russianicons.wordpress.com/tag/strastnaya/.

7   Members of the community claim that the granite from which the stone is made
     is taken from the original Cathedral of Christ the Savior. This fact is also symbolic
     because according to the interpretation of the community members, things like
     that never happen accidentally. Such a view of the world "as a constantly unfolding
     text consisting of interconnected signs-events" is, as Zhanna Kormina notes, one
     of the features of the semiotic ideology (Webb Keane) of many Orthodox believers
     (Kormina 2019, 76).

8   Parish or church feasts are feasts in commemoration of an event from sacred or church
     history, or feasts to commemorate the saint whose name a church or chapel bears.
     Therefore, in addition to every Saturday, the members of the community gather at
     the square twenty-seven more times per year. These days are devoted to eight church
     feasts and nineteen memorial dates for the monastery. The list of feasts has continually
     been changed over the past fourteen years; there are additional feasts every year.

9   See, for example, the Facebook announcement of the Openness (glasnost') Meeting on
     December 22, 2018, or the announcement for the Peace March on January 20, 2019.

10   Alexander Mikhailovich Opekushin, the creator of the monument of Pushkin, was
     a famous Russian sculptor from the end of nineteenth century.

11   In general, all groups claiming to be in the square feel the manifestation of
     "classicism" (Low 2014, 24) most strongly when rallies take place. The area
     surrounded by the fence belongs only to the authorities, not to the religious
     community, protesters, or ordinary people.

12   On the concept of the humility in the Orthodox parish subculture, see Knorre
     (2011).

13   On the idiom *namolennost* (being prayed for) of the sacred place, see Kormina
     (2019) (123–99).

Chapter 5

1 This chapter was fine-tuned amidst the Covid-19 pandemic of 2020; therefore it is mostly based on online information and digitalized data.

2 https://www.popolireligioni.it (accessed March 10, 2020).

3 http://www.moltefedi.it (accessed March 10, 2020).

4 https://www.festivalbiblico.it (accessed March 10, 2020).

5 https://www.festivaldellereligioni.it (accessed March 10, 2020).

6 https://www.ais-sociologia.it/event-items/mondoreligioni-incontriamo-le-religioni-del-mondo/ (accessed March 10, 2020).

Chapter 6

1 A somewhat different version of this chapter was published in *Religion, State and Society* 47 (4): 491–507. I would like to thank the editors of the journal for allowing me to re-publish this work here.

2 I appreciate the comments I received on drafts of this article from Stella Rock, Scott Dolff, Susie Fisher, Peter Scales, David Seljak, Paige Thombs, and two anonymous reviewers at *Religion, State and Society*. I also received useful feedback from colleagues at the Max Planck Institute for the Study of Religious and Ethnic Diversity in Göttingen, Germany, where I presented the key ideas of this chapter.

3 This concept involves a firm commitment to a scientific or naturalistic lens that leads to a broad appreciation of the region's grandeur, uniqueness, and also its fragility. The region's natural (and to a lesser extent, its human) dimensions are clearly approached in a reverential manner that is redolent of panentheism, theism, and eco-spirituality. A coedited book on this bioregion is in the works.

4 https://news.gov.bc.ca/stories/namaste-premier-announces-inaugural-international-day-of-yoga-event-in-vancouver. 2019 IDY events in India have drawn approximately 40,000 (Delhi) and 50,000 (Ranchi). See https://www.indiatoday.in/india/story/world-yoga-day-theme-yoga-for-heart-1548334-2019-06-13. About 12,000 practitioners gathered in New York City's Times Square. See https://www.efe.com/efe/english/life/thousands-celebrate-world-yoga-day-in-new-york-s-times-square/50000263-3657855.

5 For the official declaration, see http://undocs.org/A/RES/69/131. For the public-facing announcement, see http://www.un.org/en/events/yogaday/.

6 For the statement by the Indian government, see http://www.mea.gov.in/idy.htm. For the PowerPoint slide featured here, and shared via Twitter by MEA spokesperson, Vikas Swarup, see https://www.firstpost.com/photos/check-logo-international-yoga-day-finally-highlights-2219082-2.html.

7   See https://www.un.org/en/ga/69/meetings/gadebate/pdf/IN_en.pdf.

8   https://news.gov.bc.ca/releases/2015PREM0042-000861; https://news.gov.bc.ca/rele
    ases/2015PREM0039-000812.

9   https://twitter.com/SoniaSAslam.

10 What if we were to change the register of this comment: Come and look at me.
    I like to: pray/volunteer at a soup kitchen/sing in a choir/perform a *puja*/go on
    a pilgrimage? It seems hard to imagine that any politician would use prayer,
    volunteer work, devotion, or pilgrimage as opportunities to malign an adversary.

11 Jane Jacobs, famous for her powerful critique of urban planning *The Death and Life
    of Great American Cities* (1961), has been called "the mother of Vancouverism,"
    https://www.straight.com/news/vancouvers-density-debate-pits-sullivanism-
    versus-ideas-jane-jacobs.

12 As such, the concept of "visible minority" may have lost its analytical value. See
    https://www.cbc.ca/news/canada/british-columbia/visible-minorities-now-the-
    majority-in-5-b-c-cities-1.4375858.

13 By the spring of 2015, Clark's approval rating among voters was about 30 percent,
    down from a post-election high of 45 percent. See http://www.vancouversun.
    com/news/Christy+Clark+approval+rating+continues+slide+poll/11156816/
    story.html.

14 See the "Take Yoga Back" campaign of the Hindu American Foundation. https://
    www.hafsite.org/takeyogaback, an effort to remind practitioners and teachers of (in
    their view) the essentially Hindu roots of yoga. See also the cultural appropriation
    debate that unfolded at the University of Ottawa several months after the IDY
    debate: https://www.cbc.ca/news/canada/ottawa/university-ottawa-yoga-cultural-
    sensitivity-1.3330441.

15 There is an ideological irony here: the event was, or might have been, a protest of
    consumerism by a practice that is deeply enmeshed with consumer culture. As
    Andrea Jain notes (2014), yoga has adapted to the societies that have embraced it,
    and so it is not surprising to see both that yoga has become an integral feature of
    the widespread wellness culture and that it has become thoroughly commodified.

Chapter 7

1   Anti-Semitic stereotypes are deeply rooted in Spanish popular culture and are
    closely linked to religion and the history of Catholicism in the country (Baer and
    López 2012). Despite Jews representing a very tiny proportion of the population,
    stereotypes and negative attitudes toward them are prominent in jokes, popular
    festivities, the names of towns, etc.

2   The only reasons to limit these public religious expressions are security, public
    hygiene and health, and public morality (whatever that may mean).

3   G. Pisarello, "Ben Adret vuelve a casa." *Ara.cat*, November 12, 2018. Available online: https://www.ara.cat/es/opinion/gerardo-pisarello-ben-adret-vuelve-a-casa_0_2123787804.html (accessed November 27, 2019).

Chapter 8

1   Disagreement over how the Palestinian disaster (or Palestinian "Nakba") unfolded is certainly a major bone of contention between the two sides.
2   This term may be translated in various manners. In the current context it means a fortification which is set on the frontier—that is, a bastion of faith against Israeli control of the precinct.
3   Literally, platforms of learning. These stone platforms are scattered around the Haram al-Sharif and serve as places for groups to study religious issues, sponsored and encouraged by the Islamic Movement.

Chapter 9

1   See https://www.vatican.va/roman_curia/congregations/cevang/p_missionary_works/infantia/documents/rc_ic_infantia_doc_20090324_boletin7p14_en.html. The international day is March 25, but in 2018 the organizers rescheduled the celebration from March to April to avoid the days around Easter.
2   Data from the online search engine for religious entities in Spain, Justice Ministry (accessed December 3, 2017).
3   Microdata from CIS (2019) Barometro de Febrero, Estudio 3240.
4   See tweet by Doctor Gaona at https://twitter.com/doctorgaona/status/805005409463443456/photo/1.
5   Manuela Carmena is a retired lawyer and judge who won the municipal elections as a candidate of the local citizens platform Ahora Madrid (Madrid Now), in coalition with the left-wing populist party Podemos (We Can). She has described herself as agnostic (see Libertad Digital, https://www.libertaddigital.com/espana/2015-09-02/manuela-carmena-soy-agnostica-pero-me-gusta-mucho-el-papa-1276556153).
6   See Religion en Libertad coverage, https://www.religionenlibertad.com/polemicas/54245/que-paso-con-los-500-belenesprotesta-que-los-madrilenos-pusieron-.html.
7   In La Razon newspaper, https://www.larazon.es/local/madrid/llenan-de-belenes-la-puerta-de-alcala-para-exigir-la-vuelta-del-nacimiento-OC14162729.
8   There were no more than 200 figures according to our fieldwork.

9 See the coverage in Libertad Digital, https://www.libertaddigital.com/espana/2016-12-20/los-madrilenos-llenan-la-puerta-de-alcala-de-belenes-en-protesta-por-las-navidades-de-carmena-1276589156/.

10 See description and analysis in https://www.religionenlibertad.com/espana/53876/revolucion-los-belenes-original-respuesta-los-madrilenos.html.

11 Extracted from the video reportage by OK Diario, see https://okdiario.com/videos/2016/12/13/madrilenos-plantan-belenes-puerta-alcala-desprecio-carmena-597511.

12 The temporal sequence of the cases is not particularly relevant for my purposes here, so they are introduced in order from most straightforward to (theoretically) most controversial.

13 See https://www.actuall.com/laicismo/carmena-se-congratula-de-descristianizar-la-navidad-y-la-cabalgata-de-reyes/.

14 See https://elpais.com/ccaa/2016/01/06/madrid/1452098031_792632.html.

15 See http://www.abc.es/sociedad/abci-cabalgatas-mas-inverosimiles-201601070733_noticia.html.

16 See https://www.religionenlibertad.com/dos-cabalgatas-de-madrid-ostentaran-reinas-magas-sus-concejales-presumen-de-46702.htm.

17 See Matthew 2:1-12 as the only biblical source for the visit of the Magi to the Messiah.

Chapter 10

1 The notion of mediatization has been elaborated by Hepp (2012).

2 For the spatial dimension of mediatization, see Knoblauch (2020).

3 I am particularly grateful to Sezgin Sönmez, who collected data in the local organization team, Lilli Braunisch, who analyzed media coverage, and Meike Haken, who did field research in Krakow, Leipzig, and Wittenberg. I personally participated in John Paul II's visit to Vienna in 1998; for the video recordings of his visit to Berlin, we are grateful to RBB media. I am also grateful to Silke Steets, Meike Haken for comments, and Elisabeth Schmidt for corrections. As to the method of videography in religious studies, see Knoblauch (2011).

4 This follows the idea of Venturi and Brown that the materially constructed order is communicating in a way which resembles sign systems, as outlined in Steets (2015, 185ff), with the addition that the meaning of these signs is linked to communicative actions.

5 For more on the framing of religiosity, see Knoblauch (2014b).

6 Concerning politics of scale, see Brenner (2001) and Hoerning (forthcoming). The mediated encroachment of events becomes quite obvious in cases of multi-location events, such as the January 2020 European handball championships with parallel games in three European cities.

Chapter 11

1   This chapter has benefited from a research grant from the Spanish Ministry of Science and Technology. Ref. EREU—MyB: Expresiones religiosas en el espacio público en Madrid y Barcelona. Ref. CSO2015-66198-P. We appreciate the comments that we received on drafts of this chapter from Paul Bramadat and Julia Martínez-Ariño. We would like to thank all our interviewees for their kind and valuable participation, as well as Carlota Rodríguez and Teuta Stipstic for their help in the fieldwork.

2   All excerpts from interview transcripts in this chapter are translations from Catalan.

3   See also Hubert Knoblauch's chapter on the pope's visit to Berlin in this edited volume.

4   See also Becci and Okoekpen's chapter in this edited volume.

5   However, as Shapiro puts forward, not all flash mobs have a playful dimension; some are more directly political in nature and might be perceived as "threats to social order" (2017: 933).

6   The *Indignados*, also referred to as the 15-M, is the anti-austerity movement that emerged in Spain in 2011 in response to budgetary cuts to public services and other austerity policies. The movement staged demonstrations through the occupation of central city squares in Madrid (Plaza del Sol) and Barcelona (Plaça Catalunya) and the organization of local assemblies.

7   The Catalan Parliament approved a resolution which regulated the effects of the proclamation of the Catalan Republic, thus opening a constituent process on October 27, 2017. The exile of members of the Catalan government a few days later, along with the imprisonment of remaining government officials and Catalan civic activists, changed the course of the protests. The protests, therefore, changed as a result of legal measures applied by the Spanish government.

8   See https://www.omnium.cat/ca/una-vintena-dentitats-organitzen-la-2a-caminada-per-la-pau/ (accessed April 27, 2020).

9   However, this is not always the case. See Paul Bramadat's chapter in this edited volume to get a more complex picture of politics—and perceptions—of spiritual events in contemporary cities.

10 The Franco dictatorship lasted from 1939 until the establishment of a democratic system in 1978, following Francisco Franco's death in 1975.

11 Lluís Maria Xirinacs (born June 8, 1932, in Barcelona; died August 11, 2007, in Ripollès) was a Catholic priest, politician, and activist for many democratic causes. He was popular among Catalan nationalists and leftists.

Chapter 12

1   Although the names of my interlocutors have been changed to ensure anonymity, this does not change the deep gratitude I feel for the kindness with which I was received. Thank you very much for the time, teachings, and sparrings! The names of places have been made up or taken from Jorge Amado's novel *Tocaia Grande* (1984).

2   I use the term "community" (in Portuguese *communidade*) instead of favela here since this is the term mostly used by my interlocutors to refer to their settlements. The term "community" does not have the negative connotation the term "favela" has, instead emphasizing the social relations among its inhabitants. Also, the common understanding of a favela or a shantytown is characterized by the lack of public services, infrastructure, and legal status, which does not hold for many communities anymore. Reflecting the socioeconomic status of its inhabitants, the quality of the buildings in João's Hill is diverse, ranging from attractive two-story brick houses to wooden huts in danger of being swept away by landslides during heavy rainfall (see Perlman 2010, 29–36).

3   The commonly known history of Brazilian jiu-jitsu begins with the judo master Mitsuyo Maeda, who passed his knowledge on to Carlos Gracie while traveling Brazil in the late 1910s (Green and Svinth 2003). The Gracie brothers then developed the teachings of Maeda over the next decades into a "hybrid martial art" (Cairus 2012) that focused on ground combat. Anglophone academic literature has concentrated on the Gracies' contributions to the sport's development (Cairus 2020; Downey 2007; Hogeveen 2013; Penglase 2016; Spencer 2014). However, recent non-academic research coming out of Brazil indicates that the development of Brazilian jiu-jitsu has been much more complex, involving many different martial arts styles and many more innovators than only the Gracie family (Serrano 2019; Silva and Corrêa 2020).

4   The Bola de Neve church, which means snowball, is a group of megachurches present in thirty-four countries, according to their website www.boladeneve.com (accessed May 18, 2020). It also has a Facebook site dedicated to its "fight-ministry" where pictures from Brazilian jiu-jitsu groups from around Brazil are displayed ("Ministério de Lutas—Bola de Neve Church Sede"—accessed May 18, 2020).

5   A representative survey from 2013 by the Brazilian Ministry of Sports with 8,902 participants aged fourteen to seventy-five states that Brazilian jiu-jitsu is Brazil's most popular martial art, with 1.3 percent (1,907,724 persons) of all Brazilians practicing this sport (Ministério do Esporte 2015). According to this study, 2.2 percent of all men practice Brazilian jiu-jitsu; among women the percentage amounts to 0.4. While men still dominate Brazilian jiu-jitsu numerically and in decision-making positions, women are continuously conquering more spaces as

practitioners, coaches, and professional competitors in Brazil and abroad (Kavoura et al. 2015; Knijnik and de Carvalho Ferretti 2015).

6   My methodology consisted of immersive participation, participant observation, and interviews. I practiced Brazilian jiu-jitsu to gain an embodied understanding of the sport, as practiced by Loïc Wacquant in his study of boxing (2004). The acquired "carnal" (Wacquant 2015) understanding of Brazilian jiu-jitsu was deepened and contextualized by observations and interviews with practitioners, coaches, and third parties like pastors. I researched and trained mainly at two gyms in the Center and the North Zone of Rio de Janeiro, from where I followed several coaches to their respective gyms in different parts of the city.

7   In the 1980s and 1990s, Brazilian jiu-jitsu was notorious for being a brutal sport in Brazil. This was mainly because of three reasons: Brazilian jiu-jitsu athletes' involvement in the bloody *vale tudo* fights, a competition format fought without gloves (Alonso and Nagao 2014), the rivalry between different martial arts clubs which frequently challenged each other in informal fights, and the phenomenon of the so-called pitboys, a neologism combining the words "pit bull" and "playboy," used to describe upper-class delinquents infamous for their involvement in street fights (Teixeira 2007). Today, however, little is left of Brazilian jiu-jitsu fighters' notoriety for brawls. A strong indicator for the sportization (Elias 1986) of Brazilian jiu-jitsu is the fact that coaches and politicians seek to establish this sport as a pedagogical tool in Brazil (Lancenet 2018), following the example of the United Arab Emirates, where it forms part of the public school curriculum (de Sousa Pinto 2019).

8   Dojo is the Japanese term for the place where martial arts are practiced.

9   In Brazilian jiu-jitsu, the belt ranks for athletes aged between four and fifteen are white, gray, yellow, orange, and green. The belt ranks for athletes from the age of sixteen are white, blue, purple, black, red and black, red and white, and red (IBJJF 2015).

10 This discussion is reminiscent of the question of whether mixed martial arts are a sign of a de-civilizing process, limiting the validity of Norbert Elias's theory of the civilizing process (2000). The spectacular display of violence at the UFC drew much attention and sparked debates about the "civilizing" and "de-civilizing" aspects of public fights (Sánchez García and Malcolm 2010; van Bottenburg and Heilbron 2006). There is a contradiction in the fact that fighters train to harm what they value most— another trained body. Embodied ethnographic studies (Spencer 2012; Stenius 2015; Wacquant 2004) have investigated this contradiction, showing that fighters make their bodies resist the destructive impacts of fighting through a process Wacquant describes as the "building of corporeal capital" through "bodily work" (1998).

11 These signs were: "神, 光, and 活"—translating as "God, light, and living," according to the online dictionary www.jisho.org. Brazilian jiu-jitsu practitioners frequently use Japanese characters as tattoos, for example, "柔術" meaning "jiu-jitsu" or "gentle art." The athlete's tattoo seems to combine religious meaning with the fashion of using Japanese characters among Brazilian jiu-jitsu practitioners.

Chapter 13

1 This work and its conceptual underpinnings constitute an independent line of research resulting from the author's joint project with Hansjörg Dilger and Dominik Mattes (2015–19). It is carried out within the framework of the *Affective Societies* Collaborative Research Center at Freie Universität Berlin (FUB) and funded by the German Research Foundation (DFG).

2 Neukölln is a district in Berlin known for its multicultural demographic. It is the district with the highest share of residents with a "migration background," as they are called in German public discourse.

3 I use postmigrant not as a reference to being past the condition of migration, but rather to accentuate what it means to endure with or remain in the wake of historical affects of migration. For more on postmigrant research, see Römhild (2017).

4 As part of a formal "guest worker" program, migrants sought work in former West Germany from the 1950s up until the early 1970s.

5 Many followers, but not all, lived in the same neighborhood or district.

6 Excerpts included in the first section of this chapter are responses to questions such as: How do you feel during *zikr*? Why does one close one's eyes during *zikr*? What is the importance of *zikr*, in your opinion?

7 This excerpt was simultaneously translated from Turkish into German by Onur during an interview with the sheikh.

8 The gerundive form refers to a generative ontological process of worlding, not to a world that just *is*. For more on worlding, see Kathleen Stewart (2010).

9 Heterosexual intimacy is a point of reference in believers' descriptions of their feelings. That said, my contingent use of queer politics in this instance leans more toward religion's bent for troubling, testing, and resisting the normative, or a relation of being otherwise, than toward matters of sexuality in an exclusive sense.

10 Queer undertones in the reading I offer of *zikr* are in fact concerned with the potentialities of its ritual atmospheres, not the politics or identities of my interlocutors. The participation of the queer researcher in the ritual makes queerness not external to the field, but co-constitutive of it.

11 For a detailed account of my observation of the ritual, see Mattes et al. (2019).

12 Sufis consider *zikr* as an important supplement to the conduct of one's everyday life.

13 Intimacy names closeness between distinct objects, but does not extend to transcending objects or their constituting differences.

14 On the sacralizing potential of *zikr* in migration, see Pnina Werbner (1996).

Bibliography

'Ari'ar, T. M. 2002. "Al-Aqsa Is above and beyond Any Would-be Negotiator." *Sawt al-Haqq wa-l-Huriyya* (special supplement), September 15, 2002: A 9.

Abruzzese, S. 1999. "Catholicisme et Territoire: Pour une Entrée en Matière." *Archives des Sciences Sociales des Religions* 107 (1): 5–19.

Agadjanian, A. 2011. "Reforma i vozrozhdenie v dvukh moskovskikh pravoslavnykh subkul'turakh: dva sposoba sdelat' pravoslavie sovremennym" [Reform and Revival in Two Moscow Orthodox Communities: Two Kinds of Orthodox Modernity]. In *Prikhod i obshchina v sovremennom pravoslavii: kornevaia sistema rossiiskoi religioznosti*, edited by A. Agadjanian and K. Russele, 255–77. Moscow: Izdatel'stvo "Ves' Mir."

Agadjanian, A. 2012. "'Mnozhestvennye sovremennosti', rossijskie 'prokljatye voprosy' i nezyblemost' sekuljarnogo Moderna (teoreticheskoe jesse)" ["Multiple Modernities," Russia's "Cursed Issues" and the Endurance of Secular Modernity (a Theoretical Essay)]. *State, Religion and Church in Russia and Worldwide* 1 (30): 83–110.

Ahlin, L., J. Borup, M. Q. Fibiger, L. Kühle, V. Mortensen, and R. Dybdal Pedersen. 2012. "Religious Diversity and Pluralism: Empirical Data and Theoretical Reflections from the Danish Pluralism Project." *Journal of Contemporary Religion* 27 (3): 403–18.

Ahmed, N., J. Garnett, B. Gidley, A. Harris, and M. Keith. 2016. "Shifting Markers of Identity in East London's Diasporic Religious Spaces." *Ethnic and Racial Studies* 39 (2): 223–42.

Ahmed, S. 1999. "Home and Away: Narratives of Migration and Estrangement." *International Journal of Cultural Studies* 2 (3): 329–47.

Ahmetova, M. 2010. *Konets sveta v odnoi otdel'no vziatoi strane* [The End of the World in One Particular Country]. Moscow: OGI, RSUH.

Ajuntament, de Barcelona. n.d. "Les Comunitats Jueves de Barcelona Celebren l'encesa de Llums de Hanukkà." Accessed June 17, 2020. https://ajuntament.barcelona.cat/bombers/ca/noticia/les-comunitats-jueves-de-barcelona-celebren-lencesa-de-llums-de-hanukka_745318.

Alexander, J. C. 2004. "Cultural Pragmatics: Social Performance between Ritual and Strategy." *Sociological Theory* 22 (4): 527–73.

Ali, N. 2018. "The Islamic Movement in Israel: Historical and Ideological Development." In *The Palestinians in Israel: Readings in History, Policy and Society*, edited by N. N. Rouhana and A. Sabbagh-Khoury, 199–214. Haifa: Mada al-Carmel.

Alonso, J., ed. 1980. *Lucha Urbana y Acumulación de Capital*. México: Casa Chata.

Alonso, M., and S. Nagao. 2014. *Do Vale-Tudo ao MMA: 100 anos de luta*. Rio de Janeiro: Pvt Editora.

Al Sayyad, N., and M. Massoumi, eds. 2010. *The Fundamentalist City? Religiosity and the Remaking of Urban Space*. London: Routledge.

Alter, J. 2004. *Yoga in Modern India: The Body between Philosophy and Science*. Princeton, NJ: Princeton University Press.

Altglas, V. 2014. *From Yoga to Kabbalah: Religious Exoticism and the Logics of Bricolage*. New York: Oxford University Press.

Amin, A., and N. Thrift. 2017. *Seeing Like a City*. Cambridge: Polity Press.

Anderson, B. 1990. *Imagined Communities: Reflections on the Origin and Spread of Nationalism*. London: Verso.

Anderson, B. 2012. "Affect and Biopower: Towards a Politics of Life." *Transactions of the Institute of British Geographers* 37 (1): 28–43.

Antony, M. G. 2018. "That's a Stretch: Reconstructing, Rearticulating, and Commodifying Yoga." *Frontiers in Communications* 3: 47.

Anttonen, V. 2005. "Space, Body, and the Notion of Boundary: A Category-Theoretical Approach to Religion." *Temenos—Nordic Journal of Comparative Religion* 41 (2): 185–201.

Arendt, H. 1958. *Human Condition*. Chicago, IL: University of Chicago Press.

Armbrecht, A. 2009. *Thin Places: A Pilgrimage Home*. New York: Columbia University Press.

Asad, T. 1999. "Religion, Nation-State, Secularism." In *Nation and Religion. Perspectives on Europe and Asia*, edited by P. van der Veer and H. Lehmann, 176–96. Princeton, NJ: Princeton University Press.

Asch, M., J. Borrows, and J. Tully, eds. 2018. *Resurgence and Reconciliation: Indigenous-Settler Relations and Earth Teachings*. Toronto: University of Toronto Press.

Assmann, A. 2018. *Dlinnaia ten' proshlogo. Memorial'naia kul'tura i istoricheskaia politika* [Long Shadow of the Past: Memorial Culture and Historical Politics]. Moscow: NLO.

Astor, A., M. Burchardt, and M. Griera. 2017. "The Politics of Religious Heritage: Framing Claims to Religion as Culture in Spain." *Journal for the Scientific Study of Religion* 56 (1): 126–42. https://doi.org/10.1111/jssr.12321.

Astor, A., V. Albert Blanco, and R. Martínez Cuadros. 2018. "The Politics of 'Tradition' and the Production of Diasporic Shia Religiosity." *POMEPS Studies* 32. https://pomeps.org/the-politics-of-tradition-and-the-production-of-diasporic-shia-religiosity.

Augé, M. 1995. *Non-places. Introduction to an Anthropology of Supermodernity*. New York: Verso.

Augé, M. 2008. *Non-places: An Introduction to Supermodernity*. London and New York: Verso.

Aupers, S., and D. Houtman. 2006. "Beyond the Spiritual Supermarket: The Social and Public Significance of New Age Spirituality." *Journal of Contemporary Religion* 21 (2): 201–22.

Auslander, P. 1999. *Liveness: Performance in a Mediatized Culture*. London: Routledge.

Azaryahu, M., and A. Kellerman. 1999. "Symbolic Places of National History and Revival: A Study in Zionist Mythical Geography." *Transactions of the Institute of British Geographers* 24 (1): 109–23.

Azuela, A. 1999. *La Ciudad, la Propiedad Privada y el Derecho*. México: Colegio de México.

Bader, V. 2009. "The Governance of Religious Diversity: Theory, Research, and Practice." In *International Migration and the Governance of Religious Diversity*, edited by P. Bramadat and M. Koenig, 29–58. Montreal and Kingston: McGill Queen's University Press.

Baer, A., and P. López. 2012. "The Blind Spots of Secularization." *European Societies* 14 (2): 203–21.

Baer, M., and W. Seitz. 2009. *Les Verts en Suisse: Leur Politique, Leur Histoire, Leur Base*. Zurich: Editions Rüegger.

Bailey, I. 2015. "B.C. Premier Cancels Yoga Event on Vancouver Bridge Due to Politics." *Globe and Mail*. June 12. Accessed June 16, 2020. https://www.theglobeandmail.com/news/british-columbia/bc-premier-drops-out-of-yoga-day-event-on-major-vancouver-bridge/article24942720/.

Bakshi, A. 2011. "Memory and Place in Divided Nicosia." *Spectrum Journal of Global Studies* 3 (4): 27–40.

Balbier, U. A. 2010. "Billy Graham in West Germany: German Protestantism between Americanization and Re-Christianization." *Zeithistorische Forschungen/Contemporary History* 7: 343–63.

Barrionuevo, A. 2009. "Fight Nights and Reggae Pack Brazilian Churches." *New York Times*, September 14. Accessed May 18, 2020. https://www.nytimes.com/2009/09/15/world/americas/15evangelicals.html.

Barthes, R. 1981. "Semiology and the Urban." In *The City and the Sign: An Introduction to Urban Semiotics*, edited by M. Gottdiener and A. P. Lagopoulos, 87–98. New York: Columbia University Press.

Baumann, G. 2002. "Ritual Implicates 'Others': Rereading Durkheim in a Plural Society." In *Understanding Rituals*, edited by D. de Coppet, 105–24. London: Routledge.

Beaman, L. G. 2013. "Battles over Symbols: The 'Religion' of the Minority Versus the 'Culture' of the Majority." *Journal of Law and Religion* 28: 67–104.

Beaman, L. G. 2020. *The Transition of Religion to Culture in Law and Public Discourse*. London and New York: Routledge.

Beaumont, J., and C. Barker, eds. 2011. *Postsecular Cities: Space, Theory and Practice*. London: Continuum.

Becci, I., and A. Grandjean. 2018. "Tracing the Absence of a Feminist Agenda in Gendered Spiritual Ecology: Ethnographies in French-Speaking Switzerland." *Anthropologia* 5 (1): 23–38.

Becci, I., and M. Burchardt. 2013. "Introduction: Religion Takes Place: Producing Urban Locality." In *Topographies of Faith: Religion in Urban Spaces*, edited by I. Becci, M. Burchardt and J. Casanova, 1–24. Boston, MA: Brill.

Becci, I., and M. Burchardt. 2016. 'Religion and Superdiversity: An Introduction." *New Diversities* 18 (1): 1–7.

Becci, I., M. Burchardt, and J. Casanova, eds. 2013. *Topographies of Faith: Religion in Urban Spaces*. Leiden and Boston, MA: Brill.

Becci, I., M. Burchardt, and M. Giorda. 2016. "Religious Super-Diversity and Spatial Strategies in Two European Cities." *Current Sociology* 65 (1): 73–91.

Becci, I., A. Grandjean, M. Serlavos, and S. Swaton. 2018. "Une Ethnographie des Votes et Reactions sur les Scenarios dans le Cadre du Festival Alternatiba." In *Volteface: la Transition Énergétique, un Projet de Société*, edited by N. Niwa and B. Frund, 52–8. Lausanne: Editions Charles Leopold Mayer.

Becci, I., C. Monnot, and B. Wernli. 2021. "Sensing 'Subtle Spirituality' among Environmentalists: A Swiss Study." *Journal for the Study of Religion, Nature and Culture* 15 (2).

Beekers, D., and P. Tamimi Arab. 2016. "Dreams of an Iconic Mosque: Spatial and Temporal Entanglements of a Converted Church in Amsterdam." *Material Religion* 12 (2): 137–64.

Bell, C. 1997. *Ritual: Perspectives and Dimension*. New York: Oxford University Press.

Bender, C., W. Cadge, P. Levitt, and D. Smilde. 2012. "Introduction. Religion on the Edge: De-centering and Re-centering the Sociology of Religion." In *Religion on the Edge: De-centering and Re-centering the Sociology of Religion*, edited by C. Bender, W. Cadge, P. Levitt and D. Smilde. New York: Oxford University Press.

Benedict XVI, Pope. 2010. *Apostolic Letter Ubicumque et Semper*. Vatican City: Libreria Edetrice Vaticana.

Bennett, A., J. Taylor, and I. Woodward, eds. 2014. *The Festivalization of Culture*. Farnham: Ashgate.

Benvenisti, M. 2000. *Sacred Landscape: The Buried History of the Holy Land since 1948*. Berkeley: University of California Press.

Berg-Sørensen, A., ed. 2013. *Contesting Secularism. Comparative Perspectives*. London: Ashgate.

Berger, P. 1999. "The Desecularization of the World: A Global Overview." In *The Desecularization of the World: Resurgent Religion and World Politics*, edited by P. Berger, 1–19. Washington: Ethics and Public Policy Center, W. B. Eerdmans Publishing Co.

Berger, P., G. Davie, and E. Fokas. 2008. *Religious America, Secular Europe?: A Theme and Variations*. Abingdon: Routledge.

Berking, H., S. Steets, and J. Schwenk. 2018. "Introduction: Filling the Void?—Religious Pluralism and the City." In *Religious Pluralism and the City. Inquiries into Postsecular Urbanism*, 1–23. London: Bloomsbury Academic.

Berking, H., S. Steets, and J. Schwenk, eds. 2018. *Religious Pluralism and the City: Inquiries into Postsecular Urbanism*. London: Bloomsbury.

Berkovits, S. 2000. *The Battle for the Holy Places. The Struggle over Jerusalem and the Holy Sites in Israel, Judea, Samaria and the Gaza Districts*. Or Yehuda: Hed Arzi Publishing House.

Berlant, L. 1998. "Intimacy: A Special Issue." *Critical Inquiry* 24 (2): 281–8.

Bessone, P. G. 2012. "Experiencia, Aborto y Maternidad en las Católicas Feministas." *Nómadas. Critical Journal of Social and Juridical Sciences* 34 (2): 149–62.

Betz, G., R. Hitzler, and M. Pfadenhauer, eds. 2011. *Urbane Events*. Wiesbaden: Springer.

Beyer, H. 2019. "The Globalization of Resentment: Antisemitism in an Inter- and Transnational Context." *Social Science Quarterly* 100 (5): 1503–22.

Bollen, S. 2000. *On Narrow Ground: Urban Policy and Conflict in Jerusalem and Belfast*. Albany: State University of New York Press.

Borer, M. I., and T. S. Schafer. 2011. "Culture War Confessionals: Conflicting Accounts of Christianity, Violence, and Mixed Martial Arts." *Journal of Media and Religion* 10 (4): 165–84.

Bost, S. 2016. "Practicing Yoga/Embodying Feminism/Shape-Shifting." *Frontiers: A Journal of Women Studies* 37 (2): 191–208.

Bottenburg, M van, and J. Heilbron. 2006. "De-sportization of Fighting Contests: The Origins and Dynamics of No Holds Barred Events and the Theory of Sportization." *International Review for the Sociology of Sport* 41 (3–4): 259–82.

Bourdieu, P. 1978. "Sport and Social Class." Translated by R. Nice. *Social Science Information* 17 (6): 819–40.

Bourdieu, P. 1984. *Distinction: A Social Critique of the Judgement of Taste*. Cambridge, MA: Harvard University Press.

Bowman, G. 1993. "Nationalizing the Sacred: Shrines and Shifting Identities in the Israeli Occupied Territories." *Man* 28 (3): 431–60.

Bowman, M. 2009. "Glastonbury Festival and the Performance of Remembrance." DISKUS, no. 10.

Bracke, S., and D. Paternotte. 2016. "Unpacking the Sin of Gender." *Religion and Gender* 6 (2): 143–54.

Bramadat, P. 2000. *The Church on the World's Turf: An Evangelical Christian Group at a Secular University*. New York: Oxford University Press.

Bramadat, P., and M. Koenig. 2009. *International Migration and the Governance of Religious Diversity*. Canada: School of Policy Studies, Queen's University.

Brenneman, R., and B. J. Miller. 2016. "When Bricks Matter: Four Arguments for the Sociological Study of Religious Buildings." *Sociology of Religion* 77 (1): 82–101.

Brenner, N. 2001. "The Limits to Scale? Methodological Reflections on Scalar Structuration." *Progress in Human Geography* 25 (4): 591–614.

Breskaya, O. 2011. "Pravoslavnye prikhody v gorodskom prostranstve Bresta: ot obrazov k tipologii" [Eastern Orthodox Parishes in Urban Landscape of the City of Brest: From Images to Typology]. In *Prikhod i obshchina v sovremennom pravoslavii: kornevaia sistema rossiiskoi religioznosti*, edited by A. Agadjanian and K. Russele, 212–34. Moscow: Izdatel'stvo "Ves' Mir."

Brighenti, A. 2007. "Visibility: A Category for the Social Sciences." *Current Sociology* 55 (3): 323–42.

Brighenti, A. 2010. *Visibility in Social Theory and Social Research*. London: Palgrave Macmillan.

Brubaker, R. 2017. "Between Nationalism and Civilizationism: The European Populist Moment in Comparative Perspective." *Ethnic and Racial Studies* 40 (8): 1191–226.

Brusadelli, N., M. Lemay, and Y. Marteli. 2016. "L'espace Contemporain des 'Alternatives.' Un Révélateur des Recompositions des Classes Moyennes?" *Savoir/Agir* 38 (4): 13–20.

Buckser, A. 2005. "Chabad in Copenhagen: Fundamentalism and Modernity in Jewish Denmark." *Ethnology* 44 (2): 125–45.

Burchardt, M. 2015. *Faith in the Time of AIDS. Religion, Biopolitics and Modernity in South Africa*. Basingstoke: Palgrave Macmillan.

Burchardt, M. 2017. "Pentecostal Productions of Locality: Urban Risk and Spiritual Protection in Cape Town." In *Religion and the Global City*, edited by A. Strhan and D. Garbin, 78–94. London: Bloomsbury.

Burchardt, M. 2019. "Religion in Urban Assemblages: Space, Law, and Power." *Religion, State & Society* 47 (4–5): 374–89.

Burchardt, M., and I. Becci. 2013. "Introduction: Religion Takes Place: Producing Urban Locality." In *Topographies of Faith*, edited by I. Becci, M. Burchardt and J. Casanova, 1–21. Leiden: Brill.

Burchardt, M., and I. Becci. 2016. "Religion and Superdiversity: An Introduction." *New Diversities* 18 (1): 1–7.

Burchardt, M., and M. Griera. 2018. "To See or Not to See: Explaining Intolerance against the 'Burqa' in European Public Space." *Ethnic and Racial Studies*: 1–19. doi: 10.1080/01419870.2018.1448100.

Burchardt, M. and M. Griera. 2020. "Doing Religious Space in the Mediterranean City: Towards a Historical Sociology of Urban Religion." In *Religion and Urbanity Online*. Berlin, Boston: De Gruyter. Retrieved 12 Dec. 2020, from https://db.degruyter.com/view/URBREL/urbrel.13215539

Burchardt, M., and M. Westendorp. 2018. "The Im-materiality of Urban Religion: Towards an Ethnography of Urban Religious Aspirations." *Culture and Religion* 19 (2): 160–76.

Burchardt, M., and S. Höhne. 2015. "The Infrastructure of Diversity: Materiality and Culture in Urban Space—An Introduction." *New Diversities* 17 (2): 1–13.

Burchardt, M., I. Becci, and M. C. Giorda. 2018. "Religious Superdiversity and Urban Visibility in Barcelona and Turin." In *Religious Pluralism and the City: Inquiries into Postsecular Urbanism*, edited by H. Berking, S. Steets and J. Schwenk, 83–103. London: Bloomsbury.

Cairus, J. 2012. "The Gracie Clan and the Making of Brazilian Jiu-Jitsu: National Identity, Culture and Performance, 1905–2003." PhD Thesis, Faculty of Graduate Studies, York University, Toronto.

Cairus, J. 2020. "Nationalism, Immigration and Identity: The Gracies and the Making of Brazilian Jiu-Jitsu, 1934–1943." *Martial Arts Studies* 9: 28–42.

Carbonelli, M., M. Mosqueira, and K. Felitti. 2011. "Religión, Sexualidad y Política en la Argentina: Intervenciones Católicas y Evangélicas Entorno al Aborto y el Matrimonio Igualitario." *Revista del Centro de Investigación. Universidad La Salle* 9 (36): 25–43.

Carrette, J. R., and R. King. 2004. *Selling Spirituality: The Silent Takeover of Religion.* London: Routledge.

Casanova, J. 1994. *Public Religions in the Modern World.* Chicago, IL: University of Chicago Press.

Castells, M. 1996. *The Rise of the Network Society. The Information Age: Economy, Society and Culture.* Malden, MA: Blackwell.

Chukovskii, K. 1962. *Zhivoi kak zhizn'* [Living as Life]. https://www.rulit.me/books/zhivoj-kak-zhizn-read-3878-18.html.

Ciancimino Howell, F. 2018. *Food, Festival and Religion: Materiality and Place in Italy.* London: Bloomsbury.

CIS. 1965. *Actitudes Religiosas Estudio 1006.* Madrid: Centro de Investigaciones Sociológicas.

CIS. 2017. *Redes Sociales (I)/Religión (III) (ISSP) Estudio 3194.* Madrid: Centro de Investigaciones Sociológicas.

CIS. 2019. *Barometro de Febrero, Estudio 3240.* Madrid: Centro de Investigaciones Sociológicas.

City News 1130. 2015. "Premier Takes to Twitter, Fans Flames over Burrard Bridge Closure for Yoga." *City News 1130*, June 11. Accessed June 16, 2020. https://www.citynews1130.com/2015/06/11/tweet-from-the-premiers-office-responds-to-yoga-haters/.

Clot-Garrell, A., and M. Griera. 2019. "Beyond Narcissism: Towards an Analysis of the Public, Political and Collective Forms of Contemporary Spirituality." *Religions* 10 (10): 579.

Corbin, A. 2016. *Le Miasme et la Jonquille: L'odorat et L'imaginaire Social, XVIIe–XIXe Siècles.* Paris: Flammarion.

Corbin, A. 2018. *La Fraîcheur de L'herbe: Histoire d'une Gamme D'émotions.* Paris: Fayard.

Corbin, J. M., and A. Strauss. 1990. Grounded Theory Research: Procedures, Canons, and Evaluative Criteria. *Qualitative Sociology* 13(1): 3–21.

Cornejo-Valle, M., and I. Pichardo. 2017. "La Ideología de Género Frente a los Derechos Sexuales y Reproductivos. El Escenario Español." *Cadernos Pagu* 50: 1–32.

Cornejo-Valle, M., and I. Pichardo. 2020. "The Ultra-Conservative Agenda against Sexual Rights in Spain: A Catholic Repertoire to Reframe Public Concerns." In *Public Discourses about Homosexuality and Religion in Europe and Beyond*, edited by M. Van Der Berg and M. Derks. Cham: Palgrave Macmillan.

Crawford, T. 2015. "Yoga Event on Burrard Bridge Cancelled after Week of Backlash." *Vancouver Sun,* June 13. Accessed June 16, 2020. http://www.vancouversun.com/health/Yoga+event+Burrard+Bridge+cancelled+after+week+backlash+with+video/11127882/story.html.

Crespi-Vallbona, M., and G. Richards. 2007. "The Meaning of Cultural Festivals." *International Journal of Cultural Policy* 13 (1): 103–22.

Cresswell, T. 1996. *In Place/Out of Place: Geography, Ideology, and Transgression.* London: University of Minnesota Press.

Csordas, T. J. 1990. "Embodiment as a Paradigm for Anthropology." *Ethos* 18 (1): 5–47.

Cudny, W. 2016. "The Concept, Origins and Types of Festivals." In *Festivalisation of Urban Spaces.* Cham: Springer.

Das, V., and D. Poole. 2004. "State and Its Margins: Comparative Ethnographies." In *Anthropology in the Margins of the State,* edited by V. Das and D. Poole, 3–34. Santa Fe, NM and Oxford [England]: School of American Research Press.

Davis, M. 2001. *Magical Urbanism: Latinos Reinvent the US City.* New York: Verso.

De Certeau, M. 1980. *L'invention du Quotidien. Vol.1: Arts de Faire.* Paris: Union Générale d'éditions 10/18.

De Certeau, M. 1984. *The Practice of Everyday Life.* Berkeley: University of California Press.

De Michelis, E. 2005. *A History of Modern Yoga.* London: Continuum.

Dear, M. 2002. "Los Angeles and the Chicago School: Invitation to a Debate." *City & Community* 1 (1): 5–32.

Degen, M. 2008. *Sensing Cities: Regenerating Public Life in Barcelona and Manchester.* London: Routledge.

Dilger, H., O. Kasmani, and D. Mattes. 2018. "Spatialities of Belonging: Affective Place-Making among Diasporic Neo-Pentecostal and Sufi Groups in Berlin's Cityscape." In *Affect in Relation: Families, Places, Technologies,* edited by B. Röttger-Rössler and J. Slaby, 93–114. New York: Routledge.

Dixon, J., M. Levine, and R. McAuley. 2006. "Locating Impropriety: Street Drinking, Moral Order, and the Ideological Dilemma of Public Space." *Political Psychology* 27 (2): 187–206.

Dobbelaere, K., and A. Pérez-Agote, eds. 2015. *The Intimate. Polity and the Catholic Church: Laws about Life, Death and the Family in So-called Catholic Countries.* Leuven: Leuven University Press.

Dodds, J. 2002. *The Mosques of New York City.* New York: Power House Books.

Dowdney, L. 2003. *Children of the Drug Trade: A Case of Study in Organised Armed Violence in Rio de Janeiro.* Rio de Janeiro: 7 Letras.

Downey, G. 2006. "The Information Economy in No-Holds-Barred Fighting." In *Frontiers of Capital: Ethnographic Reflections on the New Economy,* edited by M. S. Fisher and G. Downey, 108–32. Durham, NC: Duke University Press.

Downey, G. 2007. "Producing Pain: Techniques and Technologies in No-Holds-Barred Fighting." *Social Studies of Science* 37 (2): 201–26.

Dowty, A. 2005. *Israel/Palestine.* Cambridge, MA: Polity Press.

Dressler, M. 2019. "Modes of Religionization: A Constructivist Approach to Secularity." *Working Paper Series of the Centre for Advanced Studies, "Multiple Secularities— Beyond the West, Beyond Modernities"* 7: 1–21.

Dunning, E. 1986. "Preface." In *Quest for Excitement: Sport and Leisure in the Civilizing Process*, edited by N. Elias and E. Dunning, 1–18. Oxford and New York: Blackwell.

Durkheim, É. 2001. *The Elementary Forms of Religious Life*. Oxford: Oxford University Press.

Dwyer, C., J. Tse, and D. Ley. 2016. "'Highway to Heaven': The Creation of a Multicultural, Religious Landscape in Suburban Richmond, British Columbia." *Social & Cultural Geography* 17 (5): 667–93.

Eade, J., and D. Garbin. 2007. "Reinterpreting the Relationship between Centre and Periphery: Pilgrimage and Sacred Spatialisation among Polish and Congolese Communities in Britain." *Mobilities* 2 (3): 413–24. https://doi.org/10.1080/17450100701597384.

Eagland, N. 2015. "Premier's Yoga Event 'Ill-conceived.'" *The Province* June 12, 3.

Elias, N. 1986. "An Essay on Sport and Violence." In *Quest for Excitement: Sport and Leisure in the Civilizing Process*, edited by N. Elias and E. Dunning, 150–74. Oxford and New York: Blackwell.

Elias, N. 2000. *The Civilizing Process: Sociogenetic and Psychogenetic Investigations*. Translated by E. Dunning, J. Goudsblom and S. Mennell. Rev ed. Malden, MA: Blackwell Publishers.

Emmel, N. 2014. *Sampling and Choosing Cases in Qualitative Research: A Realist Approach*. London: Sage.

Endelstein, L. 2017. "Lumières sur la Ville. Les Fêtes de Hanoucca entre Action Missionnaire Transnationale et Appartenance Événementielle." *Archives de Sciences Sociales des Religions* 177: 51–71.

Engelke, M. 2009. "Strategic Secularism: Bible Advocacy in England." *Social Analysis* 53 (1): 39–54.

Engelke, M. 2011. "The Semiotics of Relevance: Campaigning for the Bible in Greater Manchester." *Anthropological Quarterly* 84 (3): 705–35.

Engelke, M. 2012. "Angels in Swindon: Public Religion and Ambient Faith in England." *American Ethnologist* 39 (1): 155–70.

Environics. 2015. "Focus Canada: 2015 Survey on Immigration and Multiculturalism." Environics, June 30. Accessed June 16, 2020. https://www.environicsinstitute.org/projects/project-details/focus-canada-2015-survey-on-immigration-and-multiculturalism.

Evalúa, D. F. 2011. *Índice del Desarrollo Social de las Unidades Territoriales del Distrito Federal*. México: Consejo de Evaluación del Desarrollo Social del Distrito Federal.

Falah, G. 1996. "The 1948 Israeli-Palestinian War and Its Aftermath: The Transformation and De-signification of Palestine's Cultural Landscape." *Annals of the Association of American Geographers* 86 (2): 256–85.

Farnell, B. 2012. *Dynamic Embodiment for Social Theory: "I Move Therefore I Am."* Ontological Explorations. New York: Routledge.

Favre, O. 2014. "The International Christian Fellowship (ICF): A Sociological Analysis of Religious Event Management." In *Religions as Brands: New Perspectives on the Marketization of Religion and Spirituality*, edited by J. Usunier and J. Stolz, 47–58. Farnham: Ashgate.

Fedele, A., and K. Knibbe. 2013. *Gender and Power in Contemporary Spirituality*. New York: Routledge.

Fedele, A., and K. Knibbe, eds. 2020. *Secular Society, Spiritual Selves? The Gendered Triangle of Religion, Secularity and Spirituality*. London: Routledge.

Fernández-Mostaza, M. E., and W. Muñoz Henríquez. 2018. "A *Cristo Moreno* in Barcelona: The Staging of Identity-Based Unity and Difference in the Procession of the Lord of Miracles." *Religions* 9: 121.

Festival Alternatiba. 2019. "Website and Program." Accessed January 18, 2020. https://www.alternatibaleman.org/editions-precedentes/.

Festival de la Terre Lausanne. 2019. "Website and Program." Accessed January 18, 2020. http://www.festivaldelaterre.ch/.

Finlayson, C. 2017. "Church-in-a-Box: Making Space Sacred in a Non-traditional Setting." *Journal of Cultural Geography* 34 (3): 303–23.

Foucault, M. 1984. "Of Other Spaces, Heterotopias." *Architecture, Mouvement, Continuité* 5: 46–9, in *Dits et Ecrits*: 1571–1581.

Foucault, M. [1967] 1986. "Of Other Space." *Diacritics* 16 (1): 24–27.

Foucault, M. [1967] 2008. "Of Other Spaces." In *Heterotopia and the City: Public Space in a Postcivil Society*, edited by M. Dehaene and L. De Cauter, 13–29. London and New York: Routledge.

Foucault, M. 1998, 2000. "Different Spaces." In *Aesthetics, Method and Epistemology (Essential Works of Foucault, 1954–1984, Vol. 2)*, edited by J. Faubion and P. Rabinow, 175–85. New York and London: Penguin Books.

Foucault, M. 2009. *The Order of Things*. Abingdon: Routledge.

Foxen, A. 2020. *Inhaling Spirit: Harmonialism, Orientalism, and the Western Roots of Modern Yoga*. New York: Oxford University Press.

Francis I, Pope. 2013. *Evangelii Gaudium*. Vatican City: Libreria Edetrice Vaticana.

Frank, S., and S. Steets. 2010. "Conclusion. The Stadium—Lens and Refuge." In *Stadium Worlds: Football, Space and the Built Environment*, edited by S. Frank and S. Steets, 278–94. London: Routledge.

Freeman, E. 2007. "Queer Belonging: Kinship Theory and Queer Theory." In *A Companion to Lesbian, Gay, Bisexual, Transgender and Queer Studies*, edited by G. E. Haggerty and M. McGarry, 295–314. Oxford: Blackwell Publishing.

Friedland, R., and R. D. Hecht. 2014. "Jerusalem's Sacrality, Urban Sociology and the History of Religions." In *Jerusalem: Conflict and Corporation in a Contested City*, edited by M. Andelman and M. F. Elman, 82–113. Syracuse: Syracuse University Press.

Fuller, M. G., and M. Löw. 2017. "Introduction: An Invitation to Spatial Sociology." *Current Sociology* 65 (4): 469–91.

Gaffney, C., S. D. Wolf, and M. Müller. 2018. "Scrutinizing Global Mega-events." In *Doing Global Urban Research*, edited by J. Harrison and M. Hoyler, 124–37. London: Sage.

Gal, S. 2000. "The Arab Minority Has not Radicalized. It Has Reached the Limits of Its Endurance." *Haaretz*, October 3, 2002: A3.

Gal, S. 2002. "A Semiotics of the Public/Private Distinction." *Differences: A Journal of Feminist Cultural Studies* 13 (1): 77–95.

Gale, D. R. 2005. "Representing the City: Mosques and the Planning Process in Birmingham." *Journal of Ethnic and Migration Studies* 31 (6): 1161–79.

Gandy, M. 2012. "Queer Ecology: Nature, Sexuality, and Heterotopic Alliances." *Environment and Planning D: Society and Space* 30: 727–47.

Garbin, D. 2012a. "Introduction: Believing in the City." *Culture and Religion* 13: 401–4.

Garbin, D. 2012b. "Marching for God in the Global City: Public Space, Religion and Diasporic Identities in a Transnational African Church." *Culture and Religion* 13: 425–47.

Garbin, D. 2013. "The Visibility and Invisibility of Migrant Faith in the City: Diaspora Religion and the Politics of Emplacement of Afro-Christian Churches." *Journal of Ethnic and Migration Studies* 39 (5): 677–96.

Garbin, D., and A. Strahn, eds. 2017. *Religion and the Global City*. London: Bloomsbury Academic.

Garcia Rierola, E. 2017. "El silenci, l'ànima del diàleg." In *Creences i Religions. Llibertat, diversitat i conflicte*, edited by E. Bech and J. Puig, 39–71. Museu d'Olot: Olot.

Gardiner, M. 1993. "Ecology and Carnival: Traces of a 'Green' Social Theory in the Writings of M.M. Bakhtin." *Theory and Society* 22 (6): 765–812.

Garfinkel, H. 1967. *Studies in Ethnomethodology*. New Jersey: Prentice Hall.

Gauthier, F. 2013. "The Enchantments of Consumer Capitalism: Beyond Belief at the Burning Man Festival." In *Religion in Consumer Society: Brands, Consumers and Markets*, edited by F. Gauthier and T. Martikainen, 143–58. London: Routledge.

Gebhardt, W. 1987. *Fest, Feier und Alltag: über die gesellschaftliche Wirklichkeit des Menschen und ihre Deutung*. Frankfurt am Main: Peter Lang Gmbh, Internationaler Verlag Der Wissenschaften.

Gebhardt, W. 2000. "Feste, Feiern und Events. Zur Soziologie des Außergewöhnlichen." In *Events: Soziologie des Außergewöhnlichen*. Vol. 2, edited by W. Gebhardt, H. Ronald and M. Pfadenhauer, 17–32. Wiesbaden: VS Verlag für Sozialwissenschaften.

Gebhardt, W., H. Ronald and M. Pfadenhauer, eds. 2013. *Events: Soziologie des Außergewöhnlichen, Vol. 2*. Cham: Springer-Verlag.

Gell, Alfred. 1993. *Wrapping in Images: Tattooing in Polynesia*. Oxford: Clarendon Press.

Getz, D. 1989. "Special Events: Defining the Product." *Tourism Management* 10 (2): 125–37.

Getz, D. 2005. *Event Management and Event Tourism*. Elsford: Cognizant Communication.

Getz, D. 2007. *Event Studies: Theory, Research and Policy for Planned Events*. Oxford: Elsevier.

Getz, D. 2008. "Event Tourism: Definition, Evolution, and Research." *Tourism Management* 29 (3): 403–28.

Ghanem, A. 2001. *The Palestinian-Arab Minority in Israel, 1948–2000*. Albany: SUNY Press.

Giorda, M. C. 2019. "Geography of Religions. Introduction." *Historia Religionum* 11: 11–14.

Giorda, M. C., and S. Hejazi. 2019. "In between. Giovani musulmani ad eventi pubblici: il caso di Torino." *Protestantesimo* 74: 235–48.

Giorgi, A. 2015. "#1—Torino Spiritualità." *Directions in Religious Pluralism in Europe*. Accessed March 10, 2020. http://grassrootsmobilise.eu/1-italy-torino-spiritualita/.

Giorgi, A. 2019a. *Religioni di minoranza. Tra Europa e laicità locale*. Milan: Mimesis.

Giorgi, A. 2019b. "Feminism and Religion. Queering the Divide." *Rassegna Italiana di Sociologia* LX (4): 1–20.

Goffman, E. [1971] 2009. *Relations in Public. Microstudies of the Public Order*. London: Transaction Publishers.

Goffman, E. 1956. "The Nature of Deference and Demeanor." *American Anthropologist* 58 (3): 473–502.

Goffman, E. 1963a. *Behavior in Public Places: Notes on the Social Organization of Gatherings*. New York: Free Press New York.

Goffman, E. 1963b. *Stigma: Notes on the Management of Spoiled Identity*. New York: Touchstone.

Gökarıksel, B., and A. J. Secor. 2015. "Postsecular Geographies and the Problem of Pluralism: Religion and Everyday Life in Istanbul, Turkey." *Political Geography* 46: 21–30.

Golan, O., and N. Stadler. 2016. "Building the Sacred Community Online: The Dual Use of the Internet by Chabad." *Media, Culture & Society* 38 (1): 71–88.

Goldstein-Gidoni, O. 2003. "Producers of 'Japan' in Israel: Cultural Appropriation in a Non-colonial Context." *Ethnos* 68 (3): 365–90.

Göle, N. 2011. "The Public Visibility of Islam and European Politics of Resentment: The Minarets-Mosques Debate." *Philosophy & Social Criticism* 37 (4): 383–92.

Gómez, L., and W. Van Herck, eds. 2012. *The Sacred in the City*. London: Bloomsbury Publishing.

Goncharenko, R. 2017. "Russia Returns Cathedral to Orthodox Church." *DW*. https://www.dw.com/en/russia-returns-cathedral-to-orthodox-church/a-37374984.

Gordon, A. 2008. *Ghostly Matters: Haunting and the Sociological Imagination*. Minneapolis: University of Minnesota Press.

Gowan, A. 2014. "India's New Prime Minister, Narendra Modi, Aims to Rebrand and Promote Yoga in India." *Washington Post*, December 2. Accessed June 16, 2020. https://www.washingtonpost.com/world/asia_pacific/indias-new-prime-minister-narendra-modi-wants-to-rebrand-and-promote-yoga-in-india/2014/12/02/7c5291de-7006-11e4-a2c2-478179fd0489_story.html?utm_term=.85c4e601c1ec.

Gramsci, A. 1971. *Selection from the Prison Notebooks*. London: Lawrence and Wishart.

Grandjean, A., C. Monnot, and I. Becci. 2018. "Spiritualités et Religions: Des 'facilitateurs' pour la Transition Énergétique?" In *Volteface: La Transition*

Énergétique, un Projet de Société, edited by N. Niwa and B. Frund, 157–76. Lausanne: Editions Charles Léopold Mayer.

Green, T. A., and J. R. Svinth. 2003. "Brazilian Jiu-Jitsu." In *Martial Arts in the Modern World*, edited by T. A. Green and J. R. Svinth, 52–6. Westport, CT: Praeger.

Greenhill, M., Z. Leviston, R. Leonard, and I. Walker. 2014. "Assessing Climate Change Beliefs: Response Effects of Question Wording and Response Alternatives." *Public Understanding of Science* 23 (8): 947–65. https://doi.org/10.1177/09636625134801.

Greve, J. 2014. "Jesus Didn't Tap: Masculinity, Theology, and Ideology in Christian Mixed Martial Arts." *Religion and American Culture: A Journal of Interpretation* 24 (2): 141–85.

Griera, M. 2012. "Public Policies, Interfaith Associations and Religious Minorities: A New Policy Paradigm? Evidence from the Case of Barcelona." *Social Compass* 59 (4): 570–87.

Griera, M. 2017. "Yoga in Penitentiary Settings: Transcendence, Spirituality, and Self-improvement." *Human Studies* 40 (1): 77–100.

Griera, M., and A. Clot-Garrell. 2015a. "Banal Is Not Trivial: Visibility, Recognition, and Inequalities between Religious Groups in Prison." *Journal of Contemporary Religion* 30 (1): 23–37.

Griera, M., and A. Clot-Garrell. 2015b. "Doing Yoga behind Bars: A Sociological Study of the Growth of Holistic Spirituality in Penitentiary Institutions." In *Religious Diversity in European Prisons*, edited by I. Becci and O. Roy, 141–57. Cham, The Netherlands: Springer.

Griera, M., and A. K. Nagel. 2018. "Interreligious Relations and Governance of Religion in Europe: Introduction." *Social Compass* 65 (3): 301–11.

Griera, M., and M. Burchardt. 2020. "Governing Religious Visibilities in Urban Space: The Interaction Order of Religious Minority Rituals in Barcelona." *Ethnic and Racial Studies*.

Griera, M., M. C. Giorda, and V. Fabretti. 2018. "Initiatives Interreligieuses et Gouvernance Locale: Les Cas de Barcelone et de Turin." *Social Compass* 65 (3): 312–28.

Griera, M., A. Clot-Garrell, and A. Montanes. Forthcoming, "De la Sacralizacion del Espacio a la Secularizacion de la Religiosidad: Expresiones Religiosas en el Espacio Publico en Barcelona." In *Ciudades y Religión*, edited by H. Suarez, K. Barcenas and C. Delgado-Molina. IIS-UNAM: DF. Mexico.

Grimes, R. L. 2006. *Rite Out of Place: Ritual, Media and the Arts*. Oxford and New York: Oxford University Press.

Gruber, R. E. 2002. *Virtually Jewish: Reinventing Jewish Culture in Europe*. Berkeley: University of California Press.

Guattari, F. 1989. *Les Trois Écologies*. Paris: Galilée.

Gugutzer, R., and M. Böttcher. 2012. "Zur Einführung." In *Körper, Sport und Religion: zur Soziologie religiöser Verkörperungen*, edited by R. Gugutzer and M. Böttcher, 9–23. Wiesbaden: Springer VS.

Gunther Brown, C. 2019. *Debating Yoga and Mindfulness in Public Schools: Reforming Secular Education or Reestablishing Religion?* Chapel Hill: University of North Carolina Press.

Gutiérrez, C., R. de la Torre, and C. Castro. 2011. *Una Ciudad donde Habitan muchos Dioses. Cartografía Religiosa de Guadalajara.* Guadalajara: Colegio de Jalisco—CIESAS.

Gutiérrez, D. 2005. "Multirreligiosidad en la Ciudad de México." *Economía, Sociedad y Territorio* V (5): 617–57.

Haken, M. 2019. "Religious Emotions in Christian Events." In *Affect and Emotion in Multi-Religious Secular Societies*, edited by C. von Scheve, A. L. Berg, M. Haken and N. Y. Ural, 114–32. London: Routledge.

Hamilton, L. C. 2011. "Education, Politics and Opinions about Climate Change Evidence for Interaction Effects." *Climatic Change* 104 (2): 231–42.

Hasselle-Newcombe, S. 2005. "Spirituality and 'Mystical Religion' in Contemporary Society: A Case Study of British Practitioners of the Iyengar Method of Yoga." *Journal of Contemporary Religion* 20: 305–22.

Hayden, R. M., T. Tanyeri-Erdemir, T. D. Walker, A. Erdemir, D. Rangachari, M. Aguilar-Moreno, E. López-Hurtado, and M. Bakić-Hayden. 2016. *Antagonistic Tolerance: Competitive Sharing of Religious Sites and Spaces.* London: Routledge.

Heelas, P., L. Woodhead, with B. Seel, K. Tusting, and Bro Szerszynski. 2005. *The Spiritual Revolution: Why Religion Is Giving Way to Spirituality.* Oxford: Blackwell.

Hepp, A. 2012. *Cultures of Mediatization.* Cambridge: Polity Press.

Hernández, A. 2007. "Urbanización y Cambio Religioso." In *Atlas de la Diversidad Religiosa en México*, edited by R. De la Torre, 247–66. México: CIESAS, Colef, Coljal.

Hervieu-Leger, D. 2002. "Space and Religion: New Approaches to Religious Spatiality in Modernity." *International Journal of Urban and Regional Research* 26 (1): 99–105.

Hietzge, M. C. 2002. *Kaleidoskope des Körpers.* Wiesbaden: VS Verlag für Sozialwissenschaften.

Hilal, J. 2006. *Where Now for Palestine?: The Demise of the Two-State Solution.* London: Zed Books.

Hitzler, R. 2002. "Trivialhedonismus? Eine Gesellschaft Auf Dem Weg in Die Spaßkultur. na." In *Populäre Kultur als repräsentative Kultur*, edited by U. Göttlich, C. Albrecht and W. Gebhardt. Köln: Fiktion und Fiktionalisierung.

Hochschild, A. 1979. "Emotion Work, Feeling Rules, and Social Structure." *American Journal of Sociology* 85 (3): 551–75.

Hoerning, J. Forthcoming. "Comparing Actors and Scales: Methodological Perspectives from Political Sociology of the Re-figuration of Spaces." *Forum Qualitative Social Research (FQS)*, Special Issue.

Hogeveen, B. 2013. "'It Is about Your Body Recognizing the Move and Automatically Doing It': Merleau-Ponty, Habit and Brazilian Jiu-Jitsu." In *Fighting Scholars: Habitus and Ethnographies of Martial Arts and Combat Sports*, edited by R. Sánchez García and D. C. Spencer, 79–93. London: Anthem Press.

Höllinger, F., and T. Tripold. 2012. *Ganzheitliches Leben. Das holistische Milieu zwischen neuer Spiritualität und postmoderner Wellness-Kultur.* Bielefeld: Transcript.

Houtman, D., and S. Aupers. 2007. "The Spiritual Turn and the Decline of Tradition: The Spread of Post-Christian Spirituality in 14 Western Countries, 1981–2000." *Journal for the Scientific Study of Religion* 46 (3): 305–20.

INEGI. 2010. *Censo de Población y Vivienda*. Aguascalientes: INEGI.

Ingalls, M. M. 2012. "Singing Praise in the Streets: Performing Canadian Christianity through Public Worship in Toronto's Jesus in the City Parade." *Culture and Religion* 13 (3): 337–59.

Ingold, T. 1993. "The Temporality of the Landscape." *World Archeology* 25 (2): 152–74.

Ingold, T. 2000. *The Perception of the Environment—Essays in Livelihood, Dwelling and Skill*. London and New York: Routledge.

Ingold, T., and J. L. Vergunst. 2008. "Introduction." In *Ways of Walking: Ethnography and Practice on Foot*, edited by T. Ingold and J. L. Vergunst, 1–20. Aldershot, England and Burlington, VT: Ashgate.

Instituto Brasileiro de Geografia e Estatística. 2010. "Censo Demográfico 2010." Accessed June 17, 2020. https://censo2010.ibge.gov.br/.

International Jiu-Jitsu Federation. 2015. "General System of Graduation." Accessed June 17, 2020. https://ibjjf.com/info/graduation-system/.

Ivtzan, I., and S. Jegatheeswaran. 2015. "The Yoga Boom in Western Society: Practitioners' Spiritual vs. Physical Intentions and Their Impact on Psychological Wellbeing." *Journal of Yoga and Physical Therapy* 5: 204.

Jackson, M. 1996. "Introduction: Phenomenology, Radical Empiricism, and Anthropological Critique." In *Things as They Are: New Directions in Phenomenological Anthropology*, edited by M. Jackson, 1–50. Bloomington: Indiana University Press.

Jain, A. 2014. *Selling Yoga: From Counterculture to Pop Culture*. New York: Oxford University Press.

Jain, A. 2020. *Peace, Love, Yoga: The Politics of Global Spirituality*. New York: Oxford University Press.

Jakob, D. 2013. "The Eventification of Place: Urban Development and Experience Consumption in Berlin and New York City." *European Urban and Regional Studies* 20 (4): 447–59.

John Paul II, Pope. 1995. *Evangelium Vitae*. Vatican City: Libreria Edetrice Vaticana.

John Paul II, Pope. 1999. *Post-Synodal Apostolic Exhortation "Ecclesia in America."* Vatican City: Libreria Edetrice Vaticana.

John Paul II, Pope. 2003. *Post-Synodal Apostolic Exhortation "Ecclesia in Europa."* Vatican City: Libreria Edetrice Vaticana.

Jonas, A. E. G. 2006. "Pro Scale: Further Reflections on the 'Scale Debate' in Human Geography." *Transactions of the Institute of British Geographers* 31: 399–406.

Jones, P. 2006. "The Sociology of Architecture and the Politics of Building: The Discursive Construction of Ground Zero." *Sociology* 40 (3): 549–65.

Kasmani, O. 2017a. "Grounds of Becoming: Living among the Dead in Sehwan Sharif, Pakistan." *Culture & Religion* 18 (2): 72–89.

Kasmani, O. 2017b. "Audible Specters: The Sticky Shia Sonics of Sehwan." *History of Emotions—Insights into Research*. October. Accessed June 17, 2020. https://doi. org/10.14280/08241.54.

Kasmani, O. 2019. "Thin Attachments: Writing Berlin in Scenes of Daily Loves." *Capacious: Journal for Emerging Affect Inquiry* 1 (3): 1–36.

Kataev, V. 1978. *Moi almaznyi venets* [My Diamond Crown]. https://www.litmir.me/ br/?b=132605&p=7.

Katz, M. B. 2009. "Trademarks of Faith: 'Chabad and Chanukah in America.'" *Modern Judaism—A Journal of Jewish Ideas and Experience* 29 (2): 239–67.

Katz, M. B. 2010. *The Visual Culture of Chabad*. New York: Cambridge University Press.

Kavoura, A., S. A. Chroni, M. Kokkonen, and T. V. Ryba. 2015. "Women Fighters as Agents of Change: A Brazilian Jiu Jitsu Case Study from Finland." In *Global Perspectives on Women in Combat Sports: Women Warriors around the World*, edited by A. Channon and C. R. Matthews. Basingstoke, Hampshire and New York: Palgrave Macmillan.

Keane, W. 2008. "Market, Materiality and Moral Metalanguage." *Anthropological Theory* 8 (1): 27–42.

Kimmerling, B. 2001. *The Invention and Decline of Israeliness*. Berkeley: University of California Press.

Kister, Meir J. 1969. "You Shall Only Set Out for Three Mosques. A Study of an Early Tradition." *Le Museon* 82: 173–96.

Knijnik, J., and M. A. de Carvalho Ferretti. 2015. "Ambivalent Lives, Fighting Bodies: Women and Combat Sports in Brazil." In *Global Perspectives on Women in Combat Sports: Women Warriors around the World*, edited by A. Channon and C. R. Matthews, 253–66. Basingstoke Hampshire and New York: Palgrave Macmillan.

Knoblauch, H. 2008. "Spirituality and Popular Religion in Europe." *Social Compass* 55 (2): 140–53.

Knoblauch, H. 2009. *Populäre Religion: auf dem Weg in eine spirituelle Gesellschaft*. Frankfurt am Main: Campus Verlag.

Knoblauch, H. 2011. "Videography." In *The Routledge Handbook of Research Methods in the Study of Religion*, edited by M. Stausberg und S. Engler, 433–44. London: Routledge.

Knoblauch, H. 2012. "Körper und Transzendenz. Über den Zusammenhang von Wissen, Praxis, Sport und Religion." In *Körper, Sport und Religion: zur Soziologie religiöser Verkörperungen*, edited by R. Gugutzer and M. Böttcher, 27–48. Wiesbaden: Springer VS.

Knoblauch, H. 2014a. "Benedict in Berlin: The Mediatization of Religion." In *Mediatized Worlds: Culture and Society in a Media Age*, edited by A. Hepp and F. Krotz, 143–58. London: Palgrave Macmillan.

Knoblauch, H. 2014b. "The Communicative Construction of Transcendence: A New Approach to Popular Religion." In *Religion, Tradition and the Popular: Transcultural Views from Asia and Europe*, edited by J. Schlehe and E. Sandkühler, 29–50. Bielefeld: transcript.

Knoblauch, H. 2020. *The Communicative Construction of Reality*. London: Routledge.

Knoblauch, H., and M. Blanc. 2018. "Bilder von Benedikt: Die Mediatisierung der Papstmesse und das religiöse Gefühl." In *Das Bild als soziologisches Problem: Herausforderungen einer Theorie visueller Kommunikation*, edited by M. Müller und H. Soeffner, 57–68. Weinheim/Basel: Beltz Juventa.

Knorre, B. 2011. "Kategorii 'viny' i 'smireniia' v sisteme tsennostei tserkovno-prikhodskoi subkul'tury" [Categories of "Guilt" and "Humility" in the System of Values of Orthodox Parish Subculture]. In *Prikhod i obshchina v sovremennom pravoslavii: kornevaia sistema rossiiskoi religioznosti*, edited by A. Agadjanian and K. Russele, 317–41. Moscow: Izdatel'stvo "Ves' Mir."

Knott, K. 2005. "Spatial Theory and Method for the Study of Religion." *Temenos-Nordic Journal of Comparative Religion* 41 (2): 153–84.

Knott, K. 2015a. "Walls and Other Unremarkable Boundaries in South London: Impenetrable Infrastructure or Portals of Time, Space and Cultural Difference?" *New Diversities* 17 (2): 15–34.

Knott, K. 2015b. *The Location of Religion: A Spatial Analysis*. London: Routledge.

Knott, K., V. Krech, and B. Meyer. 2016. "Iconic Religion in Urban Space." *Material Religion* 12 (2): 123–36.

Koch, A. 2015. "Living4giving: Politics of Affect and Emotional Regimes in Global Yoga." In *Yoga in Transformation: Historical and Contemporary Perspectives on a Global Phenomenon*, edited by K. Baier, K. C. Preisendanz and P. Maas. Vienna: Vandenhoeck & Ruprecht.

Kochergina, E. 2017. "Religiosity." *Levada Analytical Center*. http://www.levada.ru/2017/07/18/religioznost/.

Koehrsen, J., F. Huber, I. Becci, and J. Blanc. 2019. "How Is Religion Involved in Transformations towards More Sustainable Societies? A Systematization." *Historia Religionum* 12 (1): 99–116.

Kolesch, D., and H. Knoblauch. 2019. "Audience Emotions." In *Affective Societies: Key Concepts*, edited by Jan S. and C. von Scheve, 252–64. London: Routledge.

Komarova, M., and L. O'Dowd. 2013. "Territorialities of Capital and Place in 'Post-Conflict' Belfast." In *Locating Urban Conflicts: Nationalism, Ethnicity, and the Everyday*, edited by W. Pullan and B. Baillie, 233–51. Basingstoke: Palgrave Macmillan.

Kong, L. 1993. "Negotiating Conceptions of 'Sacred Space': A Case Study of Religious Buildings in Singapore." *Transactions of the Institute of British Geographers* 18 (3): 342–58.

Kong, L. 2005. "Religious Processions: Urban Politics and Poetics." *Temenos—Nordic Journal of Comparative Religion* 41 (2): 225–49.

Kong, L. 2010. "Global Shifts, Theoretical Shifts: Changing Geographies of Religion." *Progress in Human Geography* 34 (1): 755–76.

Kormina, Z. 2019. *Palomniki: etnograficheskie ocherki pravoslavnogo nomadizma* [Pilgrims: Ethnographic Sketches of the Orthodox Nomadism]. Moscow: HSE Publishing House.

Kormina, Z., and S. Shtyrkov. 2015. "'Eto nashe iskonno russkoe, i nikuda nam ot etogo ne det'sia': predystoriia postsovetskoi desekuliarizatsii" ["This Is Our Original Russian, and Nowhere We Can't Get Away from It": Backstory Post-Soviet Desecularization]. In *Izobretenie religii: desekuliarizatsiia v postsovetskom kontekste*, edited by Z. Kormina, S. Shtyrkov and A. Panchenko, 7–45. St. Petersburg: izdatel'stvo evropeiskogo universiteta.

Koukal, D. R. 2010. "Here I Stand: Mediated Bodies in Dissent." *MediaTropes* 2 (2): 109–27.

Kracauer, S. [1927] 1995. *The Mass Ornament*. Cambridge, MA: Harvard University Press.

Kuppinger, P. 2014. "Mosques and Minarets: Conflict, Participation, and Visibility in German Cities." *Anthropological Quarterly* 87 (3): 793–818.

Kyrlezhev, A. 2004. "Postsekuliarnaia epokha" [Postsecular Era]. *Kontinent*, no. 12. https://magazines.gorky.media/continent/2004/120/postsekulyarnaya-epoha.html.

Lancenet. 2018. "Ex-lutador revela projeto que viabiliza o Jiu-Jitsu nas escolas de SP." *Gazeta Online*, July 16. Accessed June 17, 2020. https://www.gazetaonline.com.br/esportes/lutas/2018/07/lutador-revela-projeto-que-viabiliza-jiu-jitsu-nas-escolas-102446148.html.

Lange, B., D. Power, and L. Suwala. 2014. "Geographies of Field-Configuring Events." *Zeitschrift für Wirtschaftsgeographie* 58 (4): 187–201.

Lanz, S. 2014. "Assembling Global Prayers in the City: An Attempt to Repopulate Urban Theory with Religion." In *Global Prayers: Contemporary Manifestations of the Religious in the City*, edited by J. Becher, K. Klingan, S. Lanz and K. Wildner, 16–47. Zürich: Lars Müller Publishers.

Lanz, S. 2016. "The Born-Again Favela: The Urban Informality of Pentecostalism in Rio de Janeiro." *International Journal of Urban and Regional Research* 40 (3): 541–58.

Laqueur, W., and B. Rubin. eds. 2001. *The Israel-Arab Reader: A Documentary History of the Middle East Conflict*. New York: Penguin Books.

Larkin, C. 2010. "Remaking Beirut: Contesting Memory, Space, and the Urban Imaginary of Lebanese Youth." *City and Community* 9 (4): 414–42.

Larkin, C., and M. Dumper. 2012. "In Defense of Al-Aqsa: The Islamic Movement inside Israel and the Battle for Jerusalem." *The Middle East Journal* 66 (1): 31–52.

Latour, B. 1993. *We Have Never Been Modern*. Cambridge, MA: Harvard University Press.

Lefebvre, H. 1974. "La Production de L'espace." *L'Homme et la Société*. Anthropos: 15–32.

Lefebvre, H. 1991. *The Production of Space*. Translated by D. Nicholson-Smith. Oxford: Blackwell Publishers.

Lenhard, J., and F. Samanani. 2019. "Introduction: Ethnography, Dwelling and Home-Making." In *Home: Ethnographic Encounters*, edited by Johannes Lenhard and Farhan Samanani, 1–30. New York: Routledge.

Lijster, T., R. Celikates, and H. Rosa 2019. Beyond the Echo-chamber: An Interview with Hartmut Rosa on Resonance and Alienation. *Krisis. Journal for Contemporary Philosophy* 1: 64–78.

Lipis, M. 2016. "A Hybrid Place of Belonging. Constructing and Siting the Sukkah." In *Jewish Topographies: Visions of Space, Traditions of Place*, edited by J. Brauch, A. Lipphardt and A. Nocke, 27–41. London: Routledge.

Lipphardt, A., J. Brauch, and A. Nocke. 2016. "Exploring Jewish Space: An Approach." In *Jewish Topographies: Visions of Spaces, Traditions of Place*, edited by J. Brauch, A. Lipphardt and A. Nocke, 1–23. London: Routledge.

Liptoviesky, G. 1983. *La Era del Vacío*. Barcelona: Anagrama.

Long, N., and B. Tonini. 2012. "Les Espaces Verts Urbains: Étude Exploratoire des Pratiques et du Ressenti des Usagers." *VertigO—La Revue Électronique en Sciences de L'environnement* 12 (2) (online).

López, R. 2006. *Vestida de sol*. México: Era.

Löw, M. 2008. "The Constitution of Space: The Structuration of Spaces Through the Simultaneity of Effect and Perception." *European Journal of Social Theory* 11(1): 25–49.

Löw, M. 2016. *The Sociology of Space—Materiality, Social Structures, and Action*. New York: Palgrave Macmillan.

Löw, S. 2014. "Spatializing Culture: An Engaged Anthropological Approach to Space and Place." In *The People, Place, and Space Reader*, edited by Jen Jack Gieseking and William Mangold, 34–9. New York: Routledge.

Löw, S. M. 2000. *On the Plaza: The Politics of Public Space and Culture*. Austin: University of Texas Press.

Lucia, A. 2020. *White Utopias: The Religious Exoticism of Transformational Festivals*. Berkley: University of California Press.

Luckman, S. 2014. "Location, Spatiality and Liminality at Outdoor Music Festivals: Doofs as Journey." In *The Festivalization of Culture*, edited by A. Bennett, J. Taylor and I. Woodward, 189–205. Farnham: Ashgate.

Luckmann, T. 1967. *The Invisible Religion: The Problem of Religion in Modern Society*. New York: Macmillan.

Luckmann, T. 1990. "Shrinking Transcendence, Expanding Religion?" *Sociology of Religion* 51 (2): 127–38.

Luz, N. 2004. *Al-Haram Al-Sharif in the Arab-Palestinian Public Discourse in Israel: Identity, Collective Memory and Social Construction*. Jerusalem: Floersheimer Institute for Policy Study Achva Press.

Luz, N. 2013. "The Islamic Movement and the Seduction of Sanctified Sandscapes: Using Sacred Places to Conduct the Struggle for Land." In *Muslim Minorities in Non-Muslim Majority Countries: The Test Case of the Islamic Movement in Israel*, edited by

E. Rekhess and A. Rudnitzky, 67–77. Tel Aviv: The Konrad Adenauer Program for Jewish-Arab Cooperation, Tel Aviv University.

Luz, N. 2015. "Planning with Insurgent Religion." *Planning Theory and Practice* 16 (2): 4–11.

Lybarger, L. D. 2007. *Identity and Religion in Palestine: The Struggle between Islamism and Secularism in the Occupied Territories*. Princeton, NJ: Princeton University Press.

Machado da Silva, L. A. 2008. "Introdução." In *Vida sob cerco: violência e rotina nas favelas do Rio de Janeiro*, edited by L. A. Machado da Silva, 13–26. Rio de Janeiro: Editora Nova Fronteira.

Machado, M. 2018. "Ex-lutador, Matheus Serafim revela projeto que viabiliza entrada do Jiu-Jitsu nas escolas de São Paulo; veja." *Extra Online*, July 16. Accessed June 17, 2020. https://extra.globo.com/esporte/mma/ex-lutador-matheus-serafim-revela-projeto-que-viabiliza-entrada-do-jiu-jitsu-nas-escolas-de-sao-paulo-veja-22891529.html.

Machado, M. 2019. "Governo autoriza projeto que viabiliza prática do Jiu-Jitsu e outras artes marciais em escolas públicas do Rio." *Extra Online*, July 24. Accessed June 17, 2020. https://extra.globo.com/esporte/mma/governo-autoriza-projeto-que-viabiliza-pratica-do-jiu-jitsu-outras-artes-marciais-em-escolas-publicas-do-rio-23828918.html.

Mallinson, J., and M. Singleton. 2017. *The Roots of Yoga*. New York: Penguin Classics.

Marshall, D. A. 2002. "Behavior, Belonging, and Belief: A Theory of Ritual Practice." *Sociological Theory* 20 (3): 360–80.

Marston, S. A., J. P. Jones, and K. Woodward. 2005. "Human Geography without Scale." *Transactions of the Institute of British Geographers* 30: 416–32.

Martin, R. 2016. *The Urban Apparatus: Mediapolitics and the City*. Minneapolis: University of Minnesota Press.

Martínez-Ariño, J. 2012. "Identidades y Vivencias Judías en la Cataluña Contemporánea: Una Realidad Diversa y Cambiante." *Quaderns-e de l'Institut Català d'Antropologia* 17 (2): 73–85.

Martínez-Ariño, J. 2016. "'Being Jew Is Like Travelling by Bus': Constructing Jewish Identities in Spain between Individualisation and Group Belonging." *Journal of Religion in Europe* 9 (4): 324–49.

Martínez-Ariño, J. 2017. "Conceptualising the Role of Cities in the Governance of Religious Diversity in Europe." *Current Sociology* 66 (5): 810–27.

Martínez-Ariño, J. 2018. "The Evolution of Religious Diversity: Mapping Religious Minorities in Barcelona." In *Congregations in Europe*, edited by C. Monnot and J. Stölz, 177–93. Cham: Springer.

Martínez-Ariño, J. 2019. "Governing Religious Diversity in Cities: Critical Perspectives." *Religion, State & Society* 47 (4–5): 364–73.

Martínez-Ariño, J. 2020. "Jewish Spatial Practices in Barcelona as Claims for Recognition." *Social Inclusion* 8 (3): 240–50.

Martínez-Ariño, J., and M. Griera. 2020. "Adapter la Religion: Négocier les Limites de la Religion Minoritaire dans les Espaces Urbains." *Social Compass* 67 (2): 221–37.

Marzouki, N., D. McDonnell and O. Roy, eds. 2016. *Saving the People: How Populists Hijack Religion*. London: Hurst.

Massey, D. 1992. "Politics and Space/Time." *New Left Review* 196: 64–85.

Mattes, D., O. Kasmani, and H. Dilger. 2019. "'All Eyes Closed': Dis/Sensing in Comparative Fieldwork on Affective-Religious Experiences." In *Analyzing Affective Societies: Methods and Methodologies*, edited by A. Kahl, 265–78. New York: Routledge.

McAlister, E. 2016. "The Militarization of Prayer in America: White and Native American Spiritual Warfare." *Journal of Religious and Political Practice* 2 (1): 114–30.

McCutcheon, R. 1997. *Manufacturing Religion: The Discourse on Sui Generis Religion and the Politics of Nostalgia: Discourse of Sui Generis Religion and the Politics of Nostalgia*. New York: Oxford University Press.

MEA. 2016. "Common Yoga Protocol." Last updated June 13, 2016. Accessed June 16, 2020. https://www.mea.gov.in/idy.htm.

Mead, G. H. 1934. *Mind, Self and Society*. Vol. 111. Chicago, IL: University of Chicago Press.

Melihova, A., and R. Tsehanskii, eds. 2013. *Strasti i nadezhdy Pushkinskoi (Strastnoi) ploshchadi i Strastnogo monastyria* [Passion and Hope of Pushkinskaya (Strastnaya) Square and the Strastnoy Monastery]. Moscow: Sovero-Print.

Metcalf, B. 1996. "Introduction: Sacred Words, Sanctioned Practice, New Communities." In *Making Muslim Space in North America and Europe*, edited by B. Metcalf, 1–27. Berkeley: University of California Press.

Meyer, B. 2012. "Mediation and the Genesis of Presence: Towards a Material Approach to Religion." Inaugural Lecture. University of Utrecht, October 19, 2012.

Meyer, B. 2013. "Mediation and Immediacy: Sensational Forms, Semiotic Ideologies and the Question of the Medium." In *A Companion to the Anthropology of Religion*, edited by J. Boddy and M. Lambek, 309–26. West Sussex: Wiley Blackwell.

Meyer, B., D. Morgan, C. Paine, and S. B. Plate. 2010. "The Origin and Mission of Material Religion." *Religion* 40 (3): 207–11.

Miller, B. J. 2019. "'Would Prefer a Trailer Park to a Large [Religious] Structure': Suburban Responses to Proposals for Religious Buildings." *The Sociological Quarterly* 60 (2): 265–86.

Miller, C. 2018. "Yoga Bodies and Bodies of Water: Solutions for Climate Change in India?" In *That All May Flourish: Comparative Religious Environmental Ethics*, edited by L. Hartman, 125–55. New York: Oxford University Press.

Ministério do Esporte. 2015. "Diagnóstico Nacional do Esporte." Accessed June 17, 2020. http://arquivo.esporte.gov.br/diesporte/diesporte_grafica.pdf.

Miskolci, R., and M. Campana. 2017. "Ideologia de Gênero: Notas para a Genealogia de um Pânico Moral Contemporâneo." *Sociedade e Estado* 32 (3): 725–48.

Mittermaier, A. 2011. *Dreams That Matter: Egyptian Landscapes of the Imagination*. Berkeley: University of California Press.

Modood, T. 2013. "Multiculturalism and Religion: A Three-Part Debate. Part One: Accommodating Religions: Multiculturalism's New Fault Line." *Critical Social Policy* 34 (1): 121–7.

Molnár, V. 2014. "Reframing Public Space through Digital Mobilization: Flash Mobs and Contemporary Urban Youth Culture." *Space and Culture* 17 (1): 43–58.

Morán Faúndes, J. M. 2012. "El Activismo Católico Conservador y los Discursos Científicos Sobre Sexualidad: Cartografía de una Ciencia Heterosexual." *Sociedad y Religión* 22 (37): 167–205.

Morán Faúndes, J. M., and J. M. Vaggione. 2012. "Ciencia y Religión (hétero) Sexuadas: El Discurso Científico del Activismo Católico Conservador Sobre la Sexualidad en Argentina y Chile." *Contemporânea-Revista de Sociologia da UFSCar* 2 (1): 159–85.

Morgan, L. 2014. "Claiming Rosa Parks: Conservative Catholic Bids for 'Rights' in Contemporary Latin America." *Culture, Health & Sexuality* 16 (10): 1245–59.

Mori, L., and F. Squarcini 2019. *Nel nome dello yoga: Filosofia, disciplina, stile di vita.* Milan: Solferino.

Morris, B. 2001. *Righteous Victims: A History of the Zionist-Arab Conflict 1881–2001.* New York: Vintage Press.

Muslih, M. 1998. *The Origins of Palestinian Nationalism.* New York: Columbia University Press.

Mustafa, M. 2013. "Political Participation by the Islamic Movement in Israel." In *Muslim Minorities in Non-Muslim Majority Countries: The Test Case of the Islamic Movement in Israel,* edited by E. Rekhess and A. Rudnitzky, 95–113. Tel Aviv: The Konrad Adenauer Program for Jewish-Arab Cooperation, Tel Aviv University.

Næss, A. 1972. *Shallow and the Deep.* Oslo: Inquiry.

Office fédéral de la statistique. 2019. "Statistique des votations et des élections." Accessed July 15, 2019. https://www.bfs.admin.ch/bfs/fr/home/statistiques/ politique/elections/conseil-national/force-partis.html#-264904466.

Oosterbaan, M. 2014. "Public Religion and Urban Space in Europe." *Social & Cultural Geography* 15 (6): 591–602.

Ören, A. 1973. *Was will Niyazi in der Naunynstraße.* Berlin: Rotbuch Verlag.

Orsi, R. A. 1985. *The Madonna of 115th Street: Faith and Community in Italian Harlem 1880–1950.* New Haven, CT: Yale University Press.

Orsi, R. A. 1999. *Gods of the City: Religion and the American Urban Landscape.* Bloomington: Indiana University Press.

Palmisano, S., and N. Pannofino, eds. 2017. *Invention of Tradition and Syncretism in Contemporary Religions: Sacred Creativity.* London: Palgrave Macmillan.

Palmisano, S., and N. Pannofino. 2020. *Contemporary Spiritualities: Enchanted Worlds of Nature, Wellbeing and Mystery in Italy.* London: Routledge.

Panchenko, A. 2011. "Pushkin v sovetskom fol'klore" [Pushkin in Soviet Folklore]. In *Kul'turnyi palimpsest: Sbornik statei k 60-letiiu Vsevoloda Evgen'evicha Bagno.* St. Petersburg: Science.

Pappe, I. 2004. *A History of Modern Palestine: One Land, Two Peoples.* Cambridge: Cambridge University Press.

Pappe, I. 2011. *The Forgotten Palestinians: A History of the Palestinians in Israel.* New Haven, CT: Yale University Press.

Park, C. L., T. Braun, and T. Siegel. 2015. "Who Practices Yoga? A Systematic Review of Demographic, Health-Related, and Psychosocial Factors Associated with Yoga Practice." *Journal of Behavioral Medicine* 38: 460–71.

Patton, M. Q. 2002. *Qualitative Research & Evaluation Methods.* Thousand Oaks, CA: Sage.

Peña, E. 2011. *Performing Piety: Making Space Sacred with the Virgin of Guadalupe.* Berkeley: University of California Press.

Penglase, B. 2016. "An Oral History of Brazilian Jiu-Jitsu: Interview with Rolker Gracie." In *The Rio de Janeiro Reader: History, Culture, Politics,* edited by D. Williams, A. Chazkel and P. K. de Mendonça. The Latin America Readers. Durham, NC: Duke University Press.

Pérez, J. 2007. *History of a Tragedy: The Expulsion of the Jews from Spain.* Urbana: University of Illinois Press.

Perlman, J. E. 1979. *The Myth of Marginality: Urban Poverty and Politics in Rio de Janeiro.* Berkeley: University of California Press.

Perlman, J. E. 2010. *Favela: Four Decades of Living on the Edge in Rio de Janeiro.* New York: Oxford University Press.

Pfadenhauer, M. 2010. "The Eventization of Faith as a Marketing Strategy: World Youth Day as an Innovative Response of the Catholic Church to Pluralization." *International Journal of Nonprofit and Voluntary Sector Marketing* 15 (4): 382–94.

Philippopoulos-Mihalopoulos, A. 2019. "The Inconclusive Spatial Justice." In *Spatial Justice and the City,* edited by S. Watson, 156–63. London: Routledge.

Platt, J. 2016. *Greetings, Pushkin!: Stalinist Cultural Politics and the Russian National Bard.* Pittsburgh, PA: University of Pittsburgh Press.

Portal, M. 2009. "Las Creencias en el Asfalto. La Sacralización como una Forma de Apropiación del Espacio Público en la Ciudad de México." *Cuadernos de Antropología Social* 30 (Septiembre–diciembre): 59–75.

Pullan, W., M. Sternberg, L. Kyriacou, L. Craig and M. Dumper, eds. 2013. *The Struggle for Jerusalem's Holy Places: Radicalisation and Conflict.* London: Routledge.

Rabinowitz, D. 2001a. "The Palestinian Citizens of Israel: The Concept of Trapped Minority and the Discourse of Transnationalism in Anthropology." *Ethnic and Racial Studies* 24 (1): 64–85.

Rabinowitz, D. 2001b. "Strife in Nazareth: Struggle over the Religious Meaning of Place." *Ethnography* 2 (1): 93–113.

Rahim, L. Z. 2009. "Governing Islam and Regulating Muslims in Singapore's Secular Authoritarian State." *Asia Research Centre, Working Paper* 156.

Rainsford, S. 2019. "Activists Storm Yekaterinburg Russia Park in Protest against New Church." *BBC News,* May 15. https://www.bbc.com/news/world-europe-48276170.

Ray, J. S. 2013. *After Expulsion: 1492 and the Making of Sephardic Jewry.* New York: New York University Press.

Rebeaud, L. 1987. *La Suisse Verte. Les Premières Années du Parti Écologiste Suisse.* Lausanne: L'Age d'homme.

Reckwitz, A. 2020. *The Society of Singularities: On the Structural Transformation of Modernity.* London: Polity.

Reiter, Y. 2008. *Jerusalem and Its Role in Islamic Solidarity.* New York: Palgrave Macmillan.

Reiter, Y. 2010. "Religion as a Barrier to Compromise in the Israeli-Palestinian Conflict." In *Barriers to Peace in the Israeli-Palestinian Conflict*, edited by Y. Bar-Siman-Tov, 228–63. Jerusalem: The Jerusalem Institute for Israel Studies.

Reiter, Y., and L. Lehrs. 2013. *A City with a Mosque in Its Heart.* Jerusalem: The Jerusalem Institute for Israel Studies.

Rekhess, E. 2002. The Arabs in Israel: Localization of the National Struggle. *Israel Studies* 7 (3): 175–98.

Rivers, J. 2011. "Surprisingly Unsurprising: How Brazilian Evangelicals Work Jiu Jitsu into Their Worship Services." *The International Journal of Religion and Spirituality in Society* 1 (3): 1–21.

Rivers, J. 2016. "The Intimate Intensity of Evangelical Fighting Ministries." *Temenos* 52 (2): 215–37.

Rodríguez Rondón, M. A. 2017. "La Ideología de Género como Exceso: Pánico Moral y Decisión ética en la Política Colombiana." *Sexualidad, Salud y Sociedad-Revista Latinoamericana* 27: 128–48.

Rohy, V. 2006. "*Ahistorical.*" *GLQ: A Journal of Lesbian and Gay Studies* 12 (1): 61–83.

Rojo, L. M. 2014. "Occupy: The Spatial Dynamics of Discourse in Global Protest Movements." *Journal of Language and Politics* 13 (4): 583–98.

Römhild, R. 2017. "Beyond the Bounds of the Ethnic: For Postmigrant Cultural and Social Research." *Journal of Aesthetics & Culture* 9 (2): 69–75.

Rosa, H. 2013. *Social Acceleration: A New Theory of Modernity.* Columbia: Columbia University Press.

Rouhana, N., ed. 2004. *Citizenship without Voice: The Palestinians in Israel.* Haifa: Mada al-Karmel Center.

Rozenberg, D. 2010. *La España Contemporánea y la Cuestión Judía.* Madrid: Marcial Pons.

Rüpke, J. 2020. *Urban Religion: A Historical Approach to Urban Growth and Religious Change.* Berlin: deGruyter.

Said, E. 1978. *Orientalism.* New York: Pantheon Books.

Said, E. 2000. "Invention, Memory, and Place." In *The People, Place, and Space Reader*, edited by Jen Jack Gieseking and William Mangold, 361–6. New York: Routledge.

Saint-Blancat, C. 2019. "Introduction: The Religious Writing of Space." *Social Compass* 66 (1): 1–23.

Saint-Blancat, C., and A. Cancellieri. 2014. "From Invisibility to Visibility? The Appropriation of Public Space through a Religious Ritual: The Filipino Procession of Santacruzan in Padua, Italy." *Social & Cultural Geography* 15 (6): 645–63.

Salah, R. 2002. "Jerusalem Is above and beyond Negotiation." *Sawt al-Haqq wa-l-Huriyya* (special supplement), September 15: A 5.

Salah, R. 2015. "When Success Becomes a Doubt." *Sawt al-Haqq w-al-Huriyya*, April 24: A 4.

Salomon Cavin, J., and C. A. Kull. 2017. "Invasion Ecology Goes to Town: From Disdain to Sympathy." *Biological Invasions* 19: 3471–87.

Salzbrunn, M. 2017. "Musique, Religion, Appartenances Multiples: Une Approche de L'événement." *Sociétés Plurielles* 1: 1–23.

Salzbrunn, M., and R. von Weichs. 2013. "Sacred Music, Sacred Journeys: What Makes an Event Postcolonial?" *ThéoRèmes. Penser Le Religieux*, no. 4 (November).

Sánchez García, R., and D. Malcolm. 2010. "Decivilizing, Civilizing or Informalizing? The International Development of Mixed Martial Arts." *International Review for the Sociology of Sport* 45 (1): 39–58.

Santoro, M. 2019. "The Brutal Politics of Brazil's Drug War." *New York Times*, October 28. Accessed May 8, 2020. https://www.nytimes.com/2019/10/28/opinion/brazi-war-on-poor.html.

Sassatelli, M. 2015. "Festivals, Urbanity and the Public Sphere: Reflections on European Festivals." In *Festivals in Focus. Contemporary European Case Studies and Perspectives*, edited by C. Newbold, C. Maughan and J. Jordan, 28–39. Oxford: Goodfellow Publishers.

Sassatelli, M. 2018. "Festivals, Museums, Exhibitions: Aesthetic Cosmopolitanism in the Cultural Public Sphere." In *Routledge International Handbook of Cosmopolitanism Studies, 2nd edition*, edited by G. Delanty, 233–44. London: Routledge.

Schaefer, D. O. 2015. *Religious Affects: Animality, Evolution, and Power*. Durham, NC: Duke University Press.

Schechner, R. 1994. "Ritual and Performance." In *Companion Encyclopedia of Anthropology*, edited by T. Ingold, 613–47. London: Routledge.

Schildkrout, E. 2004. "Inscribing the Body." *Annual Review of Anthropology* 33 (1): 319–44.

Schneiderman, R. M. 2010. "Flock Is Now a Fight Team in Some Ministries." *New York Times*, February 1. Accessed June 17, 2020. https://www.nytimes.com/2010/02/02/us/02fight.html.

Sciarini, P., S. Nicolet, D. Oesch, and L. Rennwald. 2009. "Le Vote pour le Parti Socialiste et les Verts. Potentiel Électoral, Concurrence et Vote de Classe." In *Les Partis Politiques Suisses: Traditions et Renouvellement*, edited by O. Mazzoleni and H. Rayner, 279–306. Paris: Michel Houdiard.

Scott, J. 2018. *Sex and Secularism*. Princeton, NJ: Princeton University Press.

Selby, J. A., and L. G. Beaman. 2016. "Re-posing the 'Muslim Question.'" *Critical Research on Religion* 4 (1): 8–20.

Selim, N. 2015. "Healing the City: Sufi Prayers in Berlin's Towers." *Medizinethnologie: Körper, Gesundheit und Heilung in einer globalisierten Welt*. Accessed July 4, 2019. https://www.medizinethnologie.net/sufi-prayers-in-berlins-towers/.

Serrano, M. 2019. *Jiu-Jítsu 'O Túnel do Tempo': A Marinha trouxe o Jiu-Jítsu para o Brasil*. Joinville, SC: Clube de Autores.

Shapiro, A. 2017. "The Medium Is the Mob." *Media, Culture & Society* 39 (6): 930–41.

Shehadeh, R. 2010. *Palestinian Walks: Notes on a Vanishing Landscape*. London: Profile Books.

Silva, E., and E. Corrêa. 2020. *Muito antes do MMA: O legado dos precursores do Vale Tudo no Brasil e no mundo*. Kindle edition. Amazon.com.

Simmel, G. [1903] 1971. "The Metropolis and Mental Life." In *Individuality and Social Forms*, edited by D. Levine, 324–39. Chicago, IL: University of Chicago Press.

Singleton, M. 2010. *Yoga Body: The Roots of Modern Posture Practice*. New York: Oxford University Press.

Smith, A. 2015. *Events in the City: Using Public Spaces as Event Venues*. London: Routledge.

Smith, J. Z. 2004. *Relating Religion: Essays in the Study of Religion*. Chicago, IL: University of Chicago Press.

Smith, N. 1993. "Homeless/Global: Scaling Places." In *Mapping the Future—Local Cultures, Global Change*, edited by J. Bird, B. Curtis, T. Putman, G. Robertson and L. Tickner, 81–119. London: Routledge.

Smyth, M. 2015. "Shutting Down the Burrard Bridge for Yoga Day Is One of the Dumbest Government Decisions Ever." *The Province*. December 17. Accessed June 16, 2020. http://www.theprovince.com/health/michael+smyth+shutting+d own+burrard+bridge+yoga+dumbest+government+decisions+ever/11599852/ story.html.

Sointu, E., and L. Woodhead. 2008. "Spirituality, Gender, and Expressive Selfhood." *Journal for the Scientific Study of Religion* 47 (2): 259–76.

Sousa Pinto, A. E. de. 2019. "Bolsonaro assiste à apresentação de jiu-jítsu brasileiro em Abu Dhabi." *Folha de S.Paulo*, October 27. Accessed June 17, 2020. https://www1. folha.uol.com.br/esporte/2019/10/bolsonaro-assiste-apresentacao-de-jiu-jitsu-brasileiro-em-abu-dhabi.shtml.

Souza, J. 2018. *Subcidadania brasileira: para entender o país além do jeitinho brasileiro*. Rio de Janeiro, RJ: LeYa.

Spencer, D. C. 2012. *Ultimate Fighting and Embodiment: Violence, Gender, and Mixed Martial Arts*. New York: Routledge.

Spencer, D. C. 2014. "From Many Masters to Many Students: YouTube, Brazilian Jiu Jitsu, and Communities of Practice." *Journalism, Media, and Cultural Studies Journal*, 5, 1–15.

Spineto, N. 2015. *La festa*. Rome-Bari: Laterza.

Spracklen, K., and I. R. Lamond. 2016. *Critical Event Studies*. London: Routledge.

Spracklen, K., A. Richter, and B. Spracklen. 2013. "The Eventization of Leisure and the Strange Death of Alternative Leeds." *City* 17 (2): 164–78.

Spyer, J. 2017. *Social Media in Emergent Brazil: How the Internet Affects Social Mobility*. London: UCL Press.

Stadler, N. 2015. "Appropriating Jerusalem through Sacred Places: Disputed Landscape and Female Rituals at the Tombs of Mary and Rachel." *Anthropological Quarterly* 88 (3): 725–58.

Steets, S. 2015. *Die gebaute Konstruktion der Wirklichkeit.* Berlin: Suhrkamp.

Stenius, M. 2015. "Attacking the Body in Mixed Martial Arts: Perspectives, Opinions and Perceptions of the Full Contact Combat Sport of Ultimate Fighting." *Journal of Arts and Humanities* 4 (2): 77–91.

Stewart, Kathleen. 2010. "Worlding Refrains." In *The Affect Theory Reader*, edited by M. Gregg and G. Seigworth, 339–53. Durham, NC: Duke University Press.

Stolz, J. 2010. "A Silent Battle: Theorizing the Effects of Competition between Churches and Secular Institutions." *Review of Religious Research* 51: 253–76.

Stolz, J., J. Könemann, M. Schneuwly Purdie, T. Englberger and M. Krüggeler. 2014. *Religion und Spiritualität in der Ich-Gesellschaft.* Zürich: Theologischer Verlag Zürich.

Stringer, M. D. 2015. "The Future of Public Religious Ritual in an Urban Context." *Jaarboek voor liturgieonderzoek* 31: 45–59.

Suárez, A. 2000. "La Situación Habitacional." In *La Ciudad de México en el fin del Segundo Milenio*, edited by G. Garza, 390–7. México: Gobierno del Distrito Federal y El Colegio de México.

Suárez, H. 2012. *Ver y Creer. Ensayo de Sociología Visual en la Colonia El Ajusco.* México: IIS-UNAM—Quinta Chilla.

Suárez, H. 2015. *Creyentes Urbanos. Sociología de la Experiencia Religiosa en una Colonia Popular en la Ciudad de México.* México: Universidad Nacional Autónoma de México-Instituto de Investigaciones Sociales.

Suárez, H. 2017a. "La Geografía de la Práctica Religiosa en una Colonia Popular en la Ciudad de México." *Sociedad y religión* 27 (47): 12–32.

Suárez, H. 2017b. "Vida y Muerte de un Peñasco." In *La Erosión del Espacio Público en la Ciudad Neoliberal*, edited by P. Ramírez, 661–82. México: IIS-UNAM.

Swyngedouw, E. 1997. "Neither Global nor Local: 'Glocalization' and the Politics of Scale." In *Spaces of Globalization. Reasserting the Power of the Local*, edited by K. R. Cox, 137–66. New York and London: The Guilford Press.

Syman, S. 2011. *The Subtle Body: The Story of Yoga in America.* New York: Farrar, Strauss, and Giroux.

Synod of the Bishops. 2012a. "Lineamenta." *The New Evangelization for the Transmission of the Christian Faith.* Vatican City: Libreria Edetrice Vaticana.

Synod of the Bishops. 2012b. "Instrumentum Laboris." *The New Evangelization for the Transmission of the Christian Faith.* Vatican City: Libreria Edetrice Vaticana.

Synod of the Bishops. 2012c. "Final Propositions." *Synodus Episcoporum Bolletino*, 33-plurigingue, 27/10/2012.

Taneja, A. V. 2018. *Jinnealogy: Time, Islam, and Ecological Thought in the Medieval Ruins of Delhi.* Stanford, CA: Stanford University Press.

Taylor, B. 2010. *Dark Green Religion: Nature, Spirituality and the Planetary Future.* Berkeley: University of California Press.

Taylor, C. 2007. *A Secular Age*. Cambridge: The Belknap Press of Harvard University Press.

Teixeira, A. C. E. M. 2007. "Esporte e violência no jiu-jitsu: o caso dos 'pitboys.'" Master's thesis, Rio de Janeiro: Pontifícia Universidade Católica do Rio de Janeiro.

Testa, A. 2014. *Il carnevale dell'uomo-animale: Le dimensioni storiche e socio-culturali di una festa appenninica*. Naples: Loffredo.

Testa A. 2020. *Rituality and Social (Dis)Order. The Historical Anthropology of Popular Carnival in Europe*. Routledge

Todd, D. 2018. "Vancouver's Housing Crisis Revealed by Looking to China, Australia, and New Zealand." *Vancouver Sun*. January 5. Accessed June 16, 2020. https://vancouversun.com/opinion/columnists/douglas-todd-vancouvers-housing-crisis-revealed-by-looking-to-china-australia-new-zealand.

Tong, C. K., and L. Kong. 2000. "Religion and Modernity: Ritual Transformations and the Reconstruction of Space and Time." *Social & Cultural Geography* 1: 29–44.

Torino Spiritualita Durante L'Anno. Accessed March 10, 2020. https://torinospiritualita.org/.

Turner, V. 1969. *The Ritual Process: Structure and Anti-structure*. New York: Transaction Publishers.

Turner, V. 1982a. *From Ritual to Theatre: The Human Seriousness of Play*. New York: PAJ Publications.

Turner, V. 1982b. "Images of Anti-temporality: An Essay in the Anthropology of Experience." *The Harvard Theological Review* 75 (2): 243–65.

Turner, V. 1995. *The Ritual Process: Structure and Anti-structure*. New York: Aldine de Gruyter.

Umashankar, R. R. 2015. "Metropolitan Microcosms: The Dynamic Spaces of Contemporary Sufi Shrines in India." *South Asian Studies* 31 (1): 127–43.

United Nations. n.d. "International Day of Yoga 21 June." Accessed June 16, 2020. https://www.un.org/en/observances/yoga-day.

Uzlaner, D. 2013. "Kartografiia postsekuliarnogo" [Cartography of the Postsecular] *Otechestvennye zapiski*, no. 1. http://www.strana-oz.ru/2013/1/kartografiya-postsekulyarnogo#_ftnref17.

Uzlaner, D. 2019. *Konets religii? Istoriia teorii sekuliarizatsii* [The End of Religion? A History of the Theory of Secularization]. Moscow: HSE Publishing House.

Vaggione, J. M. 2005. "Reactive Politicization and Religious Dissidence: The Political Mutations of the Religious." *Social Theory and Practice* 31 (2): 233–55.

Vaggione, J. M. 2012. "La Cultura de la Vida: Desplazamientos Estratégicos del Activismo Católico Conservador Frente a los Derechos Sexuales y Reproductivos." *Religião & Sociedade* 32 (2): 57–80.

Vaggione, J. M. 2017. "La Iglesia Católica Frente a la Política Sexual: La Configuración de una Ciudadanía Religiosa." *Cadernos Pagu* 50.

Valentine, G., R. M. Vanderbeck, J. Andersson, J. Sadgrove, and K. Ward. 2010. "Emplacements: The Event as a Prism for Exploring Intersectionality." *Sociology* 44 (5): 925–43.

Vertovec, S. 2007. "Super-Diversity and Its Implications." *Ethnic and Racial Studies* 29 (6): 1024–54.

Vertovec, S. 2019. "Talking around Super-Diversity." *Ethnic and Racial Studies* 42 (1): 125–39.

Vital, D. 1975. *The Origins of Zionism*. Oxford: Clarendon Press.

Wacquant, L. 1998. "The Prizefighter's Three Bodies." *Ethnos* 63 (3–4): 325–52.

Wacquant, L. 2004. *Body & Soul: Notebooks of an Apprentice Boxer*. New York: Oxford University Press.

Wacquant, L. 2008. *Urban Outcasts: A Comparative Sociology of Advanced Marginality*. Cambridge: Polity Press.

Wacquant, L. 2015. "For a Sociology of Flesh and Blood." *Qualitative Sociology* 38 (1): 1–11.

Wagstaff, J. M. 1985. *The Evolution of Middle Eastern Landscapes: An Outline to AD 1840*. London: Rowman & Littlefield.

Watson, N. J., and B. Brock. 2018. "Christianity, Boxing and Mixed Martial Arts: Reflections on Morality, Vocation and Well-Being." In *Global Perspectives on Sports and Christianity*, edited by A. U. Adogame, 243–62. New York: Routledge.

Weber, M. 1946. "Science as a Vocation." In *Max Weber: Essays in Sociology*, edited by H. H. Gerth and C. Wright Mills. 129–57. New York: Oxford University Press.

Weber, M. 2015. *Weber's Rationalism and Modern Society: New Translations on Politics, Bureaucracy, and Social Stratification*, edited and translated by T. Waters and D. Waters. Hampshire, UK: Palgrave Macmillan.

Werbner, P. 1996. "Stamping the Earth with the Name of Allah: Zikr and the Sacralizing of Space among British Muslims." *Cultural Anthropology* 11 (3): 309–38.

White, D. G., ed. 2012. *Yoga in Practice*. Princeton, NJ: Princeton University Press.

Wilkins-Laflamme, S. 2018. *The Religious, Spiritual, Secular and Social Landscapes of the Pacific Northwest—Part 2*, UW Space. Accessed June 16, 2020. https://uwspace.uwaterloo.ca/handle/10012/13406.

Wittgenstein, L. [1921] 1987. *Tractatus logico-philosophicus*. Madrid: Alianza.

Wohlrab-Sahr, M., and M. Burchardt. 2012. "Multiple Secularities: Toward a Cultural Sociology of Secular Modernities." *Comparative Sociology* 11 (6): 875–909.

Yacobi, H. 2015. "Jerusalem: From a 'Divided' to a 'Contested' City—and Next to a Neo-apartheid City?" *City: Analysis of Urban Trends, Culture, Theory, Policy, Action* 19 (4): 579–84.

Yiftachel, O. 2006. *Ethnocracy: Land, Politics and Identities in Israel/Palestine*. Philadelphia: Penn Press.

Yiftachel, O., and A. Ghanem. 2004. "Ethnocratic Regimes: The Politics of Seizing Contested Territories." *Political Geography* 23: 647–76.

Zermeño, S. 2005. *La Desmodernidad Mexicana y las Alternativas a la Violencia y a la Exclusión en Nuestros Días*. México: Océano.

Žižek, S. 2014. *Event: A Philosophical Journey through a Concept*. London: Melville House.

Zwilling, A. L. 2015. "A Century of Mosques in France: Building Religious Pluralism." *International Review of Sociology* 25 (2): 333–40.

Contributors

Irene Becci holds a Ph.D. in social and political sciences from the European University Institute. Since 2012, she has been Professor at the Institute for the Social Scientific Study of Religion at the University of Lausanne. She has studied in Lausanne, Rome, Florence, and New York, and has worked in Germany at the Max-Planck Institute for Social Anthropology in Halle, as well as at Bielefeld and Potsdam University. In her research, she focuses on religious diversity and new spiritual practices in particular settings, such as total institutions, as well as post-socialist urban spaces and ecological activism. Together with Olivier Roy, she has published *Religious Diversity in European Prisons—Challenges and Implications for Rehabilitation* (2015). Her publications can be found in particular in *Archives des sciences sociales contemporaines, Critique internationale, Social Compass, Tsantsa,* and *Women's Studies.*

Paul Bramadat is Professor and Director of the Centre for Studies in Religion and Society at the University of Victoria. He is the author of *The Church on the World's Turf: An Evangelical Christian Student Group at a Secular University* (2000) and co-editor of several books, including *International Migration and the Governance of Religious Diversity* (2009), *Radicalization and Securitization in Canada and Beyond* (2014), *Religion and Ethnicity in Canada* (2005), and *Public Health in the Age of Anxiety: Religious and Cultural Reasons for Vaccine Hesitancy* (2017). He has published chapters in books as well as articles in *Religion, State and Society,* the *Journal of the American Academy of Religion, Studies in Religion, Ethnicities, Ethnologies,* and the *Journal of International Migration and Integration.* He recently co-edited *The Land of Tomorrow: Religion, Spirituality and Secularity in the Pacific Northwest.*

Marian Burchardt holds a Ph.D. from Leipzig University where he is Professor of Sociology. His research is about how power, institutions, and infrastructures shape urban life in diverse societies. He is the author of *Faith in the Time of AIDS: Religion, Politics and Modernity in South Africa* (2015) and *Regulating Difference: Religious Diversity and Nationhood in the Secular West* (2020). He is the co-director of the Leipzig Lab Global Health and senior research partner of the Max Planck Institute for the Study of Religious and Ethnic Diversity in Göttingen/Germany.

Anna Clot-Garrell is a postdoctoral researcher at the Center for the Study of Culture, Politics and Society (CECUPS) at the Universitat de Barcelona. She is also Research Associate at the Center for Studies in Sociology of Religion at the Universitat Autònoma de Barcelona. Since her master's thesis on the new expressions of religiosity in the city of Barcelona, awarded with the Ninian Smart Prize (Politics, Philosophy and Religion Department, Lancaster University), her research has focused on contemporary religious transformations and cultural change from a humanistic, sociological perspective.

Mónica Cornejo-Valle (Ph.D. in Social Anthropology, Complutense University of Madrid, 2007) is Associate Professor at the Social Anthropology Department of the Complutense University of Madrid. She is Director of the research group Anthropology, Diversity and Integration. Her main research topics have been popular Catholicism, contemporary spiritualities and health, religion in public spaces, and religious controversies about sexual and reproductive rights. She is the author and editor of several books (such as *La Construcción Antropológica de la Religión* and *Teorias y Prácticas Emergentes en Antropologia de la Religion*) and she also authored several papers in scientific journals and conferences.

Mariachiara Giorda is Associate Professor of History of Religions at Roma Tre University, Department of Humanities (Studi Umanistici). She is local in-charge of the international PriMED (Prevenzione e Interazione nello spazio Trans-Mediterraneo) project and her research interests focus on the spatial practices of religions, and monasticism.

Alberta Giorgi is Senior Lecturer in Sociology of culture at the University of Bergamo. Her research interests lie at the intersection of religion and politics— namely, secularism, and gender and religion. Alberta is Vice-Coordinator for the research network Political Sociology (ESA), and associate researcher of the GSRL, CRAFT, and POLICREDOS research groups.

Mar Griera is Associate Professor in Sociology and Vice-Dean at the Faculty of Political Science and Sociology in the Universitat Autònoma de Barcelona (UAB). Since 2016 she has been Director of the Barcelona-based research center ISOR focused on the study of religions in contemporary societies. She has been a visiting scholar at the University of Boston, University of Amsterdam, University of Exeter, and Université Marc Bloch (Strasbourg). Her research explores the intersection of religion, spirituality, identity, and politics in contemporary Europe.

Omar Kasmani is postdoctoral Research Fellow in Social and Cultural Anthropology at the Collaborative Research Center *Affective Societies* at Freie Universität, Berlin. Spanning the study of religion as well as queer and affect theory, his research pursues ideas of postmigrant be/longing, queer futurities, and public intimacy. His first monograph on saintly intimacies in Pakistan is forthcoming.

Hubert Knoblauch is Professor of General Sociology at the Technical University of Berlin. His fields of research are sociological theory, sociology of knowledge and communication, qualitative methods, and, of course, sociology of religion.

Nimrod Luz is a professor of Human Geography at Kinneret College on the Sea of Galilee. He specializes in cultural theories, landscape and the built environment, cities and urbanism, religion, and food. His interdisciplinary research and interests are the multiple and reflexive relations among society, culture (politics), and the built environment with a special focus on Islam and the Middle East, past and present.

Julia Martínez-Ariño is Assistant Professor of Sociology of Religion at the University of Groningen. Her main research interests are non-religion, the governance of religious diversity in public institutions and cities and the spatial strategies of urban religious groups—especially Jewish communities—and their relation to heritage. She has published in international journals such as *Current Sociology, Social Compass*, and *Comparative European Politics*. Julia Martínez-Ariño is the convener of the "Religion and Cities" research cluster of the *Centre for Religion, Conflict and Globalization* at the University of Groningen and Associate Researcher for the *ISOR—Investigations in the Sociology of Religion* research group at the Autonomous University of Barcelona.

Salomé Okoekpen is Junior FNS Researcher at the Institute for Social Sciences of Religions (ISSR) at Lausanne University. She takes part in the nationally funded project, "Towards a spiritualization of ecology? A sociological analysis of the current mediations of ecological issues in Switzerland." She wrote her master's thesis on urban music and art festivals in connection to spirituality under the direction of Professor Irene Becci.

Nadezhda Rychkova, Ph.D., Research Fellow at the Laboratory of Folklore Studies, School of Advanced Studies in the Humanities, Russian Presidential Academy of National Economy and Public Administration, Moscow, Russia.

Raphael Schapira is a Ph.D. candidate at the Graduate Institute of International and Development Studies in Geneva and a Doc.Mobility Fellow of the Swiss National Science Foundation at KU Leuven in the Faculty of Social Sciences. He is also an expert practitioner of Brazilian jiu-jitsu and German ju-jutsu. His main research interest lies in the anthropology of sport, which he approaches from the perspective of the body, skill, and religion. He has conducted long-term research in Rio de Janeiro on Brazilian jiu-jitsu for which he immersed himself into the practice of this martial art using embodiment as a topic and research method.

Hugo José Suárez received his Ph.D. from the Catholic University of Leuven in Belgium in 2001, and he currently holds a professorship position at the Universidad Nacional Autonoma de Mexico (UNAM). He has been a visiting scholar at the Latin American Studies Institute (Columbia University, New York) and at the Université Sorbonne Nouvelle Paris 3. He has published extensively on sociology of religion and culture, qualitative methodology, and visual sociology.

Sophie Watson is Professor of Sociology at Open University (UK). Previously she was Co-Director of the ESRC Centre for Research into Socio-Cultural Change. Sophie has held professorships at the University of East London, the University of Bristol, and the University of Sydney. Her recent consultancies and activities include Thames Water, and the Vienna University of Technology Fund (WWTF). Her main research interests are in urban sociology, multiculturalism, public space, the cultures of water, and street markets. She has written extensively on different aspects of cities, editing *Spatial Justice in the City* (2019), and writing *City Water Matters: Cultures, Practices and Entanglements of Urban Water* (2019).

Index